THE PROSPERITY AGENDA

To Flo Pollack —
who gets the agenda
better than most —
But

Nancy Soderberg
Aug 1.08

THE PROSPERITY AGENDA

WHAT THE WORLD WANTS FROM AMERICA—AND WHAT WE NEED IN RETURN

Nancy Soderberg
Brian Katulis

WILEY

John Wiley & Sons, Inc.

Published by John Wiley & Sons, Inc., Hoboken, New Jersey
Published simultaneously in Canada

For general information about our other products and services, please contact our Customer Care Department within the United States at (800) 762-2974, outside the United States at (317) 572-3993 or fax (317) 572-4002.

Wiley also publishes its books in a variety of electronic formats. Some content that appears in print may not be available in electronic books. For more information about Wiley products, visit our web site at www.wiley.com.

Library of Congress Cataloging-in-Publication Data:
Soderberg, Nancy E., date.
    The prosperity agenda : what the world wants from America—and what we
need in return / Nancy Soderberg and Brian Katulis.
        p.   cm.
    Includes index.
    ISBN 978-0-470-10529-0 (cloth)
        1. United States—Foreign relations—2001.   2. United States—Foreign economic
relations.   3. United States—Foreign public opinion.   4. Globalization.   5. Globalization—
Economic aspects.   6. Economic development.   7. National security—United States.
8. Security, International.   9. United States—Foreign relations—Philosophy.   I. Katulis,
Brian.   II. Title.
E902.S63 2008
327.73009'05—dc22

                                                                    2008000246

Printed in the United States of America
10 9 8 7 6 5 4 3 2 1

To Nancy's parents,
Lars and Nancy Soderberg

To Brian's wife, Kristy

CONTENTS

ACKNOWLEDGMENTS

Writing a book is almost always a collective effort. In this case, we are indebted to the many family members, friends, and colleagues who gave so generously of their minds and time as we wrote this book. We especially want to thank our respective institutions for their support of this project. The University of North Florida (UNF) afforded Nancy Soderberg course relief, research assistance from UNF students, and a wonderful group of supportive colleagues. John Podesta, Melody Barnes, and the Center for American Progress were generous with their tolerance of Brian Katulis's absence for various periods and for allowing both authors to draw on the talents of the center's researchers. We are particularly thankful to Peter Juul and Adam Hunter, whose brilliant research and unending patience with both of us have made this book far better than it would have been without their input.

We could not have written this book without the guidance offered to us by other center staff members and interns, including Matthew Forgotson, Michael Fuchs, Vanessa Gottlieb, Leah Greenberg, Andy Grotto, Jonathan Jacoby, Lawrence Korb, Peter Ogden, Dan Restrepo, Amanda Rios, Gayle Smith, and Carolyn Wadhams. Similarly, a number of students at the University of North Florida provided essential research as well, including Ruth Bacerra, Dane Boog, Alexandra Cohn, Antony Constantini, Christopher Ferrara, Tom Foran, Jason Kroiter, Mika Pitts, Mai Tran, Laura Verlangieri, and Katie Whitehurst. Others who contributed in significant ways include Deepti Choubey, Jake Colvin of the National Foreign Trade Council, Christopher Fox of Ceres, Jahn Jeffrey, Carlos Pascual, and Kate Vyborny. Nancy's friend and UNF colleague, Professor Pam Zeiser, lent her critical eye to the book and made it much better. Susan Estomin Chappelear and Link Nicoll offered helpful comments as well.

For this book, we interviewed people in the United States and abroad. Such a task could never have been accomplished without our network of friends and colleagues who put us in touch with the people who are the targets of our prosperity agenda. We want to thank the following people for introducing us to the people who made this book come alive. They include John Basso, Paul and Heather Booth, Elizabeth Shuler, Ashley Durmer of Citizens Energy Corporation, Jason Stearns and Samina Ahmed of the International Crisis Group, Jennifer Windsor at Freedom House, Juhani Grossman, Bassam Nasser, and Becky Webster. We are especially grateful to those who agreed to be profiled or quoted for this book. Nancy would also like to express a belated warm thanks to Angela Stene Mancini whom she unintentionally left out of the acknowledgments in her first book.

We are thankful to our friends and families for the support they generously gave to both of us as we wrote this book. For Nancy, her family—her parents, Lars and Nancy, and her siblings and in-laws, John and Melissa Soderberg, Sigrid and Jim Pinsky, and Lars and Jane Soderberg—has been a great source of support and a sanity check on the book (and life). Once again, Jake and Elizabeth Bistrong provided great encouragement and reminded her to take a break and have fun now and again. Nancy especially wants to thank Denise, Charlie, Kaylen, and Nick McMullin for their exquisite care of Gena during the process of writing this book.

For Brian, his wife, Kristen Katulis, read through every single line several times and made the book much better than it could have possibly been without her. Kathy and Bill Cooper, Jofi Joseph, and Kate Head all gave edits, advice, and encouragement along the way. Thanks also to Brian's parents, John and Rita Katulis; his grandmother, Madeline Katulis; his siblings, Lisa and Sean Katulis; and Sue and Bill Weed, for their support.

Eric Nelson at John Wiley & Sons, whose talents and brilliance are unparalleled, pushed both Nancy and Brian to pull it all together in the mad dash to the finish line.

Finally, we are indebted to Bob Boorstin for bringing us together.

Thank you all.

Introduction

Thirty-six-year-old Adelard Mivumba lives a decent life in Goma, on the eastern border of the Democratic Republic of the Congo in central Africa. The region's beautiful mountains, active volcanoes, Lake Kivu, and a large national park known for mountain gorillas make it a tourist destination. Businessmen from Dubai, Nairobi, and Kampala come here to buy the area's gems and minerals. Born and raised in Goma, Adelard owns a plot of land and is proud of the home he built on it. He shares his home with his wife, mother, and grandmother, and he boasts about its sitting room, bathroom, mini-corridor, two bedrooms, and kitchen. A shelter for house workers stands just outside, and a garden with fruit trees, colorful flowers, and lush green grass welcomes visitors in the front. Adelard bought the land with $5,000 that he made while working for the United Nations peacekeeping mission in the region.[1]

A college graduate with a degree in business and finance from a university in the Congo, Adelard got married recently. His twenty-seven-year-old wife also has a university degree; she studied public health. He has a steady job in the government tax office and is a small-time trader in minerals, bringing in about

1

$70 a month. His wife had the good luck of landing a job with an international organization that pays her $500 a month, which gives them a monthly income that far outpaces what most people in their country make in a year. Adelard and his family live a good life, but their prosperity is at risk and his decent life is fragile.

During the last decade, the Congo has suffered from two wars that caused the deaths of 5.4 million people, making them two of the world's deadliest conflicts since World War II.[2] Goma, a town of 400,000, has been particularly hard hit. "Life is not going well here," Adelard explained. War once again looms over the area where he lives. "People are crying, looting, and dying. Most of them are really poor, and clean water is difficult to get." Following the 1994 genocide in Rwanda, nearly a million refugees fled to Goma, straining the underdeveloped area. *Interahamwe* militiamen—remnants of those who perpetrated the Rwandan genocide—and a separate *Mai Mai* rebel group hide in the forests near Goma, plotting attacks against Rwanda and at times attacking Congolese civilians. Periodic clashes break out between the militia and Congolese soldiers, bringing with them a constant threat of a Rwandan invasion to wipe out the militias.

"We are afraid because we are on the border with Rwanda, and the war is not far from Goma, in the hills and mountains surrounding Masisi," said Adelard, referring to a town forty miles northwest of Goma. "The conflict affects us so much because people abandon their cultivation and the farmers don't know where to bring their cows. There is no more food like potatoes and vegetables coming from the villages." The Congolese soldiers also threaten the population. As Adelard described it, "Soldiers do what they want, they steal and harass and shoot people every day. So, who can we rely on? People are really afraid of war and the consequences of war."

The world is filled with billions of people just like Adelard Mivumba. Some live day to day on the bare minimum, getting just enough food and water to survive and struggling to stay out of the crosshairs of deadly conflict. Others are luckier and have more prosperous lives but worry about dangers near and far. Every day, people around the world are made aware of the fragility of their lives; they are reminded that at any instant, something could shatter their hopes for greater prosperity and a better future.

Even among the most fortunate and prosperous people in developed countries around the world, threats loom over the horizon, much as war lurks just over the mountains in the eastern Congo, whether in the flash of a breaking news banner on cable television or in the memories brought forth by the image of gaping holes in the ground in Lower Manhattan. Calamities major and minor—the blast of a roadside bomb in Baghdad, heavy rains and gusting winds of a monsoon in Bangladesh or a hurricane in Louisiana, the pink slip of a job lost to global economic changes—all can change people's lives in an instant. These threats to global prosperity know no national borders.

From the Freedom Agenda to the Prosperity Agenda

In our increasingly interconnected and interdependent world, our leaders need to present a vision that addresses these growing threats. President George W. Bush has talked about freedom and democracy as the common global aspiration of all people, but all too often, his worldview ignored the basics. Most people seek something broader than a vote at the polls. What President Bush's strategy lacks is an understanding that freedom and democracy can be achieved only if people feel secure and prosperous. People must have decent homes, enough to eat, and freedom from the threat of violence and disease. They need a sense of progress, a reason to have hope for the future.

Conservatives love to talk about big ideas—fighting communism, defeating terrorists, or promoting freedom—but in doing so, they forget about the basic elements that shape human action, the things that make people more secure and prosperous. And too few conservatives ever worry about the means corrupting their stated ends, leading them to support torture in the name of keeping

Americans secure and to cozy up to dictators who embody anti-democratic values. For President Bush, advancing a freedom agenda meant little more than the United States calling for elections as the first step toward democracy, with little regard for people's personal safety and economic well-being.

During his eight years in office, President William Jefferson Clinton also pursued a freedom agenda, heralding the milestone in the mid-1990s when, for the first time in human history, more than half of the world lived in a democracy. But Clinton understood that the freedom agenda is only one part of the larger human rights mission. That's why he set his sights on securing peace in Bosnia, Ireland, Haiti, and the Middle East, as well as across much of Africa. That's why he worked with other nations and the United Nations to try to cut world poverty in half. Clinton understood that peace depends on prosperity, and prosperity depends on peace. That's also why he increased U.S. investment around the world and slashed barriers to more trade, while seeking to help those at home who were hurt by the transition. He understood, too, the need to combat infectious diseases and tackle global warming. With the Cold War barely over as he took office, future global dynamics were uncertain. The policies he pursued were based more on principle, necessity, and pragmatism than on some grand and idealistic vision disconnected from the world's complex realities. With the Bush presidency, we have seen the folly in creating a grand vision based on a fundamental misinterpretation of these new global dynamics.

By 2008, America's leaders must understand that promoting freedom and democracy around the world requires them to address him to address the broader concerns of the world. In order to advance democracy, people must first feel safe from war, poverty, debt, and disease. They must feel hope that they will be able to provide for their families and give their children decent lives. And the more progress that is made on any one of these challenges, the easier it will be for the United States to address the others. For instance, the more conflicts come to an end, the less poverty will take hold because people will have greater opportunities to create businesses and jobs in a secure environment. The fewer barriers there are to trade and investment, the more economic growth will help to lift people out of poverty. The more people can breathe clean air and avoid contracting deadly diseases, the less untimely deaths of millions will devastate their societies. And the more people see an America working to address their priorities, the more they will be willing to work with America to address our concerns.

President Bush and his conservative backers took up the freedom agenda with gusto but abandoned the rest. They never pursued the broader agenda of working for prosperity around the world. Too many countries' citizens see the United States as a threat to their well-being, rather than the empowering force we see ourselves as being. When historians look back on President Bush's time in office, they will judge it as a period when the world had been dramatically transformed but U.S. national security strategy did not keep up with global trends.

Conservatives think that the way to make Americans safer is to bend the will of the world with raw "shock-and-awe" power. Their approach to the world relies heavily on conventional military tactics to solve problems that actually require other aspects of U.S. power. The Bush administration's primary approach was to threaten, isolate, sanction, and lecture the rest of the world. This administration operated with an outmoded win-lose, zero-sum global strategy that ended up undermining America's position and influence in the world. This approach may have worked to keep the United States safer in the previous century, but the conservative vision of the world is no longer relevant in the new millennium. The nature of what it means to be powerful in the world has been inexorably altered—how to shape and influence trends in other countries to benefit Americans' security and prosperity has fundamentally changed.

Today, America has little political capital left. The United States needs to take steps to revive its power in a world that is seeing the greatest geopolitical transformation since the collapse of the Soviet Union and the end of the Cold War. Only when this country regains its political capital and moral authority can America ensure its own safety and prosperity. Only by helping other countries to get what they want can the United States get what it needs. As in the past, America will rebound from this difficult post-9/11 period. But given the global threats to U.S. security, it is urgent that America change course. Only a broad approach that addresses these myriad challenges will keep the United States safe and secure, a new approach that we call the prosperity agenda.

The challenge for the next president will not be simply how to best promote a freedom agenda that is narrowly focused on political rights and voting. Rather, it will be how the United States can best advance a broad prosperity agenda at home and abroad. The goals for nations include ensuring physical safety—providing some shield from the effects of war, disaster, and disease—and generating economic opportunity: creating stability, growth, and the promise of a brighter future. In essence, the goal is to help other countries secure decent, prosperous lives for their people. In exchange, the benefits will be a stronger world economy, more global stability, and greater goodwill toward the United States. America will then have the political capital it needs to galvanize the world to address its main threats—the dual challenge of terrorism and deadly weapons. For this book, we interviewed people across America and around the world. And each of them wants the same thing: prosperity. Prosperity means different things to different people, but every human being dreams of decent clothes, rewarding work, a good education, a nice home, access to better technology (or any at all), and more time with his or her loved ones. Most of the obstacles to those dreams in the world's most troubled areas are things the United States is comparatively well equipped to handle: war, disease, economic decline, corruption, and a lack of start-up resources.

Since September 11, 2001, America has been engaged in a debate over its proper role in the world. How do we make Americans safer? As part of the right answer to this question, the United States must make a dramatic shift from the way it has approached its national security in recent years. We must recognize that Bush's narrow "freedom agenda" has undermined our interests in Iraq, Afghanistan, Pakistan, Egypt, and across much of the developing world. We are the most powerful nation on Earth, yet our overreliance on military might has made winning the war on terrorism harder and has alienated large segments of the world. It has also endangered the fighting strength and the military readiness of U.S. ground troops.

Seven years after 9/11, the United States is not yet winning the global battle it cannot afford to lose, and Americans deserve better. Al-Qaeda and Osama bin Laden continue to plot attacks from the rugged terrain along the Afghanistan-Pakistan border. Although President Bush identified radical ideology and extremist Islamism as central problems, his administration took steps that actually increased these dangers. Abroad, the threat posed by global terror groups has morphed and mutated, with terrorists attacking U.S. allies in Britain, Spain, Israel, Jordan, and Indonesia. Global terror networks now have more room to maneuver, as they exploit lawless zones of instability in Iraq, Afghanistan, Lebanon, the Palestinian territories, and Somalia. By mid-2006, three quarters of Americans believed that the world was more dangerous than at any other time in their lives.[3]

Making up for lost time will require a major foreign policy adjustment. Today, there are more members of the nuclear club than there were before President Bush came into office, and more want to join. Democracy is backsliding in Russia and Egypt, but the United States blindly supports both countries' leaders despite their failure to abide by democratic norms. Global warming is increasing unabated, endangering our coastlines, our way of life, and the lives of millions across the world. Infectious diseases also threaten the lives of hundreds of millions of people. On Bush's watch, the average price of a gallon of gasoline has doubled, U.S. budget deficits have spiraled out of control, and the U.S. dollar—the symbol of world confidence in the U.S. economy—is at an all-time low. As President Bush headed into his final year in office, the United States started to feel the effects of his economic mismanagement, with the country slipping into an economic downturn.

Each of these issues is now directly related to U.S. security. If the developing world fails to stem the rise of infectious diseases, deadly viruses could appear in homes across America. If new failed states arise in Africa or Asia, they may well become the next safe havens for terrorists who continue to target America. If we fail to secure stability in Afghanistan and Iraq, the terrorists will keep exploiting the lawless zones that exist in these countries. If we do not do more to rein in the spread of weapons of mass destruction, the next terrorist attack could be vastly more devastating than the one on 9/11. And if we do not wean ourselves off oil obtained from corrupt and unstable sources, we will remain shackled by their interests. The United States has the most powerful military in the world, but it must begin to use other aspects of its considerable powers—economic, diplomatic, and technological—to advance the country's interests, which are increasingly the shared interests of the entire world.

America's own prosperity depends on advancing a broad agenda that promotes a better life for people at home and abroad. At various crossroads in this nation's history, America has understood the need to engage and lead the world in helping to lift people out of poverty. We rebuilt Germany and Japan following World War II because we understood the benefits of a prosperous Europe and Japan and the dangers of faltering ones. We sent Peace Corps volunteers across the globe, certainly to counter the Soviet threat, but also to demonstrate that America understood the basic needs of the world's poor and stood ready to help them. We must start to think that way again, and we need new leadership to show the way.

A Crisis of Confidence in America's Leadership

One major consequence of President Bush's worldview and foreign policy is a growing lack of confidence in America's ability to lead in the world, among the American public and people abroad. A growing number of Americans are concluding that the world is a mess and the United States can't fix it alone. As a result, some are starting to look inward. The United States remains the strongest country in the world, but too many Americans feel as if our country is under siege. At the same time, the world has turned away from America's leadership, with anti-Americanism hitting record highs during President Bush's administration.

For the most part, Americans remain pragmatic about the need to stay involved in the world's affairs. In 2007, fully 86 percent of Americans agreed that "It's best for the future of our country to be active in world affairs"—representing only a slight decline from the start of Bush's presidency, but comparable to the same high levels of support for international engagement that existed during Ronald Reagan's presidency.[4]

But Americans show less confidence in our ability to deal with problems. The percentage of Americans who agree with the statement "As Americans, we can always find a way to solve our problems" dropped from 70 percent in 1999 to 58 percent in 2007.[5] In addition, the American public has increasing doubts about how well the government is conducting foreign policy. From 2005 to 2007, polling shows a double-digit decline in Americans' rating of how well the United States was doing in achieving its most important goals. These goals include hunting down terrorists, meeting U.S. objectives in Iraq and Afghanistan, and bringing peace between Israel and the Palestinians, according to the Confidence in U.S. Foreign Policy Index poll conducted by Daniel Yankelovich at Public Agenda.[6] The good news is that the next American president can turn these downward trends around.

A growing number of Americans are also concerned about the impact of trade and immigration on their lives and economic well-being. The percentage of Americans who think that trade is good for the country has declined nearly 20 points in the last five years, from 78 percent in 2002 to 59 percent in 2007. Support for stronger restrictions on immigration remains strong, with three-quarters of Americans in favor of them.[7] In reaction to the complicated forces of globalization, some Americans are pushing to close U.S. borders and hold back foreign trade and investment. America's economic troubles in 2007 and 2008—including a volatile stock market, the bursting of a real estate price bubble, escalating deficits and the falling dollar have further exacerbated the American public's worries about globalization.

Throughout our history, we have faced similar debates about whether and how the United States should engage in the world, and we have always pulled through. We worked ourselves out of the Great Depression and the isolationist period of the 1930s. We rebounded after World War II, and the Baby Boomer generation made America prosperous. We lifted ourselves up after the 1970s period of malaise and the Vietnam War. And we've learned from our mistakes. It was wrong to retreat from the world after World War I and to imprison Japanese Americans and close our borders to Jews fleeing the Holocaust in World War II. We must not forget those lessons. We must resist the lure of turning inward and maintain confidence in our country's ability to lead.

As Americans debate our role in the world, the world is turning away from U.S. leadership. Global polls show that favorable views of the United States declined significantly from 2002 to 2007. America has seen double-digit declines in favorable opinions among its chief allies, including Britain (from 75 percent in 2002 to 51 percent in 2007) and Germany (from 60 percent to 30 percent). Even in Poland, whose people turned to America for support during their struggle against communism and who have supported U.S. military operations in Iraq, there was an 18-point decline, from 79 percent who said they had a favorable view of America in 2002 to 61 percent in 2007.[8]

In other key parts of the world, the situation is even more dismal. Across most Muslim-majority countries, the United States has much work to do to repair its image. In the first half of this decade, regard for America has not only declined among Muslims but plummeted to staggeringly low overall numbers. Only 9 percent of the people living in Turkey, a strategic NATO ally, had a favorable opinion of the United States in 2007.[9]

People around the world—Muslim-majority countries, most parts of Latin America, and China—consider the United States their *greatest potential threat*. A third of China's citizens see the United States as their greatest threat, as do 64 percent of people in Turkey and Pakistan. Majorities in Venezuela and Argentina also consider the United States a potential threat. Worse still, in one survey of international opinions about the United States, America was named the biggest threat about as often as it was considered a close ally.[10] In addition, strong majorities around the world do not think that the United States considers the interests of countries like theirs, and they also oppose the U.S.-led war on terror.

Why does it matter if the United States has a bad image among growing numbers of people around the world? National security is not a global popularity contest, but how people around the world view America matters much more in the twenty-first century than in previous periods. If countries don't trust us, they will not help us with our priorities. As more countries become democratic, their constituents have more of a say in forming their governments' policies. In today's global media environment, what we do and what we say matters more than ever as people's perceptions of us influence their leaders and have a direct impact on our ability to get those leaders to cooperate with us. President Bush damaged America's credibility in the global arena, but the right leadership can revive America's standing in the world and get others to follow the United States once again.

Reviving American Leadership by Becoming the World's Great Persuader

A crucial reason fewer people in the world trust the United States is that countries do not see America helping them with their interests and addressing common threats. In 2007, citizens around the globe cited crime, political corruption, drugs, infectious disease, and pollution as their top national concerns. Terrorism, the poor quality of drinking water, and conflict were also high on the list.[11] Unless America is seen to be helping with these issues, the world will not help America.

American leaders tend to center U.S. foreign policy entirely on "hard power" security issues such as proliferation and terrorism (and, in all honesty, oil). This is an incomplete approach because much good can be done to benefit our own interests while helping other countries with a global campaign against crime, infectious diseases, and dirty water. The world will not follow the United States unless it is seen to be helping the world address its challenges.

In today's dangerous world, the United States must again become the world's great persuader, not only the enforcer. To do so, America must act in a way that regains the world's trust. The good news is that if it does so, America can quickly regain the political support it has lost around the world.

When America does the right thing, the world notices. For instance, favorable opinions of America in southeast Asia reached record lows during the first year after the United States started the Iraq War. Yet that image began to rebound when America used its military and economic power to help the victims of the 2004 tsunami, which set off tidal waves that wiped out communities across the coastal areas of Indonesia, Thailand, Sri Lanka, India, Malaysia, and parts of Africa. America took the lead in providing military and logistical support, including $350 million in immediate humanitarian relief assistance. (For comparison, the United States spends twice that much money *every day* in Iraq.)

The Bush administration set up a support center in Thailand and sent an aircraft carrier and a navy hospital ship to assist in the efforts. By mid-January 2005, more than 15,000 U.S. troops were providing relief, as were 25 ships and 94 aircraft. President Bush sent his brother Florida governor Jeb Bush and Secretary of State Colin Powell to assess the situation and asked former presidents George H. W. Bush and Bill Clinton to help raise funds. Almost overnight, the United States reversed the tide of anti-Americanism in the region. This is a powerful example of how America can use the full range of its powers to restore its political capital abroad.

The next U.S. president must put forward a new agenda with prosperity at its core. Certainly, there will be times when military force will be necessary. But the United States must use the full range of its strengths. There are no quick fixes to repair the damage that was done over the last seven years. But if we stick to the basics of promoting prosperity, the world will be much more prepared to work with us to counter threats to our own prosperity.

This is why it should matter to America whether Adelard Mivumba's life is ruined by a return to war in the Congo. This is why it matters to America whether the world's poor have no hope of living decent lives and whether global warming destroys people's way of life. This is why it matters whether conflicts in Africa lead to more failed states or Iraq and Afghanistan descend into further chaos. It matters whether people in Ukraine, Nigeria, or Pakistan can choose their own leaders. If we help them address their challenges, they are more likely to help us meet our own.

At their core, all people want the simplest of things. This book offers a way to put the United States on the right side of that global struggle for prosperity and to promote prosperity at home at the same time. We offer a new way to look at U.S. foreign policy and interests. It is no longer viable for the United States to define its interests as winning wars and promoting democracy, although certainly America must still do both of these important things. But now, more than ever, America must lead the struggle for the basics—the essential rights to security, health, and a good life for one's family. By engaging with real people around the world, Americans can demonstrate that we care about their problems—and give them a reason to care about ours in return.

Achieving a healthy democracy ought to be the ultimate goal for every nation, but promoting this can't be the only, or even the most important, aspect of U.S. foreign policy. It's too fragile. Progress that is made toward building a democracy can erode in the blink of an eye when a national crisis looms. Prosperity fuels democracy at the most fundamental level, and not the other way around. The foundations of a society—factors such as good governance, low corruption, and access to basic social services—must be in place before national elections can help deliver prosperity. In the case of both Iraq and Afghanistan, America lost sight of the most urgent challenge: providing the basic tenets of stability. Had we focused on improving the daily lives of citizens in both countries, our task today would be vastly less complicated.

Few can claim that we are winning the so-called war on terror. In some cases, military action will remain the right approach to keeping al-Qaeda on the run. For these hard-core terrorists, no prosperity agenda will change their extreme course. In other cases, Americans will need to do more to address the conflicts that serve as recruiting tools, such as Iraq, the Israeli-Palestinian conflict, and the simmering Kashmir conflict. Yet, the bigger challenge will be to work to improve the lives of the hundreds of millions of people who are disillusioned by the failures of their own governments to provide ways for them to prosper, to let them choose their own leaders, and to allow them to share in their nations' wealth.

We came together to write this book from different perspectives but out of similar concerns about the direction in which our country is heading. Nancy Soderberg served as an ambassador to the United Nations and as the third-ranking official at the National Security Council during the Clinton administration. She also worked on presidential campaigns, in the U.S. Senate, and for the International Crisis Group. Brian Katulis, a senior fellow for national security at the Center for American Progress, has worked in nearly two dozen countries on projects that examined how people viewed global changes that were impacting security and prosperity in their communities. Soderberg saw the dangers arising from America's reluctance to engage the world and the increase in anti-Americanism that is coming at the very time when other countries need to join the United States in a global coalition against terrorists and WMD proliferators. Katulis wanted to investigate how future U.S. leaders can revive America's power and position in the world. Together, we sought to examine the trends and set forth a better path for the United States, one that returns to America's basic values and understands that what happens in the Congo and beyond matters to Americans across the country. By promoting prosperity abroad, Americans will be safer and more prosperous at home. The next president, regardless of political party, should anchor his or her foreign policy in a prosperity agenda.

one

Making Up for Lost Time in Iraq

Army captain Brian Freeman arrived in Iraq in the spring of 2006, joining a civil affairs unit in the dusty city of Karbala, a little more than an hour's drive southwest of Baghdad. He had been working in a civilian job in Southern California when he was called back to active duty in late 2005. A standout high school athlete, Freeman graduated from West Point in 1999. By 2004, he had fulfilled his five-year active duty requirement. He was assigned to the Individual Ready Reserve, a pool of soldiers not assigned to a particular unit, to serve out the remaining two years of his commitment. He and his wife, Charlotte, had started to discuss his life after the military and how best to care for their son, Gunnar, and newborn daughter, Ingrid.

But something troubled Freeman from the time he was called to serve in Iraq. He had been trained to serve in a tank crew and assumed that his assignment in Iraq would draw on that expertise. Instead, the army activated him to serve in a civil affairs unit. Because of the army's growing manpower shortage, exacerbated by extended tours of duty in Iraq and Afghanistan, the

United States was sending troops to a war zone to do jobs that they lacked formal training to perform. Yet Freeman went and did the job, admirably and with passion. As his fellow soldier Captain Matthew Lawton explained, "Brian didn't really agree with the war, I think. But he understood, going to West Point, going to the military—that [his going to Iraq] was the right thing to do."[1]

Freeman hit the ground running shortly after arriving in Karbala, a city of more than half a million people and home to the shrine of the early Shi'a martyr Hussein ibn Ali. Karbala had been relatively quiet since the U.S.-led invasion, but violence flared up between Shi'a militias and coalition forces in March 2006. A few weeks after Freeman arrived in the country, a U.S. Special Forces operation landed helicopters on the roofs of several homes in a poor neighborhood of Karbala, causing serious damage. One of Freeman's earliest jobs was to face the Iraqis whose homes had been damaged by the helicopters. Many of the Iraqis who met him were very angry; they blamed Freeman personally for their plight. One Iraqi man told Freeman, "Through your actions, you are part of the problem. You are destroying my neighborhood, you are destroying our country."[2] As a civil affairs officer, one of Freeman's main jobs was to improve the quality of life for Iraqis.

Freeman understood the key to winning the war long before many in Baghdad's Green Zone or Washington did. After quietly listening to the residents, Freeman promised that he would make sure the problems would get fixed: that their homes would receive repairs and families would be compensated. No one believed him, but day after day, he worked to deliver on his word. "Captain Freeman demonstrated to those people and to me that he understood that this was a 'hearts and mind' fight at its core," said Colin Pascual, who served with Freeman in Iraq.[3] "He knew that helping poor people and people without political influence like those who had their homes damaged was as militarily advantageous to us as negotiating with the leaders of the provincial government. He understood that we were going to win or lose in Iraq based on our interactions with farmers and regular people, as much as with the local government leaders and others with influence." Had U.S. strategy made that goal its priority from the start, its options today would be far better, and more Iraqis and Americans would be alive.

Rather than just checking the box and doing the bare mini-mum, Freeman made sure that the civilian assistance projects had maximum impact on the lives of Iraqis. Managing millions of dollars in road and reconstruction projects, Freeman put a top priority on making the right decisions about where to place these projects to ensure that the broadest number of Iraqis benefited. "I never saw someone take as much interest in where these roads were being paved or these water systems were being installed as Freeman did," said Pascual. "He went all out on these projects because he understood how important it was to the mission—that winning the overall fight hinged on whether we did a good job helping to restore these basic services and helping to raise the standard of living for Iraqis."[4]

He often did this work without strong support from other U.S. government agencies, not even from the people sitting in the Green Zone in Baghdad. Freeman, frustrated with the lack of organization and a bureaucracy that never seemed to get things done, worried about how the overall mission was being managed, so much so that he confronted two U.S. senators on a Baghdad airfield a few days before Christmas 2006. "Senator, it's nuts over here. Soldiers are being asked to do work we're not trained to do," he told Senator Chris Dodd (D-Conn.), who was accompanied by Senator John Kerry (D-Mass.). "I'm doing work that the State Department people are far more prepared to do in fostering democracy, but they're not allowed to come off the bases because it's too dangerous here. It doesn't make any sense."[5] The mission was off track, Freeman told the senators, despite his and other soldiers' best efforts.

In the face of these problems, Freeman continued to go the extra mile. He was determined to make a difference wherever he could. His persistent efforts to help Ali Abdulameer, an eleven-year-old boy with a life-threatening heart condition, became a special mission for him. Doctors in Baghdad and Karbala could not treat Ali, but hospitals in America could. Getting advice on how to work the bureaucratic ropes from soldiers who had helped others, Freeman tracked down a fellow civil affairs officer in the U.S. embassy in Amman, Jordan, who could help Ali get a visa so that he could receive treatment for his condition. Freeman and his wife, Charlotte, worked with charities in the United States to secure funding for the boy and to get all the medical records to the doctors—no easy feat in the midst of a war zone. While at home during the two-week Christmas leave, Freeman continued to keep track of Ali's case and talked to Charlotte about how the experience inspired him to think about public service. He considered starting up a nonprofit organization to help Iraqi children get medical care.

Shortly after returning to Iraq from his holiday leave, Freeman got the good news: Ali's visa had come through and he was heading to America for his operation. Overjoyed, Ali's father thanked Freeman through an interpreter and put his arm around Freeman's shoulders, as they posed together for a photo to celebrate this happy moment. Less than a month later, Ali, accompanied by his father, made it to the United States for his operation at Schneider Children's Hospital in New York. Doctors repaired the hole between the upper chambers of Ali's heart and expected a complete recovery.

Tragically, Captain Freeman did not live to see Ali's successful surgery. Hours after his celebration with Ali's father, Freeman attended a meeting in the provincial governor's office in Karbala to discuss security procedures for an upcoming Shi'a holiday. Just after sunset, a group of armed men disguised in what appeared to be U.S. military uniforms and driving black GMC trucks drove past several Iraqi checkpoints and stormed the building. The attackers set off sound bombs and grenades, killed one U.S. soldier on the scene, handcuffed Freeman and three other soldiers, and sped away. Freeman and the three other soldiers were later found shot dead near the abandoned vehicles miles away.

Ali's surgery was performed the same week that Captain Freeman's widow received her husband's personal effects from Iraq. Charlotte, who had worked with her husband to raise money from friends and family and coordinated with the charities who helped to make Ali's surgery possible, flew to New York to meet Ali and his father, where she gave Ali her husband's hand-held Sony PlayStation. Fighting back tears, Charlotte said to Ali, "This is Brian's, so it's really his gift to you also."[6]

Forgetting the Basics of Stability and Prosperity in Iraq

Captain Freeman did his job. President George W. Bush and his top advisers did not. The Bush administration's management of Iraq from 2003 to 2007 is a textbook case of how *not* to exercise America's considerable power. It shows how the United States can squander its power and credibility, making Americans less safe and ruining the lives of others in the process.

A strategic error of unprecedented proportions, the Iraq War damaged America's reputation around the world, making it more difficult for the country to advance its interests and win over allies. The many U.S. mistakes on the ground after Saddam Hussein's ouster are well known: sending in too few troops, wasting billions of reconstruction dollars, lining the pockets of private U.S. contractors, and hiring political cronies for jobs in the U.S.-led occupation authority.[7] These strategic errors were the direct result of bad decisions made by top leaders.

Whatever one's opinion of the controversial decision to go to war in 2003, the United States did have a narrow window of opportunity to advance stability and prosperity in Iraq immediately after the invasion. The Bush administration squandered the first two years of the war by ignoring the fundamentals that were necessary to make Iraqis more secure and prosperous. In 2005, the Bush administration introduced some adjustments in an attempt to make up for lost time: creating specialized reconstruction teams that focused on local areas and putting more emphasis on diplomatic efforts to help Iraq's leaders resolve their conflicts. But, by 2007, it had become increasingly clear how difficult it would be for the Bush administration to make up for its early mistakes in Iraq.

Individual efforts to help improve the lives of ordinary Iraqis were an essential part of winning popular support and improving the chances for greater stability in the country. Most Iraqis wanted what people around the world want: jobs that paid them enough to feed their families, better schools for their kids, and a chance for a decent life. Early measures of public sentiment in Iraq found that average Iraqis put a priority on the most basic things in their hierarchy of needs. Establishing law and order, getting access to electricity, and creating jobs—these were the top concerns, even above holding elections for a national government.[8] One nation-wide poll of Iraqis in February 2004 found that regaining public security and rebuilding infrastructure outdistanced other priorities by a two-to-one margin.[9] At that early moment, less than a year after the start of the war, two-thirds of Iraqis rated jobs and services like electricity as "bad." When basic needs like these are not met, political opportunists can exploit the situation to foment violence and advance their narrow agendas.

By 2007, the United States had appropriated a total of $34 billion in reconstruction funding for Iraq, including funds for the Iraq Relief and Reconstruction Fund and building up Iraq's security forces.[10] This total sum was about the same amount of money, inflation adjusted, that the United States spent from 1946 to 1952 to rebuild Germany after World War II, and about double what the United States spent in postwar Japan.[11] Yet the progress that had been made in Iraq was nowhere close to that in postwar Germany and Japan. Despite the massive infusion of reconstruction funds by the United States, by late 2007, living conditions for most Iraqis remained dire. In addition to widespread security problems, nearly all Iraqis reported that they still lacked basic services. In a September 2007 poll, nine in ten Iraqis rated the availability of fuel and the supply of electricity as poor. Fully 79 percent gave negative ratings to their job situations, and three-quarters of Iraqis said that clean water was a problem.[12]

These dismal outcomes are the direct result of senior leadership failures to dedicate America's considerable resources to winning the peace. In the early months of the U.S. presence in Iraq, a British official described the Coalition Provisional Authority (CPA) as "the single most chaotic organization I have worked for."[13] Although there were dedicated public servants like Captain Freeman who did incredible things for Iraqis, unfortunately, too many of the individuals who worked in the CPA and served on the provincial reconstruction teams lacked the skills and the capacity to get the job done. One gaping hole was the lack of personnel with the necessary Arabic-language skills. By the end of 2006, out of more than a thousand Americans working in the U.S. Embassy in Baghdad, only six spoke Arabic fluently.[14]

The United States squandered a key opportunity to advance prosperity and stability in Iraq. Some of this was due to incompetence, but much of it had to do with the guiding philosophy of conservatives like President Bush. Although President Bush gave many speeches about the transformative power of freedom and democracy, he did not ensure that his team in Baghdad was doing its best to make life stable and more prosperous for Iraqis. At the time when the Iraqi insurgency was born and started to grow, the top U.S. administrator in Iraq, L. Paul Bremer, seemed more focused on pushing through a neoliberal economic agenda that was reminiscent of the strict "shock therapy" programs implemented by the International Monetary Fund in Russia, Central and Eastern Europe, and Latin America than he was on security. In June 2003, on a flight back to Baghdad from an international economic conference, Bremer talked with so much fervor about the need to privatize government-run factories, according to one journalist, that his voice cut through the noise of the plane's engines in the cargo hold. "We have to move forward quickly with this effort. Getting inefficient state enterprises into private hands is essential for Iraq's economic recovery," Bremer said.[15] Before leaving Iraq in 2004, Bremer pushed through a flat tax and issued decrees lowering tariffs and opening Iraq up to private foreign investment.[16] None of these measures increased the country's security or did much to improve the economic well-being of Iraqis in the near term.

The Bush administration placed more emphasis on political rights than on civil liberties or basic economic rights. Elections installed a dysfunctional government that was incapable of settling fundamental power-sharing disputes among Iraq's factions and was unable to provide security and essential services to ordinary Iraqis.

The administration was woefully unprepared to address the shift in power among the country's ethnic groups that was caused by the ouster of Saddam Hussein. While accurate figures do not exist, Iraq's main factions are roughly divided as Shi'a 60 percent, Sunni 20 percent, and Kurd 20 percent. While all three groups are Muslim, fierce opposition exists between them. Under Saddam Hussein the Sunni minority controlled most of the country's power and wealth. Under the new democracy, that control has largely shifted to the Shi'a majority. Most of the Kurds live in the autonomous northern area. In 2007, Iraq's multiple internal conflicts and campaigns of sectarian cleansing raged, claiming tens of thousands of lives and forcing more than four million Iraqis from their homes.

Despite strategic failures of leadership, there were numerous individual efforts to help improve life for Iraqis. The dominant images of Iraq—the shock-and-awe bombing campaign at the start of the war and the photographs of abused prisoners in Abu Ghraib prison—mask the quieter efforts of ordinary Americans who spent years apart from their families trying to make Iraq more stable and prosperous. These individuals, like Captain Freeman, understood how to win the war far better than Washington did: by improving the lives of average Iraqis. And through innovation and courage, many Americans taking part in the war effort did just that.

In the end, the failures of the senior leadership in the Bush administration undermined many individual contributions and small gains. But in the successes of ordinary Americans on the ground lie important lessons for our country. They show what we must do to regain the upper hand in the struggle against terrorist groups, not only in Iraq, but in places such as Afghanistan and Somalia as well.

Mosul 2003: "What Have You Done to Win Iraqis' Hearts and Minds Today?"

The support of the Iraqi people could have been won had the administration planned to implement on a regional and national scale what Captain Freeman had done one house and one child at a time. Similarly, the actions early in the war of one American general in the Iraqi town of Mosul offer a lesson in how the United States can advance stability and prosperity around the world, if it stays focused on the basics that make America safer.

Shortly after the 2003 invasion, General David Petraeus and his 101st Airborne Division arrived in Mosul, a picturesque city a few hours from Iraq's northwestern border with Syria on the banks of the Tigris River. The third-largest city in Iraq, Mosul was home to a multiethnic population of Arabs, Kurds, Turkomans, and Assyrians. The city's skyline displays Mosul's religious diversity, with a mix of mosque minarets and church steeples reaching skyward. The 101st Airborne Division took control of the city after battling through Iraq's southern cities on the way to Baghdad in the opening weeks of the war. In early April, pro-Saddam forces relinquished their positions in Mosul without much of a fight.

Mosul had a large number of Saddam loyalists, and intelligence analysts warned that radical Islamist groups had set up operations in the region. The 21,000 members of the 101st Airborne Division quickly took positions in Mosul and the surrounding areas to provide security and hunt down former members of Saddam Hussein's regime. Saddam's sons Uday and Qusay were killed in Mosul by these soldiers in July 2003.

The real success story of what the 101st Airborne Division was able to do in those first few months in Mosul did not only involve capturing and killing adversaries; instead, their early success hinged on a commonsense strategy that focused on improving the overall quality of life for Iraqis—establishing law and order, helping to create jobs, and getting services like electricity up and running—just as Captain Freeman had done in Karbala. "This is a race to win the hearts and minds of the Iraqi people," said General Petraeus, "and there are other people in this race, and they are not just trying to beat us to the finish line; in some cases they want to kill us."[17]

A West Point graduate, Petraeus had served in other postconflict stabilization and reconstruction efforts such as Haiti and Bosnia. In Mosul, Petraeus and his troops recognized that security depended not only on eliminating the enemy, but also on making sure that the people of Mosul had a chance to improve their quality of life. As Petraeus put it, "One of the tests we are constantly confronted with is: is life better than it was under Saddam?"[18] Winning over the Iraqi public was considered vital to stabilizing Iraq. "What Have You Done to Win Iraqis' Hearts and Minds Today?" read posters that General Petraeus hung on the walls of his troops' barracks.[19]

What Petraeus did was in stark contrast to the way Washington and Paul Bremer set out to handle the post-Saddam challenge of building a stable society. How Petraeus did it was different, too. He sought to involve the Iraqis in his decision-making process. Rather than issuing decrees as Bremer did from behind the walls of the Green Zone, Petraeus saw that getting buy-in and support from prominent Iraqis living in the city meant that they had a sense of responsibility and ownership in the outcome. As soon as he had set up his headquarters in Mosul, Petraeus began a series of consultations with prominent city leaders to establish local institutions that gave Iraqis opportunities to have a say in making decisions. In these consultations, he met with representatives from various ethnic groups and tribes in Mosul, listening to their concerns and finding solutions to everyday problems. He was part diplomat, part military commander.

In early May 2003, Petraeus invited community leaders— businessmen, judges, religious and tribal leaders—to a caucus to select a city council. This process also led to the selection of a mayor and a governing council for the entire province of Nineveh.

Petraeus organized these local and provincial councils well before Paul Bremer had even arrived in Iraq.[20] The councils became forums for airing community concerns and setting priorities for projects to improve life for Mosul's residents. The councils not only gave Iraqis a sense of respect, they offered Petraeus an important window into the mood on the street.

Petraeus also understood the need to show quick improvements in the daily lives of Iraqis. Rather than waiting for orders and directions to come from the national level, where the CPA was just beginning to form, Petraeus set into motion a comprehensive strategy aimed at making life better in Mosul. Since the race against Iraqi insurgents and terrorist groups was largely about improving the quality of life, job creation and economic development were key aspects of the 101st Airborne Division's approach. By the time the division's tour in Mosul had come to an end in early 2004, it had carried out an estimated 5,000 reconstruction projects worth an estimated $57 million.[21]

To fund these initiatives, General Petraeus dipped into the Commander's Emergency Response Program (CERP), U.S. military money that was used for quick reconstruction projects. Using CERP money, and in consultation with the Iraqi leaders who participated in the local and provincial governing councils, the 101st Airborne Division provided small business loans, funded neighborhood reconstruction projects to fix phone lines and sewers, implemented irrigation projects, and set up employment offices for former Iraqi military officers. The division opened an asphalt plant that had been closed for more than two decades, and it looked for ways to provide jobs and money to Iraqis. The 101st Airborne Division also helped to establish youth soccer leagues around the city, ultimately forming more than a hundred teams.

Petraeus wasn't afraid to innovate and come up with practical solutions to address problems with basic services and the economy. For instance, in an effort to boost Mosul's economy, General Petraeus and his team undertook innovative initiatives, such as working out a deal with Iraqi customs officials and tribal leaders to reopen Iraq's border with Syria by mid-May, in order to jump-start trade. Later, the 101st Airborne Division worked out a deal to trade Iraqi oil for electricity generation with Syria and Turkey. This oil-for-electricity deal helped Mosul avoid some of the blackouts that plagued Baghdad and other major cities in Iraq during the long, hot summer of 2003. Petraeus also seized on the most cost-effective ways to make Iraqis' lives better, by getting them to work and putting money in their pockets. General Petraeus told a congressional delegation visiting northern Iraq in 2003 that U.S. contractors had estimated that it would cost $15 million to get a cement plant up and running. Petraeus instead gave the job to Iraqi contractors, who did the same task for $80,000.[22]

One of the most important steps that the 101st Airborne Division took to employ Iraqis was to hire and rapidly train thousands to serve in the Iraqi Civil Defense Corps, thus providing former Iraqi soldiers with housing, medical care, and salaries. By the fall, General Petraeus said, "We have almost a division's worth of security forces. We've trained five companies of Iraqi Civil Defense Corps."[23] This initial success in establishing local security force units stood in sharp contrast to what was happening at the national level, where the efforts to hire and train a new Iraqi army and police forces floundered under the leadership of former New York City police chief Bernard Kerik. Kerik, a protégé of former New York City mayor Rudy Giuliani, had arrived in Baghdad in May 2003 to serve as the interim minister of interior for Iraq in Paul Bremer's CPA. One of his charges was to help to organize and train the new Iraqi police force, but he was slow at completing the task and stayed only a few months, departing Iraq before the end of 2003.

Petraeus understood the need to focus on the dignity of the Iraqi people. He did his best to make sure that his troops respected Iraqis' rights and abided by the Geneva Conventions, international treaties that were formulated in the first half of the twentieth century to set humanitarian standards for the conduct of war. Legal advisers to the 101st Airborne Division made certain that the actions of the unit complied with the Fourth Geneva Convention in particular, which outlined standards for people who live under an occupation force.[24] The 101st Airborne Division also made reparations to the families of Iraqis who had been killed in firefights involving U.S. troops; by early September 2003, more than $200,000 in reparations had been paid.[25] These reparations, together with the fact that Iraqis could see their lives getting better, probably headed off an escalation of the conflict in Mosul, at least temporarily.

Finally, General Petraeus understood the power of communication and the importance of getting his message to the people. He used the media to communicate with Iraqis and build community ties. The 101st Airborne Division's media strategy was an important part of the campaign to win the hearts and minds of Iraqis in Mosul. The rapid growth of satellite television bombarded Iraqis with conflicting images of what the United States was doing in Iraq, with certain Arab satellite channels, such as Al Jazeera, telling only part of the story and in some cases twisting the facts. Iraqis were experiencing a dramatic media transformation— Saddam's regime had banned all satellite television and had tightly controlled people's access to independent media sources. Rather than just criticizing the reporting of these media outlets, the 101st Airborne Division got its voice in the debate and provided avenues for Iraqis to express themselves and their concerns. General Petraeus himself appeared on radio call-in shows and set up a Mosul television station that he used to film some of the 101st Airborne Division community projects. Colonel Joe Anderson, the commander of the Second Brigade, became something of a celebrity on a local radio program that he hosted on Saturday mornings. He even got a marriage proposal from a love-struck Iraqi woman in the audience one morning.[26]

Perhaps the most famous part of the 101st's media strategy was a popular talent program for Iraqis modeled on *American Idol*, which was launched on the local television channel in early 2004.[27] The program featured Iraqis with a variety of talents: a country and western singer, traditional folkloric dance troupes, and even a comedian who impersonated Saddam Hussein.[28] Mohammed Saleh, a backup singer in the house band that played for all of the musical acts, said, "We needed new faces on television. Under the previous regime you had to pay to be on TV, even if you had talent. This show is wonderful, magnificent. It has encouraged talented people. And others are talking about it."[29] The media strategy was not only for entertainment and letting off steam. The 101st Airborne Division also employed television and radio for public service announcements that directly advanced the mission of making Mosul more prosperous and stable—announcements about basic services such as trash collection and spots promoting respect for the local Iraqi police. All of this was Nation-building 101 in the twenty-first century, with a focus on increasing the prosperity of the Iraqi people.

When edicts from Baghdad prevented Petraeus from implementing his reforms, he was not afraid to challenge Bremer's mistakes. For instance, in the spring of 2003, the CPA administrator

Paul Bremer issued orders banning former members of Saddam Hussein's Baath Party from returning to their government posts, effectively firing tens of thousands of Iraqis just when their expertise was most needed. This order hit the professional class of Mosul hard, including more than a hundred professors who had worked at the university—many of whom claimed that they had been forced to join the party under the Hussein regime to get a job. Without these professors, the university would have been forced to shut down. The commanders of the 101st Airborne Division intervened, persuading Bremer to make an exception to this ban and allow the professors to continue their jobs.[30]

Certainly, Petraeus made his own share of mistakes. For instance, his effort to reintegrate Baathists into the new provincial government was not seamless. This was a delicate process that required making sure that those with blood on their hands from the era of Saddam Hussein's brutal rule were held accountable and not brought back into power, while at the same time recognizing that many Iraqis had joined the Baath Party simply to get a job. Reintegration of Baathist elements required judgment calls, often made without sufficient intelligence and background on the individuals involved. Critics of General Petraeus and his time in Mosul cite his appointment of Mohammed Kheiri Barhawi as the chief of police. Barhawi, a former general in the Baathist regime, fled Mosul in the fall of 2004 after his police force collapsed in the face of a growing insurgency. Kurdish troops later arrested him carrying $600,000 in cash, under suspicion of collaborating with insurgent groups.[31]

But overall, General Petraeus and the 101st Airborne Division developed a strategy that was in sharp contrast to the bureaucratic bungling and corruption that took place inside Baghdad's Green Zone, and this strategy kept Mosul calm for the first six months after the invasion. By putting more emphasis on Iraqis' basic needs, the 101st was able to temporarily stabilize part of the country. Eventually, however, the Bush administration's broader strategic mistakes undermined their progress, and the country spiraled into a civil war.

By the spring of 2004, U.S.-led coalition forces were fighting major battles in Fallujah in western Iraq and in the southern Iraqi city of Najaf. The tide of violence began to engulf Mosul, too. It was no longer possible for Petraeus to pursue simple but important strategies such as letting his soldiers get out of their armored vehicles and lead foot patrols through the city's neighborhoods to send a signal that they were there to keep people safe. Now, there were simply too few troops to stem the spread of violence, and too much information was lost in the rotations of troops, so that lessons had to be relearned every twelve months.

General Petraeus would return to Iraq two more times. From 2004 to 2005, he led efforts to train Iraq's security forces in Baghdad. In 2007, he returned as the top U.S. commander in Iraq, after spending a year at Fort Leavenworth, Kansas, rewriting the military's counterinsurgency manual to update long-standing military doctrine to reflect lessons learned from the first few years of the war in Iraq and from broader battles against global terror groups.[32] Petraeus's innovative thinking and techniques contributed to declines in the overall levels of violence, but Iraqis remain bitterly divided over the core questions of how to share power peacefully.

In addition, Petraeus was handicapped by strains on U.S. ground forces that were stretched thin by extended deployments. Although the first chapter of his counterinsurgency manual called for a "force ratio" of 25 soldiers per 1,000 residents, even with the additional troops provided by Bush's so-called surge of U.S. troops in 2007, force levels were about half to two-thirds of what Petraeus's manual said was necessary to stabilize Baghdad. As in Mosul in 2003, he was doing the best he could with a flawed strategy formulated by his civilian superiors in Washington. The sins of omission and commission in the opening months of the post–invasion of Iraq had led to numerous problems, including a vicious struggle for power among various Iraqi factions, that did not have an easy military solution. The failure to focus on the basics of Iraqi security and prosperity from the outset continues to haunt U.S. efforts in Iraq.

Failed Nation-Building: Mismanagement and Corruption in Iraq

From 2005 to 2008, America's efforts in Iraq were largely attempts to correct the strategic mistakes made in the first year of the Iraq occupation and to address the fact that the overthrow of Saddam Hussein and ouster of the Sunni Baathist regime flipped the power balance in Iraq from the Sunnis to the Shi'as. The suddenly disempowered Sunnis and the newly empowered neighboring Shi'a Iran helped create the conditions behind much of the violence. However, the course adjustments to address these cataclysmic changes were little more than half-measures. President Bush failed to shore up slipping American public support for the war or marshal the full range of U.S. powers to stabilize Iraq. His misjudgments ironically contributed to the conditions that created the very terrorist havens and training grounds he warned would result if U.S. troops departed Iraq too soon.

When mistakes are made at such an early stage of the conflict, security vacuums emerge, and the genie of sectarian and ethnic rivalries comes rushing out of the bottle to fill them. Top Bush administration officials realized too late that nation-building cannot be separated from winning wars.

Nation-building and putting Iraqis' quality of life front and center emerged as central themes in the strategies the Bush administration put forward for Iraq from 2005 to 2008, at least rhetorically. President Bush put a stronger emphasis on job creation and local reconstruction in his "National Strategy for Victory in Iraq," which was introduced in the fall of 2005, and in a later version of his Iraq strategy in January 2007. In many ways, this shift in emphasis at the presidential level reflected at least a verbal commitment to truly putting Iraq reconstruction efforts at the core of the U.S. strategy. The problem remained, however, as it did with so many other Bush national security initiatives, that words were not followed up by actions. President Bush had the right instincts in talking about his policies, but the plans fell apart because of exceptionally poor execution.

A tactical measure borrowed from Afghanistan was the insertion of provincial reconstruction teams, or PRTs. PRTs are small teams ranging from sixty to ninety economic, political, legal, and civil-military affairs experts that are based throughout the country to work with Iraqis in developing institutions and implementing reconstruction and development projects. Some policy experts debate whether PRTs are a good model for sustainable development and are concerned that it blurs the line between aid efforts and military operations, thus putting aid workers at risk. But in certain parts of Afghanistan and Iraq, PRTs have helped to make life better by providing much-needed technical assistance and advice on economic development and governance. They can be a useful tool if they are part of an overall integrated strategy aimed at making life more secure and prosperous for the broader population.

The story of the provincial reconstruction teams in Iraq, however, has been one in which the PRT model has not been able to rise above the Bush administration's record of mismanagement. The instinct was correct—use American resources to give a boost to Iraq's reconstruction and economy and to make life better for Iraqis—but the execution was flawed.

It is puzzling that it took the Bush administration more than two and a half years to introduce a nationwide effort that General Petraeus had essentially developed within months in 2003 for Mosul. But in November 2005, Secretary of State Condoleezza Rice flew to Mosul to inaugurate a new PRT for Nineveh province.

The State Department initially announced that sixteen PRTs would be established: one for each of Iraq's eighteen provinces, with the three Kurdish provinces sharing one PRT.[33] There were serious delays, however, in implementing the PRTs. By the spring of 2006, nearly half a year after Secretary Rice had announced the PRTs, only three out of the sixteen teams had been staffed and sent into the field.[34]

A key reason for the delay was a disagreement between State and Pentagon officials over whether the PRTs would be protected by U.S. troops or by private security contractors. After months of this dispute, the two departments came to an agreement over the arrangements: the U.S. military would provide protection to the PRTs. The bureaucratic delay came at a critical moment in Iraq's reconstruction and transition in 2006, as a political stalemate at the national level ensued and security deteriorated throughout the country. The absence of presidential leadership in resolving these bureaucratic squabbles resulted in more time lost on the ground in Iraq as the situation spiraled out of control.

Another reason for the delay in implementation was the difficulty the State Department had in finding qualified professionals to fill the positions. Unlike the military, the State Department did not have a ready reserve of individuals to deploy who had the right skills—in this case, Arabic language fluency, postconflict reconstruction expertise, and an understanding of the political dynamics in Iraq. In addition, unlike the Pentagon, the State Department could not order its Foreign Service officers to leave for the war zone in Iraq at a moment's notice.

Secretary of State Rice had introduced a new strategy of "Transformational Diplomacy," which was ostensibly aimed at getting career employees out into the field in tougher environments like Iraq, but the wheels of bureaucracy turned slowly. For example, in Diyala province northeast of Baghdad, the U.S. government hired a Pakistani citizen who had never lived or worked in a democracy before to fill the position that was responsible for advancing democracy.[35] When President Bush announced a policy shift in Iraq in January 2007, attention was focused on the increase of troops, but less noticed was the call to add nearly 400 experts for PRTs, representing nearly four times as many specialists as were recruited and placed into the field in 2005 and 2006.[36] With the difficulties that the Bush administration had in hiring and introducing the PRTs, many skeptics raised concerns about the Bush administration's ability to implement the plan it had outlined. But by mid-2007, four years into the war, 410 PRT personnel were on the ground in Iraq, with plans to send another 200 under way.[37]

By the end of 2007, an independent auditor examined the PRT program and found that PRTs had made incremental progress in certain parts of Iraq, helping to develop local governments' abilities to create plans and manage reconstruction projects. But overall, the violence and the sectarianism prevented major gains in nearly every one of the country's provinces.[38]

The provincial reconstruction teams were only one part of a broader story of the failed efforts to get Iraq's reconstruction on track. The heavy reliance on private contractors and the associated waste and corruption also undermined the overall reconstruction effort in Iraq. The Special Inspector General for Iraq Reconstruction, or SIGIR, an independent oversight body created by Congress as a watchdog for fraud, waste, and abuse of Iraq reconstruction funds, conducted hundreds of audits and project assessments that uncovered widespread mismanagement and corruption on a large scale.

SIGIR found that only 6 of 150 planned primary health-care centers that were supposed to be constructed by the private contractor Parsons had been completed, and Parsons would ultimately end up completing only 14 more. Most of the remaining centers were only completed once U.S. reconstruction officials decided to shift the contracts to Iraqi firms.[39] Another egregious case was the Iraqi Police College in Baghdad. A $75 million project to build the new police academy failed miserably, as faulty construction caused sewage to leak between floors and threaten the structural stability of the facility. This failure necessitated a complete reconstruction.

Corruption, already endemic in Iraq under Saddam Hussein, increased in Iraq's new lawlessness and severely impeded American and Iraqi reconstruction and security efforts. As of mid-2007, there were seventy-three separate criminal investigations into more than $5 billion in contract fraud by U.S. military personnel and civilians in Iraq, Afghanistan, and Kuwait. The disappearance of thousands of U.S.-supplied weapons was under investigation. So far, twenty civilians and military personnel have been indicted as a result of these inquiries, with more investigations under way.[40]

The billions lost to waste and corruption, along with the mismanagement of key projects such as PRTs, opened the door to increased instability. By not directly helping Iraqis to improve their lives, the United States made the arguments and the criticisms of insurgents and other opponents more appealing to Iraqis. Throughout the reconstruction efforts, some leaders in the Bush administration seemed to have the right instincts: in their speeches and press releases, they acknowledged the central importance of advancing prosperity and stability. But actions speak louder than words, and the Bush administration never fully delivered on its promises regarding Iraq's reconstruction. The United States had quite simply dug itself into too deep a hole by failing in the immediate aftermath of the invasion.

Next Steps in Iraq: Salvaging Stability and Helping Iraqis to Obtain Better Lives

The United States will be dealing with the aftershocks of the mistakes made in Iraq for years to come. The simple truth is that there are no good options left today in Iraq. President Bush remains convinced that decades from now, history will show that Iraq is better off for the U.S. invasion. But at what cost in terms of blood and treasure?

The next president will have to choose between options that all have negative consequences for America, Iraq, and the region. It is now a damage-control operation to salvage U.S. interests. Only after the Republicans lost control of Congress in November 2006 was President Bush forced to admit that his policy had not succeeded and to accept the need for a new course in Iraq. Yet for more than a year he rejected the recommendations of the bipartisan Baker-Hamilton Iraq Study Group report to reinvigorate Middle East diplomacy and revive a search for peace between the Israelis and the Palestinians. Instead, he shunned diplomacy and forged ahead with a plan to send thousands of additional U.S. troops to Iraq. Announced in January 2007, this "surge" of U.S. forces was intended to provide a modicum of security to enable Iraq's national political leadership to make the difficult compromises that were necessary to reconcile Iraq's warring ethno-sectarian groups. The additional troops did, of course, help quell some of the violence during their presence, especially in Baghdad. However, the leadership failed to take advantage of that window, although a shift in strategy on the part of a number of Sunni tribal groups and a decision by a leading Shi'a militia to implement a ceasefire helped to reduce tensions in 2007. The question remains whether the Iraqis will make the political progress necessary to establish stability and security.

The first U.S. troops attached to the surge arrived soon after President Bush's speech, and General David Petraeus was sent to implement the new strategy in February 2007. As more U.S. soldiers flowed into Iraq over the next few months, Petraeus changed U.S. tactics. Troops moved out of large forward operating bases and into smaller outposts in Baghdad neighborhoods. Since the fall of 2006, Sunni Arab tribes had begun to turn away from the insurgency. Petraeus moved to capitalize on that change and worked with insurgent groups alienated by al-Qaeda in Iraq's brutal methods. More PRTs were ordered to build local economic and governance capacity. Violence remained high but declined from its late-2006 peak, and sectarian violence began to subside as neighborhoods became more and more homogeneous as a result of population displacement.

Despite the local gains brought about by new tactical alliances, the Iraqi political situation continued to deteriorate throughout 2007. By September, the U.S. Government Accountability Office assessed that the Iraqi government had met only seven of eighteen political, economic, and security benchmarks set forth by Congress, and only three of those were met completely. It became very clear that the government of Prime Minister Nouri al-Maliki was incapable of forging the political consensus necessary for progress. The main Sunni Arab parliamentary bloc withdrew over the summer. Disputes over the fundamental identity of the Iraqi state continued to grind away. Despite the sacrifices of U.S. troops, Iraq was still frighteningly far from national reconciliation at the end of 2007 than it had been at the beginning.

More than five years after the United States ousted Saddam Hussein, Iraq remains bitterly divided by multiple internal struggles for power, and a new type of instability has emerged in the Middle East: regional tensions between Sunni and Shi'a Muslims and between Arabs and Persians in Iran. One consequence of the

Bush administration's Iraq War was to alter the regional power balances, leading to a historic increase in Iran's influence. Iraq, a Shi'a-majority country that lived for decades under the repressive Sunni rule of Saddam Hussein, saw the shift of its internal power balances put its neighbors on the defensive. Jordan's King Abdullah spoke forebodingly of a "Shi'a crescent" emerging in the Middle East, and Gulf Arab countries pushed for billions of dollars in new weapons systems to defend against Iran, a Shi'a Muslim country. In this complicated mix of tensions and violence, there are no good options, but the United States can start to improve its position by going back to basics: by focusing on steps to make life better for people in the region and honor the sacrifices and the service of Americans who implemented Bush's flawed Iraq strategy.

Despite the best efforts of individuals like Captain Brian Freeman and General David Petraeus, the U.S. government was never able to orient its overall strategy toward making life better for the Iraqi people. For every individual example of public servants who were doing the best they could to make sure that resources were being delivered to the Iraqi people, there were also instances of major fraud and abuse, particularly with private contracting companies that were not held accountable by government agencies.

The American experience in Iraq from 2003 to 2008 offers many lessons of where we should go from here. These lessons can help the United States to improve the way it protects its national security by dedicating more resources to saving lives, creating opportunities for people at home and abroad, and giving more people a greater chance for a decent existence. This will require a fundamental shift in how the United States looks at threats in the world and matches its resources to meet those threats. There is a growing consensus among policy experts that the United States needs to dedicate more resources to "winning the peace"—to ensure that in postconflict stabilization efforts, the United States makes use of its considerable power to improve the lives of others. This means that people must be able to "see" the United States working to help them.

How the United States extricates its troops from Iraq will impact its broader efforts to restore its position of leadership in the world.

The pace and manner in which it does so will be one of the most important decisions of the next president and Congress. The capabilities of the Iraqi police and security forces will play a major role in that decision, as will their allegiances and motivation. However, removing troops from Iraq should be only one part of the debate. The United States also needs to determine how it will marshal its considerable economic and diplomatic powers to get Iraqi leaders, countries in the region, and other global powers to do their share and shoulder a greater part of the burden to help Iraq achieve a degree of stability and a semblance of prosperity. America's military readiness has been harmed by five years of continuous deployments, and its image is in tatters as a result of mistakes made in the Iraq War. A growing bipartisan consensus has pragmatically recognized that the United States cannot afford to simply stay the course and continue to go it mostly alone in Iraq.

The level of resources that the Bush administration dedicated to the Iraq effort did not match the high stakes and the dire warnings that it featured in speech after speech making the case for continued patience and support from the American public. Again, actions did not match rhetoric, and the result of this lack of follow-through and commitment was disastrous. At long last, the United States must change course.

STOP: Making U.S. troops shoulder the burdens of Iraq. The time is long past to begin a phased redeployment of U.S. troops. While some continued U.S. presence may be necessary to fight al-Qaeda and train Iraqi security forces that are loyal to the Iraqi state, U.S. troops should no longer be fighting Iraq's civil war. The all-volunteer U.S. military has suffered the effects of more than five years of a continuous deployment of more than 100,000 ground troops in Iraq. More than 4,000 troops have died. Sending troops for their second and third deployments has strained the national guard and the reserves, undermined overall military readiness, and put great stress on soldiers and their families. The so-called coalition of the willing, once numbering more than 50,000, has dwindled to under 15,000 by the end of 2007. U.S. forces make up more than 90 percent of the foreign military forces inside Iraq, not including the tens of thousands of foreign private security contractors. Iraq's government decides that it needs further outside military assistance, the United States should use its leadership to help Iraq get support from other countries. Numerous countries have extended offers to send forces to Iraq, including Muslim-majority countries such as Indonesia and Pakistan.

START: Honoring the sacrifices of the troops and their families with the support they deserve. Nearly 30,000 American troops have suffered serious injuries in Iraq; advances in medical technologies have helped thousands to survive injuries that were deadly in previous wars. Untold thousands more are suffering from posttraumatic stress disorders, including mental and psychological problems that directly result from their combat service. In early 2007, poor conditions and treatment of recovering soldiers at Walter Reed Army Medical Center led President Bush to appoint an independent commission that recommended broad changes, which include establishing a national system of caseworkers to help wounded troops, as well as revamping the disability system. The U.S. government needs to do a better job of helping all returning troops by giving them and their families the medical care and the economic assistance they need to reintegrate into society after serving in a war zone.

STOP: Closing America's doors to Iraqi refugees. One urgent and growing crisis the United States and the international community must address concerns Iraq's millions of refugees and internally displaced persons. It is the worst refugee crisis in the region since 1948. By the end of 2007, more than 4 million Iraqis had fled their homes in the chaos following the U.S. invasion. The United States, a nation founded by immigrants, had set a goal of taking in only 7,000 Iraqi refugees in the fiscal year that ended in September 2007. Because of mismanagement and bureaucratic delays, it didn't even make that goal, instead taking in only 1,608 in 2007. That is simply un-American. After the collapse of Saigon, more than 100,000 Vietnamese refugees were resettled in the United States without much difficulty. There is no reason Iraqi refugees, especially Iraqis who have worked with us, should not be accorded the same treatment.

START: Taking America's fair share of people displaced by the war. The United States should lead by example. Rather than accepting a paltry 7,000 Iraqi refugees a year, the United States should dramatically increase the number. America has a moral obligation to these people and must do far more than its current weak efforts to assist them. International organizations such as the UN High Commission on Refugees and the International Organization on Migration should be given greater levels of assistance to help them cope with Iraqi refugees. The United States must work with countries that have the highest concentrations of Iraqi refugees—Jordan and Syria—to ensure not only that these Iraqis receive humane treatment, but also that they do not create internal or external conflicts now or in the future. In order to be effective, we must work with regional actors and international institutions to cope with the horrendous human consequences of the violence in Iraq. If the United States leads within a comprehensive framework on the refugee issue, other countries will follow.

STOP: Reinventing the wheel on reconstruction and economic development. In Iraq, the Bush administration rejected many good lessons from the nation-building efforts of the 1990s, even shunning the career officials who have the most experience in that task. We must build on those lessons and get others to help the Iraqi government stand on its own by fulfilling donor and debt relief pledges and helping to mediate a resolution to Iraq's internal conflicts. We should not try to shoulder the burden alone of improving the lives of ordinary people in postconflict situations. In the first four years in Iraq, the Bush administration sought to maintain tight control over postwar reconstruction, ignoring a crucial lesson from the U.S. experiences in Bosnia and

Kosovo: that internationalizing the effort is a key to success. This sometimes requires tough diplomacy, but to achieve maximum success, such a strategy is essential.

START: Improving the quality of life for Iraqis. A focus on quick projects that have a high impact on Iraqis' well-being, such as wells, schools, and sewers, will demonstrate progress in action. The United States should attempt to internationalize the PRT model as it has done in the northern city of Irbil, where a multinational regional reconstruction team has been implementing projects aimed at building institutions and helping to improve quality of life. As Iraqis see tangible results from economic development and political progress, they will be less likely to rely on militias and other violent nonstate actors for basic state services. Increased international and regional engagement will be necessary to ensure that these tangible results emerge. The United States must make sure that these reconstruction efforts do not drift into gigantic projects with little or no short-term impact. Making life better for Iraqis in the wake of a political agreement will be the key to ensuring that such an agreement will last.

STOP: Thinking Iraq's police and military can achieve U.S. goals for Iraq. A program of more than five years of U.S. training and arming of Iraq's national security forces has yielded uneven results, in large part because of the Bush administration's strategic error in disbanding the Iraqi Army in 2003. Certainly, a strong Iraqi security force will be critical to ensuring stability once U.S. forces depart, but success will require military forces who are not only trained and equipped but who are also loyal to the national government.

START: Building a new program for supporting Iraq's security forces while advancing national reconciliation. Ethnic and sectarian divisions that have deadlocked Iraq's political transition have also presented serious challenges to building unified security forces that demonstrate strong allegiance to the Iraqi state. Any future U.S. security assistance should be conditioned on progress toward building more unified and coherent governing authorities at the national, provincial, and local levels. U.S. policymakers should examine the international and multilateral initiatives already functioning in Iraq. For instance, the North Atlantic Treaty Organization has provided training and mentoring for middle- and senior-level personnel from Iraq's security forces since 2004, helping build a new corps of commanders and officers in the Iraqi security forces. At the same time, as the United States shifts more of its focus to developing provincial and local capacity, and boosting the ability of police forces with oversight from those provincial and local governing authorities around Iraq, it should examine the International Law Enforcement Academies (ILEA) network started by the United States in 1995 to combat international terrorism, drug trafficking, and crime. The focus of the ILEA network is to support regional and local criminal justice institution building and law enforcement—something that is still lacking in many parts of Iraq today. It is important, however, to remember that no amount of training will succeed until the internal divisions over power sharing are resolved.

STOP: Looking for a military solution to Iraq's internal conflicts. Although violence in Iraq has declined from the high levels of 2006, the situation remains in crisis. Most of the violence in Iraq results from a vicious struggle for power among different Iraqi sectarian and ethnic groups, as well as escalating intrasectarian power struggles between political factions. The war in Iraq inexorably altered Iraq's internal power balances, removing Iraqi Sunnis from leadership and lifting Iraq's Shi'a majority into power. Although President Bush usually characterized the security challenge in Iraq as the central front in the war on terror, the simple fact of the matter is that most of the violence is Iraqi-on-Iraqi violence. During the five years of the war, U.S. intelligence agencies estimated that foreign fighters who are linked to global terror groups represent only a small fraction of the security challenge in Iraq. To build the basic foundation of security, the United States and other outside actors should listen to the military commanders on the ground, who emphasize that there is no military solution to Iraq's multiple internal conflicts—a stable Iraq requires a political settlement among the country's power brokers.

START: Achieving a political settlement to Iraq's conflicts. President Bush's 2007 military escalation was not accompanied by a similar diplomatic surge to get Iraq's leaders to settle their disputes over sharing power. For the last five years, Iraq's leaders have been debating the same issues over what Iraq is and should be, leaving aside fundamental questions about how to structure the post-Saddam system of government and other unresolved problems in the current constitution. As with most power disputes around the world, two central issues are who controls the guns and the money—which groups have a monopoly on the use of violence inside a country and how resources are distributed. Two elections and a rushed constitutional referendum in 2005 resulted in a dysfunctional political process and institutions that have left the core issues of power-sharing unresolved.

To jump-start Iraq's moribund political transition and national reconciliation, the United States must work with other global powers and neighboring countries to provide support for an emergency and inclusive constitutional convention among the Iraqi factions that is aimed at resolving these questions. Intensified diplomatic efforts require engaging Iraq's neighbors—something that the Bush administration avoided with Iran and Syria in the first three years of U.S. presence in Iraq. One key to progress in Iraq lies in its oil wealth, and the international community should work to help Iraq's warring factions settle their differences on the full range of power-sharing issues, including how to distribute its considerable oil reserves. With the second-largest oil reserves in the world, Iraq has great potential for making the lives of its people better, but only if Iraq's leaders reach a consensus on the core questions of how to share power and resources.

Going forward, the key American goal must be to move toward a political settlement that will provide lasting security. Then the United States will be able to declare victory. Given the interests of the nations in the region, we cannot unilaterally hammer out a political settlement in Iraq. Therefore, we should try to internationalize the effort to bring about political progress in Iraq. Since the United States has empowered the Shi'as and strengthened Iran, some diplomatic engagement with Iran will be necessary to limit Iran's destabilizing actions in Iraq.

STOP: Ignoring the regional dimensions to Iraq's problem. In many ways, Iraq's internal conflict has elevated regional divisions between Sunni and Shi'a Muslims and between Arabs and Persians. All of Iraq's neighbors have a clear stake in its outcome, and they will seek to assert their interests, no matter what. It is more effective to have these countries inside the tent, as difficult as that process may be, rather than stirring trouble outside it. The U.S. refusal to more actively engage Iraq's neighbors and the policy of threatening regime change in Iran have hampered efforts to advance security. As a result, antagonists of America, such as Iran and Syria, see no downside to continuing their destructive interference in Iraq, and U.S. allies like Saudi Arabia and Turkey remain on the sidelines as they perceive their own interests to be ignored by the United States.

START: Taking steps to stabilize Iraq and the Middle East through long-term international diplomacy. Iraq's problems reflect broader challenges in overall regional security dynamics, and the conservative approach to addressing Middle East security threats has undermined America's security interests and leverage in this crucial part of the world. In 2003, President Bush and his top supporters argued that the road to peace in Jerusalem ran through Baghdad: that Middle East stability would be achieved by toppling Saddam Hussein's regime. The notion was that a democratic tsunami would topple Middle Eastern dictators and autocrats who were state sponsors of terror, and freedom would defeat terrorism.

Five years later, it is clear that the exact opposite has happened: the terrorist threat remains strong in the region, Middle Eastern autocrats are more deeply entrenched in power, and the region is no more stable. The next U.S. president will have to focus considerable attention on picking up the pieces from President Bush's flawed approach to the Middle East through intensified and sustained diplomatic engagement of the sort suggested by the bipartisan Iraq Study Group. This means a renewed diplomatic effort to achieve peace between Israel and the Palestinians. The broader goal of this strategic shift is to change perceptions about the United States throughout the region—to convert widespread perceptions that the United States simply wants to dominate and occupy countries into a more constructive image that the United States is a partner for greater stability and prosperity in the region.

The sacrifices of people like Captain Brian Freeman serve as a poignant reminder of how individuals, working against all odds and trying to implement a policy without having the necessary support and resources from Washington, can still accomplish amazing things. But the strategic errors made by top officials in Washington remind us that it is simply not enough for leaders to outline policies in speeches; they need to follow up with hard work and perseverance to ensure that people risking their lives to serve their country have full access to our nation's considerable resources. Five years after the United States invaded Iraq, it is clear that our country has not met its potential—not because of a lack of service and sacrifice, but because of a failure of leadership in Washington.

two

The Centerpiece of the Battle against Terrorism

"T his country is in an absolute mess," complained thirty-four-year-old Adil of Pakistan in August 2007. "Contrary to the lies spewed forth by the current regime about Pakistan being transformed into an idyll of prosperity, the cold facts are that more people than ever before are living below the poverty line, that unemployment has increased, and that inflation has hit the roof." Adil is a lawyer living in Islamabad who makes a respectable living but worries about the future of his country. Fearing for his own safety, he did not want us to use his last name.[1]

Pakistan has become the world's most dangerous country. As one terrorism expert put it, "All of the transnational problems that threaten global peace and security come together in Pakistan: proliferation of weapons of mass destruction, terrorism, poverty, and narcotics."[2] Pakistan has fought four wars with its neighbor India, has sold nuclear technology to North Korea, Iran, and Libya, and has acquired its own nuclear bomb from stolen technology. Osama bin

45

Laden and the rest of the al-Qaeda leadership are believed to be hiding in Pakistan's border regions. Most of the recent attacks and terror plots in Europe have direct links to the al-Qaeda leaders and training camps in Pakistan.

Pakistan's nuclear arsenal means the stakes could not be higher. Although unlikely, a radical Islamist government could come to power, seizing the nuclear arsenal. Al-Qaeda sympathizers in the military could help terrorists secure a nuclear weapon or the makings of a dirty bomb. In short, Pakistan presents serious dangers on every front, and preserving U.S. security will require progress in engaging with and stabilizing this nation.[3]

The U.S. approach to Pakistan since 9/11 has focused almost exclusively on military operations along the Afghanistan-Pakistan border and on rounding up al-Qaeda operatives within the country. As Adil said, the United States "continues to prop up antidemocratic forces in Pakistan in the name of its own 'war on terror.' . . . The Americans only pay lip service to resolving the real reasons behind Pakistan's drift toward extremism, namely, poverty, illiteracy, and extended periods of unlawful military rule. If the United States is to succeed in its fight against terrorism, it must adequately address the political, economic, and societal imbalances that push people toward using terrorism as a tactic to correct those imbalances."[4] He is absolutely correct.

The fundamental challenge in Pakistan is much broader than defeating al-Qaeda. With democracy at risk, attacks from radical Islamists on the rise, and people frustrated with the lack of progress in their own lives, terrorists can find fertile ground there for support and new recruits. The challenge of promoting prosperity across Pakistan offers important insights into how the United States can make significant progress in the broader war against terrorism.

Since the end of the Cold War, the United States and Pakistan have had a difficult relationship. America responded to Pakistan's first nuclear forays by cutting off arms sales and military assistance and ending exchange programs with Pakistani military officers. After Pakistan's successful nuclear tests in 1998, the United States imposed substantial economic sanctions. President Bill Clinton pressed Pakistani president Pervez Musharraf hard to end his country's support of the Taliban and even took a risky trip to Pakistan in 2000. Musharraf turned Clinton down.

The Pakistani leader's position changed after the attacks on September 11, 2001. Throughout the subsequent U.S. invasion of Afghanistan, Musharraf allowed the United States to fly sorties from the south over its airspace, and permitted U.S. troops to use selected military bases for nonoffensive operations. He also provided force protection for U.S. troops in the Indian Ocean, logistical support for the U.S. war effort, and access to intelligence assets in Afghanistan and Pakistan. Musharraf also deployed forces to the western border in a largely unsuccessful effort to cut off al-Qaeda and Taliban fighters as they retreated into Pakistan.[5] In return, President George W. Bush began a reengagement with Islamabad. He waived the sanctions that were still in effect from Pakistan's nuclear tests, began to provide aid, and forgave $2 billion of Pakistan's substantial foreign debt. Over the last five years, the United States has given Pakistan more than $10 billion in military, economic, and development assistance and probably as much, if not more, in covert military and intelligence funds.

Yet the United States has largely ignored the fundamental ills of Pakistani society. President Bush fell into the trap of seeing a false choice between fighting terrorism and standing up to President Musharraf's repressive, undemocratic actions. We need to do both. It's common to think that we can either work with a regime or against it. We created a similar false choice during the Cold War when we assumed we had to choose between fighting communism and opposing dictatorships. In both cases, American security suffered.

The truth is, the United States can work to make the lives of normal Pakistanis better right now while continuing to fight terrorist groups and in a way that makes a future stable democracy more likely. Allowing people to hope for a better life doesn't require us to endorse a regime or vow to end it. But it will help to prevent more al-Qaeda recruits.

Pervez Musharraf is the latest in a long string of Pakistani leaders who have not been ideal allies to the United States.

Musharraf took control of the government in a coup in 1999 and then appointed himself president in 2001. He bypassed the regular method of presidential election by engineering a 2002 referendum that confirmed him as president for a five-year term. In 2007, he was reelected by methods that many viewed as unconstitutional.

While securing his power, Musharraf failed to adequately address the terrorist threat. There are long-standing ties between militant movements and the Pakistani army and Pakistan's Directorate for Inter-Services Intelligence (ISI), which is believed to still be providing some support to Afghanistan's insurgent groups. To help consolidate his own power, Musharraf made a deal in 2006 with tribal leaders in North Waziristan, which virtually freed the area from Pakistani government control. In exchange, the tribal leaders agreed to stop attacks into Afghanistan and against Pakistani troops. It is in this region, the Federally Administered Tribal Areas (FATA), that Osama bin Laden is believed to have found a new safe haven.[6] Intelligence officials assert that bin Laden's deputy, Ayman al-Zawahiri, and other principal members of al-Qaeda operate freely from these areas.

From that perch in Pakistan, al-Qaeda has vastly improved its communications. It sent out a record seventy-four videos to the international media in the first nine months of 2007, an average of three a day.[7] Since 2000, al-Qaeda has run its own media production company, al Sahab, or "the clouds" in Arabic (after Afghanistan's misty mountains). Thus, it no longer needs to risk sending runners to deliver videotapes but rather can use an anonymous global network of webmasters to cover its electronic tracks.[8]

In addition to a mixed record as an ally in the war on terror, Pakistan has a weak democracy. In recent years, prodemocratic forces in the country have begun to fight back. In March 2007, they challenged President Musharraf's efforts to dismiss Supreme Court chief justice Iftikhar Chaudhry. The chief justice had shown real independence from Musharraf in ruling on various habeas corpus petitions for "disappeared" citizens who were abducted by the ISI.[9] When Chaudhry unexpectedly refused to resign, Musharraf suspended him. As protests mounted (mostly by lawyers dressed in suits), Chaudhry spent months touring the country, calling for justice and a return to the rule of law. The Supreme Court further bucked Musharraf by ruling that Chaudhry should be reinstated—which he was in the summer of 2007.

The security situation in Pakistan has since worsened. In July 2007, President Musharraf ordered the storming of the Lal Masjid, or Red Mosque, the headquarters of radical clerics who had been blatantly defying the government's authority for months. The weeklong standoff at the mosque came to a bloody end on July 10, when Musharraf sent in Pakistani security forces, killing more than a hundred people.[10] Although this action met with approval from much of the mainstream political establishment, it set off a violent reaction among Pakistan's religious extremists, with more than three hundred people killed in upheavals over the next month.[11]

By the fall of 2007, Musharraf's grip on power was weakening as he maneuvered to remain president past the two terms that were permitted by the constitution. Prodded by the United States, he negotiated with exiled former prime minister Benazir Bhutto, then the leader of the secular opposition Pakistan People's Party (PPP), for a power-sharing deal that was intended to stem the plummeting of his popular support. The move was controversial. Nawaz Sharif, the exiled former prime minister whom Musharraf had deposed in 1999, blasted Bhutto for negotiating with Musharraf, declaring, "How can a democrat share power with a dictator?"[12] Musharraf was reelected by the parliament in October 2007, and Benazir Bhutto returned to the country shortly thereafter.

Adil had harsh words for the U.S. backroom dealing. "The recent U.S. decision to cobble together an alliance of perceived 'enlightened moderates' like Benazir Bhutto and General Musharraf has also not gone down well with the people of Pakistan who obviously resent American interference in their domestic politics. Instead of rooting for and, indeed, imposing its own favorites, the United States needs to push for a pluralistic and inclusive democratic system in Pakistan where elections are free and fair and in which politicians of all shades of opinion are allowed to contest—not just those acceptable to the United States."[13]

Musharraf declared emergency rule in late 2007, largely to repress his democratic opposition and maintain his grip on power. Tragically, Benazir Bhutto was assassinated at a campaign rally in Rawalpindi on December 27, 2007, and her murder sparked violence and plunged the country into greater uncertainty. Parliamentary elections in February 2008 resulted in a stunning rebuke of political parties associated with President Musharraf. Whether his political defeat provides an opening for a peaceful transition to democracy remains to be seen.

The central problem in U.S. policymaking, particularly as it relates to the country's approach to Pakistan, is the inclination to connect U.S. strategies to individual leaders and their personalities. A strategy that is dependent on specific leaders is one that is built on a shaky foundation, especially in volatile countries like Pakistan.

Adil explained the risks of U.S. policy partnerships with dictators, saying that the youths of Pakistan, "bereft of an inspirational and visionary leadership, have been left alienated and isolated by a system that promotes mediocrity and discourages independent thought, that practices nepotism and disregards merit, and that stifles and suffocates where it should nurture and nourish. It is this sense of alienation from the system that is compelling young people in this country to resort to extremist or terrorist activity in order to remove perceived injustices within society. . . . The writ of the state is nowhere to be seen in many parts of the country, and suicide bombings have become virtually a norm even in major cities like Islamabad and Karachi."[14]

Pakistan is not the only troubled country where the U.S. has looked to an individual leader to safeguard its interests, instead of investing in making life better in the country itself. It was a mistake many U.S. leaders made during the Cold War, when they supported autocrats and dictators who took a stance against the Soviet Union. This strategy is inherently unstable. Instead the United States should look to use the full range of its considerable powers—both economic and diplomatic—in policies that expand stability and prosperity in troubled countries in order to fight the threat posed by terrorists and extremists. Targeted military action and the integrated work of intelligence and law enforcement agencies are essential in addressing the immediate threats posed by terrorist networks, but focusing on a comprehensive prosperity agenda in places like Pakistan is what will eliminate the conditions that allow terrorist groups to thrive.

Even though the country had an annual growth rate of 7 percent and more than $10 billion in U.S. assistance, Pakistan failed to become more stable and prosperous, in large part because the Pakistani people did not see tangible benefits from these funds. At the end of 2007, several U.S. officials said that much of the money that had been sent to Pakistan to support operations against terrorist groups did not make it to the right units. It was instead diverted to finance weapons to counter Pakistan's regional rival, India.[15]

When the United States does the right thing by focusing on policies that benefit the people of the world, other countries notice. Following the devastating 2005 earthquake in Pakistan, which killed more than 76,000 people, the Bush administration pledged more than $500 million for earthquake relief and sent U.S. helicopters and soldiers to help deliver emergency assistance. Immediately afterward, polls showed that the number of Pakistanis with a favorable opinion of the United States had doubled to more than 46 percent, up from 23 percent before the earthquake. The poll also found that opposition to terrorist attacks against civilians had doubled after the earthquake, with 73 percent saying that such attacks were never justified.[16]

The next American president must deploy all of the weapons in the U.S. arsenal to make life better for ordinary Pakistanis. Unless the Pakistani people begin to feel a steady improvement in their daily lives, Pakistan's stability and America's security remain at risk.

The challenges are daunting. More than a quarter of Pakistan's population still lives in poverty. More than a third of children under five are underweight. Half of the population are illiterate, with women's literacy rates trailing those of men. Only 51 percent of girls attend school.[17]

The value of focusing on these basic building blocks of society is a lesson we are learning in Iraq, which also applies to the effort to promote democracy and fight terrorism worldwide. The former head of the U.S. Central Command, General John Abizaid, recognized the link. "The question for us," he said in September 2007, "is whether people will have an opportunity for more prosperity. . . . I believe that's probably the centerpiece of the battle."[18]

Abizaid is right. Should the United States fail in helping to provide the opportunity for prosperity, the extremists may well gain a foothold on power, as they have already done in Lebanon and the Palestinian territories. There, the terrorists have seized the prosperity agenda and are gaining influence as a result.

Hezbollah and Hamas Have Found the Key

With his long, gray-flecked beard and traditional black turban, Hassan Nasrallah, the forty-six-year-old leader of Hezbollah in Lebanon, was in a buoyant mood. Speaking in August 2006 on al-Manar's television station, which the United States had designated as a terrorist entity two years earlier, the cleric claimed credit for a "strategic and historic victory" for Lebanon.[19] In July, Nasrallah's Hezbollah forces had launched rocket attacks into Israel and kidnapped two Israeli soldiers, baiting Israel into a bloody war. During thirty-four days of Israeli shelling of Lebanon and an invasion by Israeli ground troops, Lebanon suffered more than 1,000 deaths, with nearly a million Lebanese civilians displaced. Israel sustained 163 deaths, with more than 300,000 people displaced.[20] Hezbollah quickly claimed victory and moved to rebuild the areas in Lebanon destroyed by the violence.

Nasrallah understands the power of promoting prosperity. He made sure that Hezbollah was at the forefront of the reconstruction effort after the war with Israel. In his speech declaring victory, he promised to deliver enough cash to pay for a year's rent for those whose homes and furniture had been destroyed in the conflict. "In order to complete the victory, we should begin the reconstruction, especially building the houses exactly as they were built—and even better so that those honorable people would return to them. Without the steadfastness of those people, we would not have been able to achieve this victory," Nasrallah proclaimed.[21] Altogether,

Hezbollah planned to spend $150 million on reconstruction, with funds provided by Iran.

Hundreds of Hezbollah members spread out across southern Lebanon following the war to survey the extent of the destruction. In the southern Lebanese town of Khiam, Hezbollah fighters outnumbered the residents, and these men who had been fighting the Israeli army the day before turned into relief workers overnight.[22] A local whose house was destroyed praised the effort, saying, "Everything coming in, Hezbollah puts an eye on it, makes sure it is all given out the proper way. It is all in the hands of Hezbollah."[23] Through its own efforts and the subtle co-opting of nongovernmental efforts, Hezbollah managed to take ownership of the reconstruction effort in the south.

Its quick and effective action stood in sharp contrast to the seemingly feckless reaction by the Lebanese government. The government waited two weeks for an international donor package of $500 million to come through. Although its compensation package to individuals who lost houses in the war was ultimately far more generous than Hezbollah's—$33,000 to Hezbollah's $10,000 to $15,000—the government lost the propaganda campaign in the war's immediate aftermath.[24] A Shiite woman in the south remarked, "Where is the government? Do you see anyone from the state here? [Nasrallah] is our state." An older man emphasized Hezbollah's image of competence: "The party works correctly. . . . And the state? We don't know anything about the state."[25] By the end of 2006, Hezbollah felt politically strong enough to challenge the Siniora government with street protests that boiled over into violence in January 2007.

The failure of the Lebanese state to provide decent lives for its people paved the way for Hezbollah to build support by providing those basic services. Both the organization's leaders and its foot soldiers have recognized the political power of improving people's prosperity.

Hezbollah understands what people think will improve their lives—a sense of progress, whether that means a new home or an attack on Israel—and they're happy to deliver it. The model is a dangerous one for weak states around the world. Nasrallah's support in the Arab world has never been higher.

In Egypt and the Palestinian territories, people praised Nasrallah for standing up to Israel. "The Hawk of Lebanon," a song praising Nasrallah that was written by a Palestinian band from the northern West Bank town of Jenin, became one of the most requested songs at weddings in the second half of 2006. The lyrics praised Nasrallah's leadership: "Here you come, one who has become victorious with the help of God. Nasrallah, you brave man. You responded to our call for revenge as the Arab blood becomes hotter and hotter." The song was circulated widely on the Internet, and some people even used the tune as their cell phones' ring tone.[26]

Hezbollah today is the most technically capable terrorist group in the world. Created in 1982, the group seeks to establish a Shiite theocracy in Lebanon, destroy Israel, and eliminate Western influences from the Middle East. Hezbollah is closely aligned with Iran and has been involved in some of the world's bloodiest terrorist attacks against Israelis and Americans. Prior to September 11, 2001, Hezbollah was responsible for more American deaths than any other terrorist group. Its suicide truck bombings of the U.S. Embassy and the U.S. Marine barracks in Beirut in 1983 killed 241 Americans, and its bombing of the U.S. Embassy annex in Beirut in 1984 killed 17. The group remains a threat to U.S. national security; a 2007 U.S. National Intelligence Estimate assessed that Hezbollah "may be more likely to consider attacking the Homeland over the next three years if it perceives the United States as posing a direct threat to the group or Iran."[27]

Over the last few decades, Hezbollah has not only professionalized its military capabilities, it has also joined Lebanon's political process and enmeshed itself into the fabric of Lebanese society. The organization's militia controls most of southern Lebanon and is a significant force in the Lebanese parliament, with 14 of 128 seats. In addition to its ruthless and deadly terror tactics, it has found the key to surviving: building support among ordinary people by responding to their basic needs.

The terrorist organization Hamas, an outgrowth of the Muslim Brotherhood, has taken a similar approach to legitimacy in the Palestinian territories. Founded in 1987 during the first Palestinian intifada, Hamas's main objective is to destroy Israel and replace the Palestinian Authority with an Islamic state. Its armed faction conducts anti-Israeli attacks, including suicide bombings against civilian targets inside Israel. Since 1987, Hamas has killed an estimated 600 people. Both Iran and Syria support Hamas, and the extremist head of the group, Khaled Mishal, resides in Damascus.

While training suicide bombers to strike inside Israel, Hamas has also developed an effective social services system. Its *dawa,* or ministry activities, run charities, schools, and fund-raising events that help to meet the vast needs of the Palestinian people.

Extreme poverty keeps the Palestinian territories ripe for supporting terrorism. While terrorists themselves tend to be from comparatively well-off homes, the communities that support them are usually downtrodden. At the same time that public approval of suicide bombings and other forms of violence against civilians has dropped in the Muslim world, 70 percent of Palestinians still believe that such violence can be "often or sometimes justified." Since 2003, overall Muslim confidence in bin Laden has fallen. But in the Palestinian territories, 57 percent still have confidence that bin Laden will do the right thing in world affairs.[28] As much as the United States ought to worry about al-Qaeda's operations in the short term, that statistic is indicative of a greater long-term problem.

Hamas has successfully played on the incompetence and the corruption of Yasser Arafat's Fatah movement, which failed to provide for the most basic needs of the Palestinian people. The United States estimates that Hamas's spending on social welfare in 2005 was somewhere between $40 and $75 million, which includes funding for schools, orphanages, mosques, health clinics, soup kitchens, elderly care, education centers for women, and libraries.[29] After the United Nations, Hamas is the largest food donor in Gaza and the West Bank.

It came as a surprise only to the Bush administration when the Palestinians voted Hamas into office in the 2006 elections. The Hamas victory stopped any hope of resumed Israeli-Palestinian negotiations dead in its tracks. And although the United States suspended its aid, other outside actors, such as oil-rich Gulf countries, stepped in to fill the void. In June 2007, Hamas executed a violent takeover of Gaza, gaining control of Palestinian Authority institutions that were previously held by the Fatah Party. Hamas now controls some significant Palestinian ministries, including the Ministry of Interior, and continues to endorse terrorism as a means to achieve its objectives. Neither Hamas nor Hezbollah shares the goal of al-Qaeda to establish an Islamic caliphate across the Middle East. The groups have narrower, yet still dangerous, agendas, aimed at undermining the security of Israel. Their entrance onto the political stage should serve as a wake-up call to the United States and the broader international community.

Again, we see that the people of a troubled nation will follow whichever organization holds out the promise of a better life, be it a terrorist organization, a dictator, or a principled democracy.

Why Money Doesn't Equal Prosperity

When people think of Saudi Arabia, the first image that comes to mind is an oil-rich kingdom overflowing with palaces and Rolls-Royces. Certainly, Saudi Arabia is doing very well. Although poverty exists in the country, it is less common than in other Arab countries, particularly those with little or no oil resources. Why, then, did fifteen of the nineteen hijackers on 9/11 come from Saudi Arabia?

Despite its vast wealth, the Saudi government has failed to share its riches equitably or to make the long-term investments in the society that are necessary to ensure the prosperity of its nearly twenty-five million people. The tight control over political power maintained by the ruling House of Saud has denied the majority of the people a place at the table. While such policies may have been sustainable decades ago when the country was booming, today these policies are undermining the regime.

If you define prosperity as life, liberty, and the pursuit of happiness, as we do in the United States, then Saudi Arabia is one of the least prosperous nations on Earth. Since 1981, the country's per person gross domestic product (GDP) has been falling. In the

1970s and the early 1980s, high oil prices drove GDP to a peak of $16,650 in 1981.[30] Today, it is down to $13,800. The wealth is held by a small minority in the country, with an estimated 120,000 millionaires controlling assets of $400 billion.[31] Power and wealth belong to an oligarchy that is run by the male descendants of the kingdom's founder, King Abd al-Aziz, and his forty-four sons by seventeen wives. The late King Fahd is believed to have had a personal fortune of $20 billion.

Today, the country faces systematic problems stemming from an overdependence on oil, a population explosion of more than 2 percent a year, and massive unemployment, with estimates ranging between 13 and 25 percent. Immigrants make up a large part of the Saudi workforce and are often subjected to cruel working conditions.[32] The petroleum sector accounts for roughly 75 percent of government budget revenues, 45 percent of GDP, and 90 percent of export earnings. Indeed, only about 25 percent of GDP comes from the private sector.[33]

How Saudi Arabia uses its vast financial resources can tip the geopolitical balance in the broader fight against global terror networks. On this front, Saudi Arabia plays a strategic, yet controversial, role. Although the Saudi government has cooperated with varying levels of enthusiasm in the war on terror, Saudi Arabia's oil wealth, repressive state apparatus, and radical religious streak have made it a reliable source of manpower and financial support for international terrorist networks, especially al-Qaeda. Not only did the majority of the 9/11 hijackers come from Saudi Arabia, an estimated 45 percent of foreign militants now targeting U.S. troops in Iraq are Saudis.[34] Fighters from Saudi Arabia have carried out more suicide bombings in Iraq than have fighters from any other country. Yet Saudi officials have shown little interest in cracking down on militant traffic from Saudi Arabia to Iraq, perhaps believing that they can simply export the problem.

Saudi Arabia knows firsthand the costs of terrorism. Osama bin Laden has made the overthrow of the Saudi government his highest priority, and in recent years, there have been a number of attacks within the kingdom, including the 2003 Riyadh compound bombing by al-Qaeda, which killed 35 people, and a 2004 attack on an Al-Khobar compound, which killed 22.

The Saudi government has taken important actions to disable al-Qaeda cells in Saudi Arabia and has regularly killed al-Qaeda members and sympathizers. In December 2006, the government announced that it had captured more than 130 suspected terrorists. In April 2007, it announced the arrest of another 172 men in a plot to blow up oil installations.[35]

Saudi Arabia has taken some steps to combat extremism in cultural and religious settings as well, starting a National Campaign to Counter Terrorism, revising some curricula in schools, and monitoring mosque sermons and religious leaders' statements for extremism. It has also increased its cooperation with the United States in law enforcement and intelligence sharing. Despite these steps, the State Department concludes that Saudi Arabia "still has significant ground to cover to address these issues."[36]

Funds from wealthy Saudis continue to flow to terrorist networks. While there is no proof that the government or senior officials have directly funded al-Qaeda, there is significant evidence that al-Qaeda has raised funds from Saudi individuals and charities. The Saudi government has renewed efforts to enforce anti–money laundering laws and regulations in recent years but has been reluctant to examine fully, much less denounce publicly, the roles played by Saudi charities in funding terrorist networks. The kingdom has done little to rein in the Saudi-based charities that control billions of dollars and has failed to prosecute Saudi-based individuals who are known to have financed terrorist groups.[37]

Well-connected Saudis are managing to skirt financial controls to continue their support of terrorist networks. For instance, a Saudi multimillionaire, Yassin Qadi, has managed to use his friendship with the Turkish prime minister Recep Tayyip Erdogan to free up millions of dollars in assets frozen by the United Nations and the U.S. Treasury Department after 9/11. An architect by profession who trained with the Chicago-based firm Skidmore, Owings & Merrill, Qadi speaks fluent English and has a son who is an American citizen. Most of his business empire is in Saudi Arabia, but he is also invested in a large supermarket chain in Turkey, where he allegedly does business with known financiers of al-Qaeda, such as the al-Qaeda logistics coordinator

Wael Julaidan. After many of his assets were frozen after 9/11, Qadi transferred other assets to his business associates, including individuals with known ties to al-Qaeda. His friend the Turkish prime minister is sticking by him and declared in 2006, "I trust him the same way I trust my father."[38]

Saudi Arabia also remains a global exporter of the extreme Islamism adopted by terrorists around the world. Its Wahhabi brand of Islam encourages violence against anyone who does not adhere to its strict interpretation of Islam and also treats women as little more than property. Saudi leaders have spent millions of dollars supporting Wahhabism in mosques, cultural centers, hospitals, and madrassas in places like Pakistan and Afghanistan. Radical clerics are trained and sent abroad by Saudi Arabia to spread this religious ideology. As one expert put it, this massive, unregulated spending to promote Wahhabism "constitutes a paramount strategic threat to the United States."[39]

Saudi Arabia can tip the balance against al-Qaeda. In the fight to address the threat posed by global terror networks, U.S. relations with Saudi Arabia will be of paramount importance. As the respected International Crisis Group put it, "Saudi Arabia is at a critical stage in both its struggle against terrorism and its on-again, off-again efforts at reform, and Islamism is at the heart of both. The success or failure of the moderate Islamists in providing social, religious and political responses to the country's predicament will, probably as much as anything, determine the ultimate fate of their radical rivals."[40]

So we find ourselves again in that forced and false dichotomy: must we choose between working with an ally to fight terrorism or promoting democracy? How do we help Saudi citizens secure their rights, while having a good-enough relationship with their leaders to continue to work together to combat the extremist threat? With the prosperity agenda, we can do both.

The United States can press harder for reforms in Saudi Arabia and across the Arab world. The political, economic, and societal dysfunctions of the Arab world fuel sympathy for terrorists' aims. Changing Arab societies will take generations, but the terrorist threat will continue to grow unless reforms begin now.

$1 Trillion and Seven Years Later: Are We Winning the War on Terror?

Following 9/11, President Bush declared that all aspects of U.S. power would be put to use in combating terrorism, including "diplomatic, economic, law enforcement, financial, information, intelligence, and military" instruments. Yet the administration's emphasis has been on military operations, ignoring the crucial role of soft power in winning that war. In October 2001, the United States overthrew the Taliban in Afghanistan, destroying all known al-Qaeda training sites and killing or detaining numerous al-Qaeda and Taliban leaders. Nearly a year and a half later, the Bush administration invaded Iraq, arguing that the potential threat posed by Saddam Hussein and his alleged nuclear program was so great that the United States could not afford to wait for weapons inspectors to do their work. In the ensuing chaos, al-Qaeda in Mesopotamia established itself in Iraq.

Certainly, the United States has made important progress in some areas in the fight against global terror groups. Numerous attacks have been disrupted, such as the airliner plot in the summer of 2006, when al-Qaeda hoped to blow up British airliners en route to the United States over the Atlantic Ocean. Leading al-Qaeda operatives have been killed or captured, such as Khalid Sheikh Mohammed, Hambali, and Abu Musab al-Zarqawi. New counterterrorism partnerships have been fostered internationally and communications improved between the CIA, the FBI, and other intelligence, homeland security, and law enforcement agencies.[41]

But Americans are not yet secure. U.S. security interests remain at risk from a wide variety of threats. Bin Laden may be living in a cave, but his organization is not. From their safe haven along the Afghanistan-Pakistan border, Osama bin Laden and senior al-Qaeda leaders continue to plot attacks against the United States and its interests. Iraq is now a magnet and a recruiting tool for terrorists. Anti-Americanism is at an all-time high, while al-Qaeda exploits that backlash to recruit more followers. Democracy, the antidote to the ideology of terrorism, is backsliding in the Middle

East, Russia, and Latin America and has yet to take hold in Afghanistan and Iraq. Pakistan is at risk from radical Islamists. Al-Qaeda and other terrorist networks continue their attacks, including in Europe. Nonproliferation efforts are stalled, if not losing ground. Iran and Syria continue to support terrorists. U.S. armed forces are strained to the breaking point, with no end in sight. Together with enhanced security measures, the cost of the wars in Iraq and Afghanistan, as well as the broader war on terror, will top $1 trillion in fiscal year 2008.[42]

Conventional military approaches—fighting them over there so we don't have to fight them here—became a central organizing principle for the Bush administration. U.S. military operations also became one of al-Qaeda's biggest recruiting tools. As the terrorism expert Bruce Hoffman pointed out, al-Qaeda's ability to continue its struggle is "predicated on its capacity to attract new recruits" by highlighting U.S. military actions.[43] We must make a clear distinction between the core al-Qaeda terrorists and their potential sympathizers. For the former, military defeat is the only way to win; for the latter, we must get at the reasons why they consider joining al-Qaeda or other terrorist groups in the first place. This means that America's approach must be smarter and broader and must use the full range of its superpower strengths to stop al-Qaeda in its tracks, to make progress in the simmering conflicts that fuel al-Qaeda's recruitment efforts, and to put America once again on the side of progress and prosperity. When the world sees that the United States is working to address global concerns, the terrorist recruiting pool will be seriously diminished.

Since the initial setbacks following the U.S. invasion of Afghanistan in 2001, al-Qaeda has regrouped, adapted, and expanded its reach. By the summer of 2007, top U.S. government intelligence analysts concluded that al-Qaeda was the strongest it had been since the aftermath of the September 11, 2001, terrorist attacks. And it still has America in its crosshairs. The July 2007 National Intelligence Estimate concluded that al-Qaeda is "the most serious threat to the Homeland," and that the United States will "face a persistent and evolving terrorist threat over the next three years." Al-Qaeda remains intent on "producing mass casualties, visually dramatic destruction, significant economic aftershocks, and/or fear among the U.S. population."[44]

The al-Qaeda threat has metastasized like a cancer, spreading throughout the Muslim world, where it has developed a large cadre of operatives, and in Europe, where it can claim the support of some disenfranchised Muslim locals. Because of the global al-Qaeda movement's decentralized nature, estimating its size is difficult, but it is believed to range from several hundred to several thousand members.

Hoffman described four different layers of al-Qaeda: al-Qaeda Central, consisting of the leadership based on the Afghanistan-Pakistan border; al-Qaeda Affiliates and Associates, mainly composed of already established terrorist groups in Central Asia, Indonesia, Morocco, and the Philippines; al-Qaeda Locals, which are dispersed cells that have some direct connection to al-Qaeda, including the homegrown bombers who attacked the London transport system in the summer of 2005; and finally, al-Qaeda Network, a loose network of radical, self-generating cells in Western countries that have little direct connection to al-Qaeda beyond an ideological bond.[45]

Although Osama bin Laden still influences the direction and gives guidance or specific instructions to much of al-Qaeda, he has less direct control. To survive and ensure the movement's ability to conduct attacks, it can no longer risk direct command and control of operations. Al-Qaeda has regenerated itself, becoming even more global and diffuse. As it grows more decentralized, it is linking up with other terrorist organizations and sharing people, knowledge, and plans. The organization has some links to Jemaah Islamiya (JI), the main terrorist Islamic network that is seeking to establish a pan-Islamic state in Southeast Asia. JI has been responsible for several major terrorist incidents in the past years, including the 2002 Bali nightclub bombing that killed more than 200 people and another series of Bali attacks in 2005, as well as allegedly targeting U.S. and Western interests throughout the region. Extensive arrests have weakened the organization, but the State Department still considers it a "serious threat." JI links to al-Qaeda include Hambali, a JI leader captured in 2003 who served as an intermediary between JI and al-Qaeda. Evidence obtained from Khalid Sheikh Mohammed also suggests that JI has supported al-Qaeda in the period following 9/11, including a plan to attack sites in California.

Other areas in Asia to watch are the Philippines, which suffered nearly a hundred bombing incidents in 2006, mostly by the Abu Sayyaf Group, a militant organization seeking a separate state for the Philippines' Muslim population.[46] Thailand also remains an area of concern, especially following the 2006 military coup ousting the elected government. The country faces an ongoing Muslim separatist insurgency in the south, which does not pose a major international threat at this time. But the continued mishandling of unrest could lead to further instability. Some officials fear that conditions in southern Thailand are ripe for JI and perhaps even al-Qaeda intrusion. Thailand, in any event, has long had a bad track record against terrorism, both international and otherwise. Groups like Hezbollah have operated effectively from Thailand for years, as have the Tamil Tigers, and the JI leader Hambali was apprehended in a city just north of Bangkok in 2003.[47]

Africa, too, is of growing concern. The State Department's 2007 global terrorism survey noted that a number of al-Qaeda operatives and affiliates are based in the eastern part of the Horn of Africa and the northwest of the continent. Somalia is a particular problem because the internal chaos and the floundering peace process have left the country open to al-Qaeda influence. The northwest region of Africa is witnessing a resurgence of terrorist activity. The Salafist Group for Preaching and Combat, an Algeria-based organization that has sent jihadis to Iraq and staged numerous attacks in the region, has renamed itself al-Qaeda in the Islamic Maghreb and is now claiming to be a local franchise for al-Qaeda.[48]

As al-Qaeda's tentacles spread, the United States must increase its efforts to make the lives of would-be recruits and terrorist sympathizers in these countries more prosperous. Our efforts in Afghanistan will be particularly pivotal.

The Unfinished Job in Afghanistan

More than seven years after the United States invaded Afghanistan to remove the Taliban from power and destroy al-Qaeda's safe haven, the daily lives of average Afghans have not improved on key fronts. Afghanistan remains one of the poorest countries in the world. Life expectancy at birth is forty-six years old, the adult literacy rate is only 28 percent, and about 20 percent of Afghan children die before their fifth birthday.[49] Reconstruction and economic development have stalled, opium production has skyrocketed, and the Afghan government is weak, often corrupt and, in many areas of the country, simply not present.

As prosperity flounders, members of the Taliban have flooded back into Afghanistan and are now the de facto authority in much of the Pashtun south and east. The Taliban operated in squad-sized units in 2003 and increased the size of these units to 400 or more men by 2006.[50] By 2007, the Taliban moved once again in smaller units following air assaults on the larger units.[51] Confrontations and casualties have increased, with greater numbers of people (more than 8,000) killed in 2007 than in any year since the 2001 invasion.[52] The Taliban is taking advantage of the weaknesses of the government and the exploding drug trade to reestablish itself. In the same territories, al-Qaeda is providing the Taliban with funding and training, while relying on the safe haven that is created by the Taliban's activities.[53]

Most alarmingly, the Taliban is now working with several different forces in Afghanistan, establishing a true insurgency that is bent on overthrowing the government. This includes the forces of several Afghan warlords, against whom the United States fought in 2001, such as the Jalaluddin Haqqani network, the Hizb-i-Islami network, and the Jamiat Ulema-e-Islam network, as well as foreign jihadists and Pakistani militants.[54] Al-Qaeda has helped train these forces, teaching tactics such the use of improvised explosive devices and suicide bombings.

U.S. military forces and reconstruction efforts are insufficient to meet this challenge. First, prosperity cannot be restored in Afghanistan without security. Yet the United States has only

25,000 troops in Afghanistan falling under two commands: the U.S.-led Operation Enduring Freedom (OEF) force and NATO's International Security Assistance Force (ISAF).[55] Although Afghanistan is the larger of the two countries, the United States has nearly 170,000 troops in Iraq.[56] Without enough troops to perform effective counterinsurgency operations, forces in Afghanistan have to rely on air strikes and large army sweeps. These types of operations inevitably incur high levels of civilian casualties, which in turn anger and alienate the population.

Second, reconstruction efforts are faltering and Afghans do not see their daily lives improving. The gaping hole in the international strategic approach to Afghanistan has been the failure to make life better for ordinary Afghan citizens. Perhaps the highest priority for the international community is to strengthen the Afghan government. President Hamid Karzai has attempted to build the authority of the government, and Afghanistan has passed a new constitution and held elections for a parliament. Karzai sought to co-opt the warlords and tribal leaders and bring them into the government via governorships, cabinet positions, and other senior appointments.[57] But chronic abuse of these positions has simply put a government façade on the continued exploitation of the Afghan population, which has damaged popular faith in the government.

In addition, the government faces an explosion of opium production. Afghanistan now produces more than 90 percent of the world's opium, and opium revenues make up approximately a third to half of Afghanistan's GDP.[58] Eradication efforts often backfire against the local population, allowing insurgents to portray themselves as protectors of ordinary Afghans by defending local fields. A smarter strategy is needed, one that recognizes that the solution cannot simply be an effort to eradicate an industry that provides half of the country's economic well-being. Some realistic alternative source of income will first need to be developed.

Even though President Bush promised a "Marshall Plan" for Afghanistan, aid and economic development assistance to date have fallen far short of that promise. Aid per capita to Afghans in the first two years after the overthrow of the Taliban was approximately one-tenth of that given to Bosnians at the end of their civil war.[59] In 2006, the United States sent $1.6 billion to Afghanistan, well below the $4.8 billion it gave to Iraq, a country rich in oil.[60] Meanwhile, worsening security conditions are threatening aid operations, whose workers are increasingly seen as targets. This limits the areas in which aid groups can operate, particularly in the south and the west.[61]

In order to make the United States safer, we need to do more to make sure that Afghanistan—the country that hosted the headquarters of al-Qaeda during the September 11 attacks—does not continue to spiral downward into greater instability and poverty. That will require more troops to counter the growing insurgency that threatens to put the Taliban back in power. And it will necessitate more and smarter aid to build up Afghan security forces and strengthen the government's reach throughout the country. The people of Afghanistan do not see their lives getting better. Until they do, America remains at risk.

When Muslims Find Prosperity

Muriel Degauque, a pretty thirty-eight-year-old blond woman from Belgium, traveled to just north of Baghdad in 2005 and detonated explosives that she had attached to her body, becoming the first European woman to stage a suicide attack in Iraq.[62] Degauque had converted to Islam after marrying a Belgian of Moroccan origin, who was shot by U.S. troops after his explosive belt failed to detonate when he attempted his own suicide bombing. She became a face for the threat of homegrown terrorists across Europe.[63]

Terrorist attacks in Madrid in 2004 and London in 2005 killed more than two hundred people. The London attacks were conducted by four British young men, three of Pakistani origin, who previously had given little indication that they were involved with extremist ideology, let alone terrorist plots. As citizens of their country, such homegrown terrorists can travel freely. They pay their bills on time and attract little notice. On the surface, even budding terrorists live normal, relatively prosperous lives.

Five percent of the European Union's 425 million people are Muslim, and that number is expected to double by 2020. Another 70 million will be added if Turkey joins the European Union. Many of Europe's 23 million Muslims live on the fringes of their societies. As the second-generation immigrants reach maturity, they resent the barriers they face—too many European Muslims do not feel integrated, accepted, or given an equal opportunity to succeed. The greatest concern among Muslim minorities in Great Britain, France, Germany, and Spain is unemployment, despite the prosperity across much of Europe.[64]

This "second-generation backlash" is fueling the homegrown terrorist phenomenon in Europe. As one French academic put it, "[N]either the blood spilled by Muslims from North Africa fighting in French uniforms during both world wars nor the sweat of migrant laborers, living under deplorable living conditions, who rebuilt France (and Europe) for a pittance after 1945, has made their children . . . full fellow citizens."[65] The alienation of the Muslim community in France burst to the surface in the summer of 2006, when suburbs of Paris burned in protest after two French Muslim youths were killed by the police.

Europe must meet the challenge of fully integrating its Muslim immigrants and citizens into its society. Unless European Muslims have a sense that if they work hard, they—and, most important, their children—will prosper, al-Qaeda and other extreme terrorists can gain a foothold in these countries.

So far, the threat of homegrown terrorists is less in the United States than in Europe. While we are not immune to a homegrown threat—we do have John Walker Lindh, Adam Yahiye Gadahn, Daniel Maldonando, and the foiled plotters who targeted Fort Dix and JFK Airport—terrorist incidents on the home front have been few and far between. Relative to Muslims in many European countries, American Muslims are integrated and prosperous. Half of them attend college, and their income is on a par with people in the rest of America. Although pockets of bigotry certainly exist, overall, American Muslims feel accepted in their own communities. They know they can raise their families and prosper as well as their neighbors from other backgrounds.

For instance, a 2007 Pew Research Center poll found that the American Muslim community is highly diversified and decidedly American in its outlook, values, and attitudes. Nearly two-thirds (63 percent) do not see a conflict between being a devout Muslim and living in a modern society. Also, seven in ten (71 percent) American Muslims agree that most people who want to get ahead in the United States can if they work hard.[66]

But America is not an island. The United States, for example, is increasingly concerned about the potential links to terrorism of Britain's Pakistani population, which, like all British citizens, can visit the United States without a visa. In May 2007, the United States tried to impose travel restrictions on British citizens of Pakistani origin, many of whom travel back and forth to Pakistan, but Britain rejected the idea. The concern, of course, is broader than British Pakistanis. The U.S. visa waiver system allows citizens from twenty-seven countries to travel to the United States without a visa for up to ninety days.[67]

Winning Hearts and Minds with the Prosperity Agenda

In order to gain an upper hand in the worldwide battle against terrorists and to undermine terrorists' ability to appeal to new recruits, the United States needs to deploy one of the strongest weapons in its antiterror arsenal: its power to give people around the world a stake in their own prosperity and stability. The United States must couple its military actions against al-Qaeda and other terrorist groups with more active steps to address the underlying magnets for terrorism and help people around the world feel safer and more prosperous. That means America needs an army of diplomats and aid workers to effect on-the-ground change for the world's poor, disenfranchised, and marginalized.

Winning the war on terror will require demonstrating to the world that America understands the needs of those denied democracy in Pakistan, those repressed by the Saudi oligarchy, and those struggling to feed their families in Afghanistan. And it will require the United States demonstrating that it can help to bring prosperity to the citizens of these countries.

But for too much of the last seven years, the United States has not done nearly enough to advance the prosperity of disadvantaged people in these countries. Instead, the United States has relied on conventional twentieth-century military approaches to address an unconventional twenty-first-century national security threat. The military actions of the United States in Iraq and Afghanistan have failed to bring prosperity to those lands and continue to fuel resentment against the United States in those countries and beyond.

A global counterinsurgency approach would suggest that about 80 percent of U.S. efforts should go toward political, diplomatic, development, intelligence, and informational activity and 20 percent should go to military activity. Today, the Defense Department budget is 210 times larger than those of the Agency for International Development and the State Department combined.[68] Nonmilitary counterterrorism programs have budgets in the millions, rather than billions, and the funding for counterterrorist efforts outside the Pentagon and a few intelligence agencies remains flat.[69]

In some areas, the United States has already redirected its efforts, such as in the Horn of Africa. In October 2002, the U.S. military formed the Combined Joint Task Force—Horn of Africa, a 1,800-strong task force that operates out of a former French Foreign Legion base at Camp Lemonier in Djibouti.[70] The task force's work is vital to the fight against terrorism in the long term. It has been focused on civil affairs missions: building schools and improving roads and medical facilities. Since 2003, the task force has drilled more than a hundred wells and assisted in eleven humanitarian relief missions.[71]

As Captain Patrick Myers, the task force's director of plans and policy, described the effort, our "mission is 95 percent civil affairs. It's trying to get at the root causes of why people want to take on the U.S."[72] American troops also reach out to local residents on a one-to-one basis, often playing games of soccer with local youths. But U.S. military officials in Djibouti acknowledge that theirs is a long-term effort: "Our target group is today's children, so we're not going to know for 10 or 15 years. But we hope that, in the long run, we could be saving lives."[73]

Recognizing that the U.S. military cannot shoulder this burden alone, the Bush administration has begun to pull together the various U.S. government agencies into an integrated regional effort that will be more flexible and effective in fighting terrorist groups. These Regional Strategic Initiatives seek to establish America's own regional networks to counter those of terrorist groups. In addition to the Trans-Sahara Counterterrorism Initiative, the State Department is in the process of forming regional networks in the eastern Mediterranean to work against the influence of Hezbollah, the Kurdistan Workers Party (PKK), and al-Qaeda, and in Southeast Asia to tackle the Islamist terror groups plaguing the Philippines, Indonesia, and other countries.[74] Although the budget of $1 million is hardly adequate to the challenge, the effort recognizes the need to combine all of the United States' assets—political, economic, and military—to make progress against terrorism.

The Clash of Faltering Civilizations

Classrooms in Islamabad, street corners in poor Muslim immigrant neighborhoods in France, the garment factories of Dhaka—these are the places where the real fight against terrorist extremism is taking place. But many terrorists do not lack material needs. Why, then, would they turn to violence?

Understanding the answer is crucial to devising a successful effort to address the threat that people among us may turn against us. President Bush in his speeches referred often to a clash of civilizations when he sought to rally the American people. For instance, on the fifth anniversary of 9/11, in speaking about the fight for freedom, he said, "This struggle has been called a clash of civilizations. In truth, it is a struggle for civilization. We are fighting to maintain the way of life enjoyed by free nations. And we're fighting for the possibility that good and decent people across the Middle East can raise up societies based on freedom and tolerance and personal dignity."[75]

Is the threat of terrorism, as President Bush claimed, "the decisive ideological struggle of the twenty-first century"? Or is it a real life struggle for prosperity? In essence, the challenge today is for the United States to be seen as working for a broad view of prosperity in which everyone can hope for a better life, more opportunities, justice, and control over the direction of his or her destiny. The United States is competing with the terrorists over who can best meet the basic needs of the people. These needs include feeling a sense of belonging to a community and of being treated fairly among their peers. Whether "we" or "they" provide prosperity may well become the defining issue of the twenty-first century. Whether "they" be dictators, terrorists, resurgent communists, pseudo-socialists with petrodollars, or radical clerics matters little to people who are denied decent lives. Most people who are excluded from prosperity will follow leaders who offer to provide it.

Rather than a clash with Islam, terrorism today is more a clash with the downsides of globalization. Much of terrorism is due to a failure to secure prosperity for Muslims who are hit by the effects of globalization. Migration, the export of Wahhabism, and the U.S. invasion of Iraq and Afghanistan have all played into the terrorist narrative and helped to fuel resentment against the United States. Large segments of the Muslim communities in the West feel alienated. Couple this with ongoing conflicts between Israel and its neighbors, in Kashmir, and, most important, in Iraq. The result is a simmering cauldron of resentment that threatens the United States.

The problem is not the Islamic world; Americans and Europeans are not in a struggle with most of the Muslim world. Terrorists are not seeking us out from the world's most populous Muslim nation: Indonesia. Nor are they seeking to kill us in Bangladesh, Nigeria, or most of Muslim Central Asia. Certainly, there are groups of hard-core terrorists who want to kill us. They must be dealt with decisively. Yet they are only a small portion of the Arab world and an even smaller portion of the Muslim world. There is no question that increasing numbers in the Muslim world are discontented, however, and unless we deal with the causes of their discontent, the terrorist threat will continue to rise.

Truly winning the war on terror will require progress on all the fronts discussed in this book. We must distinguish between the hard-core terrorists and their potential sympathizers who may or may not join a terrorist movement. Stopping them before they do is an essential task.

Any comprehensive counterterrorism effort will have at least the following six broad areas of focus, packaged into one grand strategy: better intelligence; an effort to win the war of ideas; addressing conflicts that fuel the terrorist fires in Iraq, in Kashmir, and the Arab-Israeli conflict; stabilizing problem states, such as Iraq, Afghanistan, Pakistan, and Somalia; improved homeland security; and diversification of America's energy supply. Particularly important is the recognition that much of the war against terror involves repairing a breakdown in key societies (Saudi Arabia, Iraq, Afghanistan, and Pakistan) that cannot be solved quickly or by military force alone. The United States must press for a broader, long-term effort to address the root causes of the instability within these societies and must advocate for political reform. Only then will people see their lives improving and choose a path other than terror.

The United States must once again be seen as working to make individuals around the world safe, secure, integrated, and able to care for their families. What America does and does not do matters. To put America firmly on the side of prosperity and security, U.S. leaders must take the following clear, decisive steps:

STOP: Ignoring the threat of new recruits and sympathizers. Defeating al-Qaeda is the central challenge in the war on terror, but we will never win that battle if our sole focus is on al-Qaeda. As the threat of al-Qaeda grows, we must look at where al-Qaeda is getting its recruits and why people are attracted to its narratives. In other words, distinguish between the terrorists and their potential sympathizers and devise a strategy to keep them apart.

START: Undermining political support for the terrorists. Today, al-Qaeda has roots in the societies that are failing to deliver on the broad prosperity agenda. Those failures lead to support for terrorism, either directly or in spirit. This means that America must begin to look at the corrupt oligarchy of Saudi Arabia and the repressive, undemocratic regime in Pakistan as direct threats to the United States. We must recognize that the war in Iraq serves as a recruiting tool for al-Qaeda and that Afghanistan remains very much at risk of falling to the insurgency. Even in Europe, more effort must be made to integrate the growing Muslim population and ensure that they have opportunities to prosper.

STOP: Putting a target on Americans' backs. U.S. actions over the last seven years have fed right into the terrorists' narrative that the United States wants Arab oil and territory and does not respect the Muslim religion. Certainly, the war in Iraq has given fodder to al-Qaeda's propaganda. The human rights abuses, such as those at Abu Ghraib and Guantánamo, do as well. We must respect the basic rules that have governed wars and helped to keep our soldiers safe abroad. Special care must be given not to alienate the Muslim American population.

START: Growing prosperity by giving aid that actually makes a difference. Rather than simply supporting democracy in principle, the United States must do more to demonstrate to people on the ground that it is interested in helping them meet their basic needs. Giving money, weapons, and loans with lots of strings attached doesn't do it, but handing out vaccines, disaster relief, and $100 laptops does. The United States also needs to move beyond a narrow focus on elections and devise a strategy that promotes broad political and economic reform in the Middle East and the developing world. These U.S. policies should strengthen the rule of law and the judiciary, support broad civic education, advance women's rights, and protect the rights of religious minorities. It will be such democratic institutions, civil society, and rule of law that will in the end defeat terrorism.

STOP: Ignoring the underlying conflicts that fuel violence. As long as the northwest territories of Pakistan, Kashmir, southern Afghanistan, central Iraq, southern Lebanon, the Palestinian territories, and Somalia fester, terrorists will have havens from which to operate. Although we cannot solve these crises overnight, we need to invest more in bilateral, multinational, and international efforts to bring order and prosperity to these parts of the world. Targeted military actions by the United States and its allies will continue to be necessary to address immediate security threats posed by terror groups. Yet the United States must also dedicate more diplomatic resources to ending these conflicts and to demonstrating the tangible benefits that peace can bring. The United States must once again lead in the search for peace between warring factions.

START: Putting the full force of American diplomacy toward resolving these conflicts. These continuing conflicts help fuel the terrorists' claim that America is helping their enemies. While they are often not the cause of terrorism, these conflicts fuel much of the hatred that promotes it.

If the United States takes these steps to promote prosperity, people like Adil will understand that the United States is on his side—and on the right side of history.

three

Freedom Stumbles
without Prosperity

Vitaliy Moroz was fed up with the way things were run in his country. Ukraine, which had become independent from the Soviet Union in 1991, had suffered from corrupt and autocratic rulers. A graduate student in political science at the University of Kiev's Mohyla Academy, Moroz became an activist for change by taking a job in the spring of 2004 with Freedom House, a U.S.-based organization that promotes freedom and democracy. His new job involved building networks of support for Ukrainian civic activists who wanted to push for political change and monitor against electoral fraud.

The winds of political change were blowing in 2004. Ukraine's president, Leonid Kuchma, tried to control the media, ignored the rule of law, and continued to collaborate with the Russian Kremlin. He and his cronies took part in criminal business deals that made them rich at the expense of others. Kuchma was also implicated in the 2000 abduction and subsequent beheading of a journalist, Georgiy Gongadze. Barred by law from another term in office, Kuchma put forward a governor, Viktor Yanukovych, to replace him, with Russia's backing.[1] The leading opposition candidate was Viktor Yushchenko, who had emerged five years earlier as a reformer, imposing fiscal discipline, fighting inflation, and taking on corruption while prime minister. Yushchenko also sought to assist struggling Ukrainians by giving wage increases to teachers, health-care workers, and other state employees. He helped the elderly to obtain decent lives by increasing pension payments. His reforms proved too far-reaching for Kuchma, who forced him out after only eighteen months in office. Despite his dismissal, more and more Ukrainians flocked to Yushchenko's "Our Ukraine" reformist party.

As discontent with the old political order bubbled up, Ukraine saw the simultaneous development of an economic middle class. Between 1999 and 2004, prodded partly by Yushchenko's reforms, GDP growth for Ukraine's 48 million people more than doubled, from a little more than 5 percent in 2002 to 12.5 percent in 2004. This growing middle class would no longer tolerate being ruled by a few rich cronies who were backed by Russia, and the middle class's rising prosperity was an important ingredient in the mix that led to change in Ukraine.

Throughout the 2004 presidential election campaign, the government put up one obstacle after another to Yushchenko's candidacy. Air traffic controllers denied landing rights to Yushchenko's plane moments before campaign events were scheduled to occur. State security agents trailed him and eavesdropped on his conversations. Government-controlled media outlets issued a steady stream of negative and distorted stories about him. Despite these efforts, Yushchenko's support continued to grow, prompting the old political order in Ukraine to take more extreme measures. A few months before the elections, someone tried to murder Yushchenko by poisoning him with dioxin. Gravely ill, he stepped off the campaign trail in September, his face scarred and bloated from the poisoning. The government tried to say that he had contracted the disease by eating contaminated sushi, getting herpes, or undergoing botox treatments at age fifty to preserve his good looks.[2]

Despite such rumors, polls put Yushchenko ahead of Kuchma's choice, 52 to 43 percent on the eve of the presidential elections.

Voter turnout was high, and the initial tallies showed strong support for Yushchenko. But at the last moment, Viktor Yanukovych was declared the winner by 800,000 votes. Estimates are that the government rigged nearly 3 million votes in favor of Kuchma's candidate.[3]

Ukraine's middle class had had enough, and millions took to the streets to demand their right to choose their own leader. A sea of protestors gathered in the main squares of major cities and towns around the country, dressed in orange, which became the symbol of the push for political change in Ukraine's Orange Revolution. "Together, we are many! We cannot be defeated," chanted protestors in Kiev's main square on cold nights through the early winter of 2004. "During the Orange Revolution, the people of Kiev lived two lives—an official one during the day and an unofficial one at night," said Vitaliy Moroz, the young Ukrainian working with Freedom House. "People went to their jobs during the day, but after work they would join the protestors gathered in tents that had been put up around the main squares of the cities and in front of government buildings."[4]

People from all walks of society came to the streets to protest and offer their support. At the height of the protests, Moroz remembered seeing an elderly man dressed in the clothes that were typical of Ukraine's rural areas. The man had come to give all that he had to support the protestors—ten liters of honey from his village. He had brought the honey to help treat the sore throats of protestors who were outside in the freezing cold Ukrainian nights. Other people came to Moroz with money from their own pockets, hot food, and warm clothes. "Especially in the morning—as people were going to work—they would stop by Khreschatyk Street, the main street in Kiev, with hot dishes for the protestors," Moroz recalled. People were investing their own assets in the protestors against electoral fraud and in favor of fundamental political change.

On November 27, Parliament voted by a clear majority to declare the presidential vote invalid. The following week, the Supreme Court annulled the results and called for new elections. Yushchenko won the presidency in late December—with more than 12,000 international monitors present—by 52 to 44 percent, almost exactly what the polls had predicted. As he declared victory, Yushchenko, with his badly scarred face, went before the nation and declared, "We are free. The old era is over. We are a new country now."[5]

Change came to Ukraine, and the recipe for change had a longer list of ingredients than simply holding an election or two. Other essential ingredients included long-term efforts to build independent institutions such as the judiciary, the media, and civil society, all of which played a crucial role in ultimately tipping the balance toward greater change. As the former U.S. ambassador to Ukraine Carlos Pascual explained, "The Orange Revolution was backed by fifteen years of training—by the U.S. government and others. By 2004, we had already had 26,000 Ukrainians visit the United States for training programs. There already was an emerging sense of a Ukranian civil society where people were standing up and saying they weren't going to let the elections be stolen from them."[6] As Pascual said, it is one thing to develop civic engagement but another to create responsible governance. He detailed three fundamental factors behind the revolution. First, Ukrainian democracy did not happen overnight. There were years of long-term training and support for civic institutions of the sort that Vitaliy Moroz and his colleagues at Freedom House provided.

Second, the United States and other outside powers had engaged the ruling party officials, especially Kuchma, which helped to push him to give way to the democratic forces. "Part of the democracy promotion strategy was to work with Kuchma to allow space for these civic institutions to grow." While Pascual was ambassador from 2000 to 2003, he developed an honest, open relationship with Kuchma. That dialogue was crucial in convincing Ukraine's president to give the opposition some space. So, too, was engaging the broader range of business leaders and oligarchs. For instance, a key player who influenced Kuchma's decision not to use force in the Orange Revolution and to cede the election was his son-in-law, Victor Pinchuk. Pascual had pressed Pinchuk to get involved in the broader foreign policy community, including the nonprofit International Crisis Group based in Brussels. That international exposure helped to motivate Pinchuk to secure the right outcome for Ukraine.

A third important factor was Ukraine's growing prosperity: the economy was prosperous enough that most people's basic needs were being met. As Pascual explained, after 2000 the economy started to grow, and "people weren't thinking about the next meal but rather could think about civic institutions." Ordinary citizens were able to spend their evenings with the protestors and bring hot food and honey because of greater economic growth and opportunities. But Ukraine's struggle for democracy and prosperity did not end with the Orange Revolution.

Infighting and policy disputes between Yushchenko and the then prime minister Yulia Timoshenko led to another political stalemate. A few short months after the Orange Revolution, some Ukrainians wondered what had actually been achieved. One young man in Kiev said, "There are no grounds to hope for a better life just because the president or the prime minister changed. We ourselves have not changed—that's the problem."[7] The overriding concern in the immediate aftermath of the Orange Revolution was economic: many people worried about wages not keeping up with escalating prices for essential goods—in particular, gasoline, sugar, and meat.

Economic concerns were most pronounced in the eastern part of the country, which had closer ties to Russia and faced greater economic challenges than western Ukraine did. In Donetsk, one older Ukrainian described the economic situation and life in general: "We work in the coal industry. Miners are strained again and ready to strike. And every month you think, will there be wages? Or will there not? Will the salary be delayed? We don't know what to expect. The last salaries came in May. It is frightening. It is just frightening."[8] Even in western Ukraine, which was relatively more prosperous than the east, several Ukrainians expressed concerns about selling off factories and companies, including one older person in Lviv, who said, "Now it is very difficult to change the economy for the better. How can you give jobs to people if all of the factories are shut down, destroyed, and plundered?"[9]

For many Ukrainians, the tussles between the political elites remained disconnected from the personal lives of ordinary citizens whose focus was on getting better jobs and better education for their children. By September 2005, people felt that the country was on the wrong track, and Yushchenko dismissed the entire government. New parliamentary elections in 2006 further solidified internal divisions, and Yanukovych, the main rival in the 2004 presidential elections, became prime minister. In September 2007, emergency parliamentary elections, sparked by continued deadlock among Ukraine's political elite, marked the fourth national elections that were held in Ukraine in less than three years. Elections alone could not resolve Ukraine's political deadlock, but the country's citizens continued to move forward, motivated in large part by the engine of prosperity.

"We joke that as long as all of these disputes are going on, [politicians] don't have time to interfere with business," said Taras Kutovyy, the chief financial officer at XXI Century Investments, a leading financier for developing new hotels, apartments, and other projects.[10] Ukraine still has a long way to go in the struggle to advance prosperity and freedom; its average annual income remains only half of Russia's and less than 10 percent of Britain's per capita income. The strong rates of economic growth have lifted many Ukrainians out of poverty, but more needs to be done to build the institutions that are necessary to sustain and expand prosperity. This is where the freedom and the prosperity agendas become intertwined. "The political crisis has derailed structural economic reforms: pension reform, tax reform, judicial reform— which Ukraine badly needs as a post-Soviet state," said Ukraine's finance minister, Mykola Azarov.[11]

The former U.S. ambassador to Ukraine Carlos Pascual gave Ukraine's progress a "B or B minus. The country is still democratic, there is still strong civic engagement. It has an eight percent growth rate and a free press. Is it lost? No. If you look across states that have gone through these changes and ask, is Ukraine growing, delivering a better life, creating more jobs, allowing for freedom of expression, and is the press free? The answers are all yes." The healthy economic growth rate today is a strong indicator that Ukrainians will continue to feel prosperous and remain on the democratic path.[12]

Bush's Stalled Freedom Crusade: Freedom without Security and a Decent Life

Ukraine was one of the few positive exceptions to global democratic trends during President George W. Bush's time in office, one of only a handful of examples of progress. Despite his rhetorical use of the words *democracy* and *freedom*, as we near the end of his two terms in office, the global march toward freedom has effectively stalled: President Bush witnessed fewer democratic transitions than either of his two predecessors had. Ironically, despite Bush's central rhetorical focus on freedom, few real and sustainable advances for democracy were made on his watch. According to *Freedom in the World*, the annual global index of political rights and civil liberties produced by Freedom House, the number of countries rated as "free" nearly doubled in the twenty years from 1976 to 1996, from 42 to 79.[13] Throughout the 1990s, freedom spread in key parts of the world. Globally, people who had formerly been oppressed by communism in Central and Eastern Europe openly protested in the streets and black South Africans lined up for their country's first free elections in 1994 following the collapse of apartheid. Decades of military rule in Indonesia came to an end in 1998 after widespread protests against corruption led to Suharto's resignation and free elections in 1999.

By the time President Bush entered office in 2001, the trend toward greater freedom in the world had begun to stall. Although the overall number of countries that were ranked "free" grew from 79 to 90 in the ten years between 1996 and 2006, most of those gains occurred before 2001. Waves of democracy began to ebb in the face of new countertrends—undertows of repression and a backlash against unfettered free market globalization that increased inequalities between the powerful and the powerless.

President Bush put the promotion of freedom and democracy at the center of his approach to national security. His freedom agenda was perhaps best articulated in his second inaugural address on January 20, 2005, when he presented a sweeping argument that the survival of liberty in America depends on the success of liberty in other lands. "America's vital interests and our deepest beliefs are now one. . . . Advancing these ideals . . . is the honorable achievement of our fathers. Now it is the urgent requirement of our nation's security, and the calling of our time."[14]

In some respects, there was nothing new about Bush's call for freedom. U.S. presidents have defined the promotion of democracy around the world as a core national security objective for decades. Since the time of Woodrow Wilson, the United States has used democracy promotion as an argument for military intervention around the world: to "make the world safe for democracy." The goal of the Marshall Plan was to secure democracy in post–World War II Japan and Germany. Over the last thirty years, democracy promotion has become a core goal of U.S. foreign policy. President Jimmy Carter focused on human rights, President Ronald Reagan used democracy as a bulwark against communism, President George H. W. Bush sought to consolidate the democratic gains after the collapse of the Soviet Union, and President Bill Clinton promoted democracy as a buffer against instability in the tumultuous post–Cold War era.

But in other respects, President George W. Bush elevated the freedom-and-democracy rhetoric to a level well beyond that of his predecessors. In word, if not always in deed, President Bush presented himself as nothing less than a true believer in the power of freedom to transform the world. In the four corners of the world, he delivered speeches on freedom, calling for religious freedom while on a trip to China, meeting with democracy advocates and civil society leaders when visiting Russia, and making freedom the focal point in a number of other state visits. Bush is such a strong believer in the importance of freedom and democracy that he has indicated that his post-presidency plans include heading a new institute aimed at promoting freedom around the world.

Perhaps the most distinctive feature of President Bush's approach to promoting democracy and freedom is that he closely tied these efforts to his unpopular and ineffective so-called global war on terror, as well as to the war in Iraq. By 2005, the administration sought to make the case that its invasion of Iraq was advancing the cause of democracy in the Middle East and the fight against terrorism. "As Iraqis make progress toward a free society, the effects are being felt beyond Iraq's borders," Bush proclaimed. "In the last few months, we've witnessed elections in the Palestinian Territories and Lebanon. These elections are inspiring democratic reformers in places like Egypt and Saudi Arabia. Our strategy to defend ourselves and spread freedom is working. The rise of freedom in this vital region will eliminate the conditions that feed radicalism and ideologies of murder, and make our nation safer."[15]

Yet in each of these cases in the Middle East, the conservative vision that freedom would defeat the forces of terrorism and extremism has backfired or has never gotten off the ground. In Iraq, conservative and, in some cases, extremist Shi'a and Sunni political parties garnered popular support. In other instances, terrorist organizations such as Hamas seized the reins of power. Rather than defeating terrorism, the conservative vision of democracy—narrowly defined as electoral processes—actually empowered extremist forces. Outside the Middle East, democracy stalled in Russia, with President Vladimir Putin's increasingly autocratic behavior, and in Pakistan, as President Pervez Musharraf ran roughshod over democratic institutions in a blatant bid to retain power. In all cases, two pivotal factors were missing: one was the long-term integrated approach to help build the governing institutions and the civil society structures that are needed for true democracy and freedom to take root; the second was prosperity.

As President Bush headed into his final year in office, the global trends in freedom continued to spiral downward. At the beginning of 2008, Freedom House's annual *Freedom in the World* report declared that freedom was in retreat and that "the year 2007 was marked by a notable setback for global freedom." One-fifth of the world's countries—including large and politically important nations such as Pakistan, Russia, Nigeria, and Venezuela—saw reversals in political rights and civil liberties.[16] Kenya, which was long a standard of stable democracy in Africa, erupted in violence following irregularities in its 2007 presidential election.

Why did the global march to freedom stumble and limp just as President Bush increased his advocacy of it? Studies and polls conducted across the globe with ordinary citizens in Asia, Africa, Europe, and Latin America uncovered a crucial ingredient in the struggle for advancing democracy and freedom in the world: prosperity and the need to focus on helping more people obtain decent lives. Voting and elections are only one essential part of a functioning democratic and free society. All too often, more fundamental rights, including economic and social rights, were overlooked in the push to advance democracy. The failure to recognize that democracy is broader than holding an election has undermined Bush's democratic crusade.

President Bush's approach to advancing democracy also became too closely associated with his Iraq policy, and the chaos that enveloped Iraq in 2006 and 2007 was hardly the sort of thing that people living under repressive regimes wanted for themselves. Because of Iraq, Bush's global freedom strategy lacked credibility. Many people around the world saw democracy promotion as a code word for regime change by force, and this undermined the sense of security that all people crave. Speaking about Iraq, one Syrian human rights activist said, "What happened in Iraq makes the entire region afraid. People don't want to risk occupation, chaos, and sectarian bloodshed. And the Syrian regime is playing on those fears."[17]

Another factor that contributed to the stalling of the global march toward freedom was the perception that the United States did not practice what it preached, particularly when it came to the abuse of prisoners in the Abu Ghraib scandal in Iraq, as well as the open-ended detention of terrorist suspects in Guantánamo Bay, Cuba. The world saw fewer checks and balances and a decline in the rule of law in Bush's policies, as terror suspects were sent to secret prisons or detained by regimes that have poor human rights records. New initiatives to wiretap phone calls without sufficient judicial oversight, as well as legislation supported by Congress and the Bush administration to allow certain forms of torture in interrogations, raised questions about American credibility in promoting freedom and democracy around the world. "Do as we say, not as we do" became the world's cynical interpretation of U.S. rhetoric on advancing freedom.

American actions can help to inspire or undermine democratic change around the world. But ultimately, the internal conditions within a nation will determine its march toward freedom. And in many cases, Bush's push for democracy left out a critical ingredient: the strengthening of the central pillars of democracy. These include rule of law, justice, and a balance of power between different branches of government. Other indispensable ingredients include the need for individual economic well-being and prosperity, for personal safety from conflict and terror, and for access to a decent job and health care.

The two most vivid examples of the failure of the Bush-style promotion of democracy are in Iraq and Afghanistan. After removing two of the most repressive regimes in the world from power, the Bush administration worked to quickly hold elections and empower a new set of leaders in both countries. But these leaders did not feel in control in large part because of their inability to deliver material security and services to their people. Free participatory elections may have bestowed a temporary degree of legitimacy on these leaders, but they were unable to sustain it because they simply could not give their people what they needed and wanted. Where the main pillars of democracy are not in place, democracy cannot flourish. For instance, Afghan president Hamid Karzai lamented, "We are still among the poorest in the world. While we have better roads, we are still the worst in the world. While we have improved our supply of electricity, we are still the worst in the world. While our education has picked up a lot, we are among the worst. We still have the lowest literacy rates in the world. We are still the worst in child mortality."[18]

Nearing the end of his term in office, President Bush has not achieved tangible advances toward democracy in Afghanistan and Iraq, the two countries where his administration has spent nearly one trillion dollars. Both countries had elections, and both had started to build the institutions that were necessary to help democracy take root. But neither has become the glowing success story that President Bush had hoped they would, in inspiring a new global wave of freedom.

A Backlash against Democracy in Latin America and Russia

Latin America is a prime example of a place where freedom's march has stalled, in large part due to declines in the quality of life. A United Nations report found in 2004 that income inequalities, poor economic growth, and poverty were undermining confidence in democracy. Although 60 percent of the people in the region still believed that democracy is preferable to any other system of government, troubling trends lie beneath that belief. For instance, a 2004 survey found that more than half of the people supported the replacement of a democratic government with an authoritarian one if it could produce economic benefits. Fully 58 percent agreed that leaders should "go beyond the law" if they have to. More than half (56 percent) said that economic development was more important than maintaining democracy.[19]

Today, Latin America has overcome the Cold War era of proxy wars and human rights violations. During the "lost decade" of the 1980s, much of Latin America was mired in meager economic growth. The external debt crisis, hyperinflation, and macroeconomic stagnation or decline forced a fundamental rethinking. Since that period, Latin America has liberalized trade, welcomed foreign investment, and privatized many state-owned entities, including utilities and banks. It has also achieved better fiscal and monetary management. The hyperinflation of the past is now reduced to single digits and trade is increasing. But inequalities are also growing across the region.

Latin America has some of the highest rates of inequality in the world. Fully 40 percent of the region's population lives below the poverty line. The richest 10 percent receive nearly half of the total income in Latin America, while the poorest 10 percent receive only 1.6 percent. The problem is not just income inequalities but also inequalities of access to public services, including education, health care, utilities, and law and order.[20] The indigenous populations are especially hard hit. In countries with significant indigenous or Afro-descendant populations, such as Brazil, Bolivia, and

Guatemala, the incomes of these sectors of society are half those of whites. Such populations are beginning to fight back and demand equal rights and access to wealth. The indigenous leaders Evo Morales in Bolivia and Alejandro Toledo in Peru effectively drew on indigenous support in their election bids.

Latin America lags in other key areas. Education falls behind other regions, especially at the secondary level. To succeed, Latin America must break out of its slow growth, high poverty, inequality, poor education levels, and slow technological progress. Its diverse nations will need more effective ways to narrow the divide between the haves and the have-nots.

Over the last decade, more people in Latin America saw democracy as a system that failed to deliver, and they turned to populist leaders, even if they were demagogues intent on consolidating their power. A democracy or any other system of government is only as good as the benefits it delivers to its people, and antidemocratic leaders have used the economic card to boost their power and crack down on political dissent. In Venezuela, President Hugo Chavez, who launched a failed coup attempt as a military officer in 1992 and later won the presidency in 1998 running on a populist, anticorruption, antiestablishment platform, gradually took steps to increase his power and institute tighter controls over the media, the judiciary, and independent opposition groups. Chavez used the country's vast oil wealth to fund new social service programs and boost his personal popularity and his grip on power. In the Western hemisphere, then, President Bush's freedom agenda never really got off the ground because of his administration's lack of focus on the region and its disregard for the basic building blocks of prosperity.

It did not do well in Russia, either. As economic growth increased, Russian president Vladimir Putin used this additional wealth, much of it driven by a surge in global oil and gas prices, as leverage to expand the government's powers and squelch political opposition. The Russian economic recovery had begun at the end of the previous decade, and from 2001 to 2005, Russia experienced robust annual economic growth averaging 6 percent.

Just as economic growth was increasing, political rights and civil liberties declined. Russia saw its political transition endangered by Putin's moves to dismantle press freedoms and weaken independent institutions. Pluralism slowly shifted toward a consolidated state control of power. As the Russian observer Stephen Sestanovich put it, "Russia's institutions are less transparent, less open, less pluralist, less subject to the rule of law, and less vulnerable to the criticism and restraints of a vigorous opposition or independent media."[21] By 2004, Russia had backslid so far that Freedom House assessed that it had fallen back into the "not free" category of countries, and it continued to experience declines in freedom through 2007.

Putin jailed his political opponents, and others fled into exile. For instance, he jailed Mikhail Khodorkovsky, the head of Yukos, the world's fourth-largest oil company and a potential political rival. The suspicious murders of the prominent investigative journalists Anna Politkovskaya and Ivan Safronov, as well as the London murder of the former Russian intelligence officer Alexander Litvinenko, who was poisoned by the heavily restricted polonium-210, raise questions about how far Putin and his successors may go to consolidate power and squelch dissent. As he cracked down on democratic freedoms, Putin's public approval ratings increased well above 70 percent by 2007.[22]

With Putin's second term coming to an end, the highly popular president arranged to keep his hands on the reins of power. His handpicked, obscure successor, Dmitri A. Medvedev, won the March 2008 elections by a landslide, and the two have agreed that Putin will serve in the powerful position of prime minister.

The examples of countries such as Venezuela and Russia demonstrate that prosperity and economic growth are a double-edged sword: leaders can use prosperity to undermine democratic reforms and consolidate their hold on power. Democracy will take hold only if the pillars—independent institutions such as the judiciary and the media—exist alongside prosperity. Only with the proper checks and balances in place can democracy deliver on core human rights: personal security, law and order, food, clothing, shelter, and health care.

Why Egypt Did Not Have Its Own
Orange Revolution

For the last fifty years, Egypt has been ruled by a strong presidency that has effectively used the military, the security services, and state resources to maintain a tight control over all meaningful forms of political authority. The ruling National Democratic Party (NDP) dominates the political scene in Egypt, holding a strong majority in the People's Assembly and maintaining dominance over regional and local government structures. Opposition political parties exist, but they are weak and lack broad-based support. The government has banned the Muslim Brotherhood and other Islamist parties from establishing formal political organizations and formally competing as a slate in elections.

Just as President Bush became increasingly vocal in his push for democracy, there were hints of political reforms emerging in Egypt. Street protestors demanded more competitive elections, and Egypt's judiciary, which is considered one of the most independent and impartial judiciaries in the Arab world, issued demands for even greater independence in its oversight of the electoral process. In 2005, the Egyptian regime responded to these demands for change with limited tactical reforms, amending the election law to allow competitive presidential elections for the first time in Egypt's history.

To seize on a possible opening to advance democracy in Egypt, Secretary of State Condoleezza Rice flew to Cairo in June 2005 and delivered a speech at the American University of Cairo that contained a "to-do" list for Egypt: "The Egyptian Government must fulfill the promise it has made to its people—and to the entire world—by giving its citizens the freedom to choose. Egypt's elections, including the Parliamentary elections, must meet objective standards that define every free election. Opposition groups must be free to assemble, and to participate, and to speak to the media. Voting should occur without violence or intimidation. And international election monitors and observers must have unrestricted access to do their jobs."[23] The speech received mixed reviews, in part because of the perception that Rice was issuing demands and lecturing to Egypt.

Nevertheless, some democracy proponents who had worked for decades for political reform were heartened, including activists who had formed the "Kifaya" movement—"Enough!" in Arabic. The group had clamored for political change in the summer of 2004 and had organized protests against President Hosni Mubarak's running for a fifth term of office. But in the end, no mass movement emerged. Unlike Ukraine, which had received decades of support from outside groups to help build independent pillars for democratic reform, Egypt's repressive government had placed severe restrictions on the assistance provided by outsiders. And even though Egypt had seen some economic growth, the gap between the haves and the have-nots was much greater than it was in Ukraine. Subsequently, it was hard for mostly elite movements like Kifaya to organize broad-based grassroots support. Unlike in Ukraine, few Egyptians brought food and material support to the relatively small number of protesters after the election. In addition, Egyptians faced brutal and sometimes violent responses from the country's security services. The combination of repression and lack of broad-based economic growth had lulled the vast majority of Egyptians into an apathy that was hard to break.

Most Egyptians did not care about what was happening in the formal political system; they were deeply disengaged in large part because they were focused on more basic needs: jobs, education, and the chance for better lives. President Bush and his administration may have seen freedom's clarion call as the way to win over the rest of the world, but for far too many Egyptians, the type of freedom Bush was pushing was irrelevant if the formal governing structures could not deliver what they wanted. Egyptians' dominant preoccupations were with their country's economic troubles: recent price increases, unexpected currency exchange fluctuations, unemployment, and the perception of a growing division between the rich and the poor. People worried about meeting their families' basic needs. As one middle-aged man in Alexandria said, "These days . . . people don't even care about Palestine. They just care about providing their families with their daily food."[24]

Interviews conducted in 2004 with Egyptians from all walks of society confirmed the pervasive nature of economic concerns. There was a strong sense among the public that Egypt's long-standing social contract was disintegrating; people had become more selfish and did not look out for one another, and the government no longer guaranteed the provision of essential services. Some Egyptians worried that weakened social bonds and economic troubles were contributing to other problems like crime, drugs, and a general loss of values. As one man in Cairo said, "Our major problem in Egypt is that people only think of themselves—everyone is thinking 'me, me, me,' and they don't care about others. If we stop this selfishness, things would be better."[25]

Some Egyptians, particularly those living in cities, complained about Egypt becoming a country of *wasta*—a corrupt favoritism based on personal and family connections. They saw *wasta* as playing too strong a role in relations and affecting all types of decisions, from selecting players on Alexandria's football team to hiring for everyday jobs. As one young man in Alexandria said, "I got a job in government only because I had *wasta*. Without this *wasta*, I would not have been able to get the job."

Furthermore, most Egyptians considered political rights meaningless under their current political system. Many saw formal politics as an elite game and viewed debates among political leaders as irrelevant to their lives and concerns. Few Egyptians said that they have ever voted in elections, confirming reportedly low rates of voter participation. Reasons that were cited for not participating in formal politics included people not seeing a direct impact on their lives, the perception of electoral fraud and cheating, and bureaucratic inefficiencies that made it difficult to obtain voter identification cards. One young woman from a Nile Delta village outside of Tanta said, "If I felt that things would change or would be affected by my voting, then I would definitely do it." One woman in Cairo added, "They keep discussing the bread crisis in the People's Assembly and they keep condemning the bread price increases, but then nothing is done." A man from a rural village in Upper Egypt near Asyut said, "After a candidate wins, nothing happens. You cannot even reach him again—they don't have time for us."

Despite their widespread disengagement from formal politics, some Egyptians still held out hope that changes could make their political participation more meaningful. When asked about their views of democracy, Egyptians' associations were largely positive, with freedom of speech and opinion and equality coming in as top responses to the question of how they define democracy. Some people stated that democracy was an essential part of Islam. As one young man in Cairo said, "We have this concept of *shura* [consultation] in Islam, and *shura* means democracy. I should listen, respect what I am listening to, and discuss it." Not everyone, however, was a fan of democracy. One college-educated young man in Cairo was particularly forceful in his objection, saying, "This concept of democracy is being exported to us as part of the intellectual war they [the people of the West] are waging against us."[26]

Such suspicions about democracy, as well as the broader apathy about formal politics in Egypt, help to explain why Egypt did not experience its own Orange Revolution. In fact, Egypt's old order found itself more deeply entrenched after the rumblings for democratic reform in 2004 and 2005. On September 7, 2005, President Mubarak was reelected for a fifth term, rivaling the time in office of most pharaohs of ancient Egypt. Mubarak won with more than 88 percent of the vote. The official tally of voter turnout was low at 23 percent, and some people thought that it was probably even lower. The runner-up, Ayman Nour, who received a little more than half a million votes,[27] was convicted of forging signatures on his party's registration papers and sentenced to five years in prison, where he has remained at the start of 2008.[28]

After the arrest of the opposition figure Ayman Nour in 2005, the United States put talks about a free trade agreement with Egypt on hold, but the United States took no other major steps to press the Egyptian government on reform, even though Nour's imprisonment marked the beginning of a new phase of restrictions imposed by the Mubarak government. In 2006, the Egyptian government cracked down on judges who protested against electoral irregularities and for greater judicial independence. Greater press restrictions were imposed, and several independent journalists were arrested for various crimes, which included insulting the president. Emergency law was extended, and a referendum in the spring of 2007 passed a series of measures that expanded the powers of the presidency.[29]

Unlike Ambassador Pascual in Ukraine, U.S. diplomats dealing with democracy promotion in Egypt were operating without a coherent strategy that incorporated the full range of U.S. interests that were in play in Egypt; these included the Arab-Israeli peace process and the fight against global terror groups. Perhaps most important, the relationship was mishandled at the very top.

Although President Mubarak had a close relationship with every U.S. president during his quarter century in power, he has had no such relationship with President Bush. The relationship first soured following Mubarak's visit to Bush's ranch in Crawford, Texas. Before Mubarak had even left U.S. airspace, President Bush made a public statement that represented a shift in the U.S. stance on the Arab-Israeli conflict. Mubarak was humiliated before he got home. The Iraq War further damaged the relationship, and Mubarak has not been back to the United States since. Even the infrequent transcontinental phone calls are short and not very friendly.

Despite the soaring rhetoric about freedom, the Bush administration's policies on democracy did not make much of a long-term impact in Egypt. "It was not clear what . . . the United States accomplished or intended to accomplish," said Issandr El Amrani, a journalist based in Cairo since 2000 who watched the Egyptian political developments closely, first as a journalist and later as an editor in a leading independent weekly newspaper.[30] Two years after Secretary Rice had made her impassioned plea for expanding freedom and democracy in Egypt, with no serious follow-up policy actions, she traveled back to Egypt and barely mentioned the freedom agenda. Instead, she spoke of "common interests" between Egypt and the United States.[31]

As Hisham Kassem, a prominent Egyptian publisher and democracy activist who won an award in 2007 from the National Endowment for Democracy, explained, "George Bush made the first serious U.S. attempt on democratization in Egypt. . . . Now we've seen this U-turn take place—and believe me, this U-turn was very damaging—people who put their necks out on the line and risked their lives and reputations. There are a lot of disappointed people."[32]

The march toward freedom in Egypt had not only stalled, it had sputtered out. As Kassem lamented, "It's really sad—we did see tangible results. And we're seeing now a counterattack from the regime—they are taking back the territory that was gained in this democratic opening. The minute the United States backed off, Mubarak went back to take more power."[33]

The United States talked a good game but did not actually develop the policy instruments to advance its goals. The end result was a net negative: U.S. credibility was harmed, no real democratic progress was achieved, and no substantial changes were made in the quality of life for ordinary Egyptians. As the Bush administration headed into its final year of office, it had substantially downgraded its focus on and expectations for democratic reform in Egypt. Freedom had not marched, and the lives of ordinary Egyptians had not improved. Ukraine's Orange Revolution had stood on strong democratic pillars supported by the United States and others and thus was able to move forward. Egypt's push for democracy collapsed, in part because of an incoherent and inconsistent approach to democracy promotion by outside powers, including the United States.

Bangladesh: A Democracy That Fails to Deliver Prosperity Collapses

While democracy never really got off the ground in Egypt, another Muslim-majority country that had experienced a democratic transformation slid back into authoritarianism. Bangladesh, one of the world's poorest and most populous countries, is a prime example of the dangers of focusing on political rights and elections without paying sufficient attention to more important needs such as security and economic development. Bangladesh has more than 150 million people living in an area about the size of the state of Wisconsin. It became independent from Pakistan in 1971. Although the country periodically held elections in its first two decades of independence, it came under military rule in 1982 when General H. M. Ershad seized power in a bloodless coup, declared martial law, and suspended the constitution.

Ershad used the democratically elected government's corruption and ineffectiveness as his rationale for seizing power.

But by the 1990s, democracy seemed to take root in Bangladesh. In 1991, the country passed a referendum that transformed its political system from a strong presidential system into a parliamentary democracy. It held four national parliamentary elections: one in 1991, two in 1996, and another in 2001. Bangladesh seemed to be a model to the world of a secular Muslim democracy.

But in 2007, military rulers in Bangladesh again seized control and declared a state of emergency just as Bangladesh was preparing for its fifth election. What happened? A major factor was the inability of the government and the two main political parties—the Bangladesh Nationalist Party (BNP) and the Awami League—to work together to deliver on promises to the people. Both parties were guilty of political violence, and Bangladesh topped global lists of the most corrupt countries in the world. Boycotts of Parliament by the opposition party and strikes, or *hartals*, that closed down major cities all contributed to a deadlocked political system that had the features of democracy and allowed most freedoms but simply did not deliver on basic needs.

A series of interviews and a poll conducted in 2004 offered signs of the brewing trouble, demonstrating strong public discontent with the deadlock in Bangladesh's political system and growing dissatisfaction with the government. One woman in the eastern city of Chittigong said, "One party always blames the other. The party in power blames the party that used to be in power. We don't understand all of these things." Some ordinary citizens directly blamed democracy. A young man, also from Chittigong, a supporter of the then ruling BNP Party, blamed democracy for creating anarchy: "Because of democracy, the opposition is given the chance to destabilize the government. Democracy could create anarchy—the opposition tries to destabilize the government two hours into its tenure."[34]

As prosperity stalled, the public's enthusiasm for democracy waned. The Bangladeshi government failed to provide for the needs of its people, which were so fundamental that when asked what they understood by the term *human rights*, the second leading response among Bangladeshis was "basic needs": food, shelter, and clothing. (The leading response, 44 percent, was "don't know.") For ordinary citizens in Bangladesh, human rights meant social and economic rights, rather than political rights and civil liberties, which underscored the dominance of material concerns. One woman living in the rural area of Laksam, when asked whether she thought that men and women were equal, responded, "Yes, if I am starving, my husband will also starve. So we are equal."[35]

Although voter turnout was consistently high in Bangladesh's elections, public disenchantment with the government was growing. A series of terrorist bombings inside Bangladesh in 2005 heightened security concerns, and more Bangladeshis worried about their personal security as crime increased, economic woes continued to plague the country, and endemic corruption remained unaddressed.

Fifteen years of democratically elected but ineffective governments in Bangladesh opened the door for the military to reassert control. The military rulers who seized control in 2007 arrested the two previous prime ministers and charged them with corruption. The new military leadership sought to clean up Bangladesh and restore order, but the way the leaders did it led to questions about how far they would go to limit freedoms. Although it remains unclear whether this is just a temporary slide back into military rule for Bangladesh, one primary lesson from the decade and a half of its most recent democratic period is that an electoral democracy that fails to provide people with prosperity is not likely to remain in place for long.

The Way Forward: Promoting Democracy with Prosperity

After three decades of advances for global freedom, democracy has stalled around the world.

What caused this global trend toward greater freedom to stall? It was not a lack of vocal support and advocacy on the part of President Bush, nor was it a lack of funding. The Bush administration matched its rhetoric with increased funding for democracy promotion, doubling the funds for the National Endowment for Democracy, introducing a new Middle East Partnership Initiative at the State Department to promote reform in the Middle East, and creating the Millennium Challenge Corporation, a new development fund that provided development assistance to countries on a competitive and conditional basis.

Many factors explain the pause in the upward trend toward greater democracy and freedom in the world, and they offer lessons for a better way forward. Some backsliding was related to measures undertaken by governments globally in response to the threat from terror groups such as al-Qaeda. Some represented a crackdown by authoritarian governments. In other cases, the pressures of globalization created a backlash against reform. Until the United States changes course and begins to lead the effort to address the concerns that people have that can trump their desire for democracy or freedom—their need for decent, safe, and prosperous lives—no freedom agenda will prevail. Certainly, the United States cannot on its own deliver democracy abroad. But it can help the forces of democracy work to strengthen the pillars essential to creating democracy.

STOP: Making democracy promotion a crusade. When democracy is viewed as a crusade to advance U.S. interests, it is likely to backfire. The next U.S. leader must stop pushing democracy abroad with a "Made in America" label on it. America's strong support for the highest human rights and democratic standards must remain a top priority, but U.S. leaders need to stop creating impractical expectations. We must stop trying to impose a system and recognize that people understand when their system, whether democratic or not, delivers on their most basic needs. Overselling the freedom agenda can create unrealistic expectations and can also leave the impression that democracy is part of a broader American crusade to dominate other countries.

START: Practicing what we preach about democracy and human rights. If it is to successfully promote democracy abroad, the United States must ensure that it respects democracy and its own Constitution at home. The sad truth is that in fighting the war on terror since 2001, the United States is guilty of some of the human rights violations that are outlined in the State Department human rights reports on other countries. Independent human rights monitors and journalists point out abuses by U.S. troops against detainees in Iraq, Afghanistan, and Guantánamo Bay, Cuba. These reports of violations make the task of promoting democracy abroad all the more difficult. This is not only a philosophical or moral consideration; it has practical implications. Many countries in the region are pointing to America's diminished record on civil liberties as an argument against reform. Our moral authority and capacity to actually encourage change and reform may be hampered by actions we have taken in the name of fighting terror.

STOP: Narrowly focusing on elections. Elections in a vacuum can make things worse. By pushing early elections in the Palestinian territories, the Bush administration brought Hamas to the fore. A myopic focus on elections in Iraq has exacerbated tensions among the various factions. The Iraq experience serves as a vivid reminder that rapid democratization can exacerbate conflict and tensions within societies. Democratization changes the prevailing power structure, threatening the political status and the gains of established elites, who then seek to protect their position and access to power. In doing so, they may appeal to religious or ethnic differences to mobilize support or to create a climate of disorder and violence that discourages any further change in favor of maintaining the status quo.

START: Building institutions that are necessary for democracy to take root. In making sure that popular support for democracy grows, the United States must place greater emphasis on building credible governing institutions that are responsive to societal concerns. In post–Saddam Hussein Iraq, no government has yet provided Iraqi citizens with basic security and services. Egypt's government, too, has failed to provide for the people or plant strong roots for the pillars of democracy. Yet both countries have had elections. Unless governing institutions provide for the material needs of the people, the government will lack political authority and legitimacy, and citizens will turn to alternative mechanisms to meet their essential needs for security and services. People must see that a democracy can deliver better lives for them.

In advocating for elections, the United States must ensure that the fundamental structure and framework for political competition exists. The United States must improve its capacity to help other countries develop the institutions and the processes that Americans take for granted: a functioning tax system, a department of motor vehicles that is free from corruption, a public education system that grants equal opportunities, and all sorts of everyday things that actually help people improve their standing in life. Although elections are indispensable for helping societies choose their top leaders, it is the long-standing institutions that have been too often overlooked in the Bush administration's push for democracy and freedom.

STOP: Using threats of force and regime change. The threat of military force against countries such as Iran is actually counterproductive to efforts made by human rights advocates. Threats of war will undermine ordinary people's sense of security and stability. Now that the world has seen the aftermath of the Iraq invasion, this scenario will not motivate reformers—and, more important, ordinary citizens—to support changes to the power structures in their countries. On the contrary, a "regime change by military force" approach to democracy promotion is likely to backfire by giving less space to reformers in other countries and unifying people against possible military aggression.

START: Resolving conflicts that undermine the foundations for democracy. This means investing more in diplomatic efforts than we have to date to work with other global leaders to help divided factions in other countries to agree on the core principles for building cohesive political institutions. In countries that are divided along ethnic and sectarian lines like Pakistan, Iraq, and Nigeria, this means helping leaders negotiate new compacts and internal power-sharing agreements to create the space for democratic competition that does not destabilize.

STOP: America's go-it-alone approach to promoting democracy. With its focus on shunning international institutions, the United States has undermined the global resources that can help build democratic institutions across the world. The United States should coordinate democracy and governance strategies with European institutions and international organizations such as the World Bank and the United Nations Development Program, which also support political reform.

START: Promoting democracy with long-term coordinated strategies to improve daily lives. Helping people obtain a right to vote is only one part of ensuring that their government is responsive to their needs. As the examples of Bangladesh, Iraq, Egypt, and Pakistan indicate, holding elections without concurrently making a strong and effective push toward improving citizens' quality of life can undermine the overall freedom promotion project. It is vital that the United States work closely with and help coordinate the many different countries and multilateral organizations that are dedicating their resources to advancing economic development, as well as democracy and good governance. The next U.S. leader must work with other countries, as well as with leading multilateral institutions like the World Bank, to ensure that political reform efforts are implemented with a close eye to the overall standard of living and quality of life of ordinary citizens.

The next U.S. leader should look for ways to encourage multilateral forums to set standards and create clear benchmarks for simultaneously improving democratic governance and the economic well-being of citizens. During the Cold War, the OSCE's (Organization for Security and Cooperation in Europe) Helsinki Process did just this, and it was an effective way to encourage the expansion of democracy and the respect for human rights in central and eastern Europe.

Finally, patience is required. Sometimes democracy and prosperity require generations to take hold. In some cases, as in the Arab world, the progress in making fundamental structural changes to societies will be a slow evolution, rather than a quick revolution. If the United States understands the necessity of a nuanced approach and for various programs tailored to the needs of each country, progress can truly be made. Only then will prosperity be achieved for people around the world—Vitaliy Moroz in Kiev, Hisham Kassem in Cairo, the journalists in Moscow who work under threatening conditions, the indigenous people of Latin America struggling to make ends meet, and the young man in Chittigong who is concerned that democracy may create anarchy. To stop the recent backsliding in global freedom, the United States needs to return to its core values, move beyond the Bush administration's narrow freedom agenda, and put a more comprehensive prosperity agenda at the heart of its strategy.

four

Energy: Leading the World Where It Needs to Go

E verything seems to be going up except income," lamented
fifty-two-year-old Randy Bobula of Iron River, Michigan.
Married with two grown children, he struggles to make
ends meet on his $800 monthly disability check from Social
Security, supplemented by his wife's part-time work at a local
drugstore. Randy was injured on his job taking care of apartments eight years ago, and now he has trouble heating his home,
filling his car's gas tank, and living a normal middle-class life.
"We can't go on vacation, we can't go out to eat like normal
people do," he explained. "Everyone else has a steak, we have to
have hot dogs."[1]

Heating his home—a fixer-upper he got through his mother-in-
law—is a particular challenge, given cold Michigan winters that
average little more than 21 degrees Fahrenheit. Randy estimated
that he needs to fill his house's fuel oil tank between four and six
times to make it through the winter, but at $900 a tank, he can-
not afford to heat his home. Although help during the previous
year came from the Citizen's Energy Corporation, a nonprofit

group that provides fuel assistance to lower-income individuals, he does not know how long he can count on that.

Randy is not alone in his struggle. The price of gas reached record levels in the summer of 2007, and Americans across the country took an estimated $20 billion hit.[2] Gas prices hovered well over $3 a gallon in most parts of the country for the past year. In the summer of 2005, approximately 40,000 Massachusetts residents couldn't pay their electric bills and faced possible power and heat cutoffs as they headed into the colder months. One mother in Boston stopped cooking dinner to conserve energy and save money; instead, she gave her kids peanut butter and jelly sandwiches to eat.[3] With millions in state and federal energy subsidies slashed from the budget in 2007, even more people are now struggling to pay their bills. Yet too many politicians in Washington seem blissfully unaware of the pain inflicted on hardworking middle-class American families by the rise in energy prices. These high energy prices are one acute symptom of America's flawed and shortsighted energy strategy. We are paying more for energy sources that pollute the planet and strengthen the hand of dictatorships and autocrats in dangerous countries around the world.

Some people have argued that the United States is facing the biggest challenge in a generation: providing affordable energy to a growing economy without destroying the environment or relying on oil imported from unstable parts of the world. This problem isn't only an American one; it is a global challenge shared by all people. In the developing world, the rising cost of energy keeps millions from making the transition to the middle class. And as the developing world industrializes, it is using the dirtiest sources of energy: oil and coal. This reliance on fossil fuels contributes to the global warming crisis and puts much of the prosperity of the developing world at risk. Millions struggle to breathe clean air in major metropolitan areas, from Beijing to São Paulo and Mexico City to Mumbai, where unregulated vehicles and unclean coal and oil pollute the air. China and India are especially dependent on coal, with no changes in sight to relieve the ever-growing haze of pollution over their cities. Millions more will be displaced as coastal water rise and wipe out their farmlands and homes.

Many people in other countries blame the United States, the largest contributor to global warming over the last two centuries. Even though former vice president Al Gore was ridiculed by some people when he first sounded the alarm, the facts are now clearly on his side. Human burning of fossil fuels is heating the atmosphere, putting the health of the planet and its people at risk. Unless the United States—and the world—changes its collective approach to energy, there is no doubt that the planet will face hotter temperatures, rising sea levels, more severe storms, greater disruptions, and increased conflict. Water scarcity is already a major issue in Africa and Central Asia. We need smart government and U.S. leadership to change this dangerous course.

Global dependence on oil is undermining global prosperity and security. Oil saps America's power as surely as kryptonite does Superman's. To meet its growing energy needs, China is investing heavily in the developing world, supporting corrupt and repressive regimes throughout Africa in its bid to secure long-term contracts. Venezuela's president is using his petrodollar wealth to undermine the country's democracy and economic stability. Russia is playing hardball with its oil, reasserting government control, and keeping investors out.

Yet the U.S. government is not smart about addressing these challenges. Despite President George W. Bush declaring in his 2006 State of the Union address that "America is addicted to oil," it has been decades since the federal government has taken serious steps to address the crisis. The United States has no real policy to reduce its oil and gas consumption; to help Americans pay their rising energy bills; to shift away from our current dependence on imported oil from unstable areas of the world, such as Saudi Arabia and Venezuela; and to transition to cleaner sources of energy. Even worse, Washington has largely rejected international efforts to move toward cleaner energy sources or to address global warming.

Anyone who is familiar with twelve-step programs that help people with addictions knows that admitting you have a problem is the first step toward recovery. By admitting the oil addiction, President Bush helped the country take the first step toward dealing with this growing global security problem, but his policies did little to change America's behavior. Twelve-step programs have eleven more steps for a good reason.

We must confront the triple challenge of energy: its growing costs, which have made the American dream more elusive for more Americans; the national security threats posed by many of the countries that are chief sources of oil and gas; and the global threat posed by pollution and global warming.

Pundits and presidential candidates have called for an Apollo space program or a Manhattan Project on energy. What the conservative-led government has delivered on energy is more like a bridge to nowhere.

America's addiction to oil is weakening U.S. security at home and abroad. Today, much of the world sees the United States as a gas-guzzling, polluting breaker of international agreements, and a friend of corrupt oil-exporting nations. That image undermines America's efforts to lead the global fight against the myriad challenges it faces, such as terrorism and nuclear proliferation. The United States must change course now by turning away from a conservative agenda that has done little more than boost the profits of oil companies while harming the environment and the economic well-being of ordinary Americans.

Driving: America's Way of Life Now Produces Sticker Shock

Americans' love affair with gas-guzzling cars is perhaps the most vivid example of our failure to admit the need for change. Two hundred twenty million adults spend, on average, an hour and a half in their cars each day. The average household owns two cars, trucks, or sport utility vehicles; one-quarter owns three or more.[4] This is a big country, with four million miles of roads and highways from sea to shining sea, and Americans both want and need to drive. This addiction to automobiles may explain why the United States as a country does a poor job of making public transportation a convenient and affordable alternative. Among Americans, 93 percent prefer to travel by car even if public transportation is available, and 56 percent believe that it is less expensive for them to drive than to take public transportation, even as the price of gasoline has skyrocketed.[5]

If we're not going to change the way we get to work, then we'll have to change the cars themselves. The addiction to gas guzzlers is gutting our prosperity. In 1973, the price of gas in today's dollar was $1.48, rising to $2.77 in 1981 before dropping down again in 1986 to $1.59. It hovered between $1.40 and $1.80 until the turn of the century, when it began a steady increase, reaching $2.75 in 2006.[6] The rise in the national price for regular gas to a record $3.22 a gallon in the summer of 2007 cost the American people another $146 per year for each car they drive.[7]

The price of gas will continue to rise. While many critics have sought to blame oil companies for price gouging, most analysts attribute the rising costs to broader geopolitical and geo-economic shifts. A leading factor in the rising price is growing demand, particularly from countries like China and India that are experiencing rapid economic growth as more people work to pull themselves out of poverty and into a middle-class lifestyle. As more people improve their lives, the increased global demand for fuel drives down inventories of oil and gas. Other factors contributing to higher prices are continued Middle East instability and the rising costs of production as cheaper sources are depleted.[8]

Sixty-eight percent of the oil used in the United States today is for transportation, and 97 percent of our cars still run on it. After Congress imposed Corporate Average Fuel Economy (CAFE) efficiency standards following the gas crisis in the early 1970s, automotive fuel economy rose from 13.5 miles per gallon in 1975 to 18 miles per gallon in 1978, to 23 miles per gallon in 1985. Yet in the two decades since, efficiency has stalled. Washington has kept standards constant at 27.5 miles per gallon since 1990.[9] Long-overdue congressional efforts to raise CAFE standards were introduced at the end of 2007. Congress passed legislation that President Bush signed into law on December 19, 2007, to boost average fuel efficiency standards from 25 miles per gallon to 35 miles per gallon by 2020, with the new standards taking effect for 2011 model cars.[10]

Even though Washington finally moved forward on increasing these standards, the U.S. auto industry was hurt by the government's slowness, which cost American workers their jobs. In fact, according to 2007 reports, U.S. car manufacturers for the first time accounted for less than 50 percent of the U.S. market, in part because Americans are demanding more fuel-efficient cars that are made overseas.[11] Chrysler today has only half the plants that it did in the 1950s and is closing even more. The bankrupt auto supplier Delphi Corporation wants to close 21 of its 29 U.S. plants, while Ford Motor Company plans to close 16 plants by 2012 and General Motors Corporation will shut down 12 factories by the end of 2008. The mayor of Newark, Delaware, Vance Funk, lamented the closing of the Chrysler plant in his town: "It's not the fault of the workers. People are demanding cars that get better fuel economy and they're only building a full-size SUV."[12] Ford did not even introduce the first American hybrid until 2004, four years after the Toyota Prius began to sell in the United States. U.S.-made flex-fuel vehicles that are capable of running on E85 ethanol fuel were introduced around 2000, although most of them still run on gasoline.

Solving the national, much less the global, energy crisis will take a lot more than fuel-efficient cars, however. It will require a revolution in thinking and innovation across the energy field. Public-private partnerships will be needed to spur new technologies. The United States must diversify its sources of energy and find ways to secure its energy supplies in an age of terrorism and global warming.

After 9/11, Americans looked to their leaders to make major changes to bring about a new, safer world. Energy policy should have been one of the main pillars of change. But the conservative agenda espoused by President Bush failed to meet the new challenges of energy security. He relied on twentieth-century solutions to a twenty-first-century problem. This is a new type of problem that requires a renewed focus on global prosperity. A strategy to improve our country's energy security is directly linked to advancing prosperity abroad.

How Our Oil Addiction Undermines International Stability and Prosperity

Since the middle of the last century, U.S. consumption of oil has grown steadily, except for a brief period in the 1970s and the early 1980s when fuel-efficiency standards and high oil prices caused a reduction in use.[13] Today, 40 percent of our total energy consumption comes from oil, 60 percent of which we import, leaving us dependent on an energy source that pollutes the environment and links the United States to unstable, repressive regimes. Unless we change course, we will leave our children an energy policy that prevents them from achieving the prosperity they deserve. The legacy of our energy approach could connect our children's well-being even more closely to the world's least stable regions. Steps must be taken now to relieve this burden; solutions won't be easy and won't come overnight, but the right leadership can ensure that future generations enjoy at least the same chance of having a safe, prosperous, and healthy life that previous generations have had.

The U.S. occupation of Iraq has led some people to charge that Americans are giving their blood for Iraq's oil. Importing Arab oil fuels Osama bin Laden's false but popular narrative that the United States is stealing the Arabs' resources. Bin Laden has used oil as a rhetorical weapon in his attempts to foster hatred toward America, calling on his fighters to stop the export of Arab oil— "the greatest theft in history"—and to "focus operations on [oil] production, especially in Iraq and the Gulf areas, as this will cause [the Americans] to die off."[14] America's close relationship with Saudi Arabia's authoritarian government, in particular, is one of the top reasons that bin Laden and other terrorists seek to attack Americans. The largest oil producer in the world, Saudi Arabia is the birthplace of bin Laden and the state patron of the extremist Wahhabi sect of Sunni Islam that has fostered instability across the globe. Its ruling royal family is increasingly unpopular at home as the per capita income of many Saudis has declined during the last two decades.

The top countries that the United States imports oil from include Canada, Mexico, Saudi Arabia, Venezuela, Nigeria, Iraq, Angola,

Algeria, Ecuador, and Kuwait.[15] Of these, only Canada, Mexico, and Ecuador are not members of the Organization of Petroleum Exporting Countries (OPEC), a global oil cartel that controls more than 70 percent of the world's proven oil reserves.[16] Venezuela, Nigeria, Angola, Ecuador, and Algeria all face considerable threats to their internal stability that could threaten the supply of oil in the United States, most notably poverty, crime, and corruption.

Oil-hungry nations cozy up to oil-rich regimes to secure a steady supply of oil. As one study found, the policies that develop from such symbiotic relationships include protecting oil-rich regimes from international sanctions and investing in large infrastructure projects as part of various deals to secure oil concessions. One reason that Europeans have been reluctant to follow the tough U.S. lead in opposing Iran's nuclear ambitions is that they fear losing Iran's 2.5 million barrels per day of oil exports.[17] This dynamic is no secret to the oil-rich regimes of the world.

Oil also provides problematic regimes with vast resources with which to advance their policies—policies that are often at odds with U.S. interests, its allies' interests, and even the interests of the regime's own people. For instance, Russia, rich in oil and natural gas reserves, can tilt toward more authoritarian rule without fear of outside criticism, and its influence will only grow as it exports increasing amounts of oil and gas to Japan and China. Russia has already used oil as a weapon to play hardball with Ukraine, shutting off its energy exports in 2006. Venezuelan president Hugo Chavez is using his oil wealth to buy influence and spread his populist anti-Americanism throughout the hemisphere. He has lent billions of dollars to Argentina since its economic collapse in 2001, funded schools in Brazil, lavished trade deals on neighbors, and purchased $25 million in Ecuadorian debt. He has funded a Bank of the South to counter the influence of the International Monetary Fund—and the United States—on the continent.

Because our close relationship with oil-rich regimes has served as a recruiting tool for terrorists, our energy infrastructure here at home is vulnerable. As the energy expert Daniel Yergin pointed out, America's energy security has been about managing a disruption of oil supplies from producing countries. The United States must broaden that policy to include protecting the entire energy supply chain and infrastructure. Tankers are an especially vulnerable part of the supply chain. Every day, 40 million barrels of oil cross the oceans in tankers, with chokepoints along the way that are easy for terrorists to target.[18]

America's Prosperity and the World's Rising Middle Class: Win-Lose or Win-Win?

The days of bargain gas are gone forever, for two reasons. First, the cheapest oil has already been extracted—future reserves will come only at higher economic and environmental costs. In August 2007, the Russian explorer Artur Chilingarov planted the Russian flag on the seabed floor of the North Pole, signaling that the competition for the region's oil and gas was well underway. Experts have identified oil and gas deposits in northern Canada and under the Barents Sea near Russia and Alaska. But the remoteness of the area and the extreme climate conditions are likely to increase production costs, and some of the technology that is needed to extract the region's hydrocarbons will likely remain unavailable until midcentury.[19]

Second, the growing global aspirations for prosperity are pushing energy demand to record levels. People in the developing world are beginning to travel more as they earn more and move to the cities. As gross domestic product (GDP) grows, increased trade by trucking and freight transportation will add to the demand. The choices that the developing world makes in meeting its growing energy needs will affect not only American prosperity in the years ahead, but the billions around the world who also seek to live healthy lives. China, Indonesia, and Brazil now rank just behind the United States in the amount of greenhouse gas they emit, according to the World Bank.[20]

Coal is China's biggest polluter, while deforestation and poor land management put Indonesia and Brazil at the top of the list of emitters.[21] Burning and cutting down forests releases greenhouse gases such as carbon dioxide and also removes trees and plants that would otherwise absorb carbon dioxide. Brazil's government has resisted foreign involvement in the management of its massive

Amazon rainforest and has been reluctant to participate in carbon markets, insisting that industrialized countries need to shoulder the burden of responding to climate change, given wealthier nations' contribution to the buildup of greenhouse gas pollution over the previous two centuries of industrialization. It took a severe 2005 drought, which ruined crops, kindled forest fires, dried up transportation routes, and wrought economic havoc, for Brazil's leaders to reconsider their opposition and begin to crack down on deforestation.[22]

The biggest factors, however, will be the energy choices made by China and India, the two largest developing countries which will make up the world's greatest growth in energy demand, especially for the dirtiest sources, coal and oil. China is on track to pass the United States as the world's largest absolute emitter of greenhouse gases by 2009, although not on a per capita basis.[23] Some believe China may have already done so. As a result, the health of the Chinese people is suffering. Simply breathing the air in Beijing on some days is equivalent to smoking two packs of cigarettes a day.

By December 2007, global oil consumption had reached 84 million barrels per day. This is an increase of 7 million barrels per day since 2000, of which China accounted for 2 million barrels daily. China had been self-sufficient in oil until 1993 but now imports almost half of the oil it consumes. India's demand is growing, too, at about 40 percent of China's rate. India is also undergoing a coal boom, with its use expected to increase fourfold by 2030. India's per capita energy consumption rates remain low in comparison to the rates of countries like the United States and China. But India, the world's fifth-largest energy consumer, is projected to surpass Japan and Russia to become the third-largest energy consumer by 2030.[24] Like Brazil, both China and India do not feel that it is their responsibility to combat climate change, despite direct threats to their environments and economies.[25] Chinese leaders note that much of their emissions are the result of manufacturing products for export to the United States—cheaper products that American consumers love.

As China's demand for oil grows, its energy policies may increasingly influence its foreign policy decisions and may indirectly fuel global conflict. China's quest for energy has already started to affect the lives of people around the world. A notable example is China's energy interests in Sudan and its impact on the Darfur conflict. Since the crisis in Darfur began in 2003, 400,000 people have been killed, with another 2.5 million displaced. In 2006 alone, more than 2,500 rapes were reported in Darfur. And despite pledges of "never again" following the genocides of World War II and Rwanda, the world has stood idly by. The reasons for this conflict are complex, but they include environmental degradation and Sudanese oil.

The environmental role is indirect but real, helping to form the conditions for conflict. The United Nations reports that there is a very strong link between land degradation, desertification, and conflict in Darfur, noting that rainfall in northern Darfur has dropped by one-third over the last eighty years.[26]

Oil is a major factor in perpetuating the conflict. The world has the power to force an end to the crisis, yet in large part because of China, it has refused to put any significant pressure on Sudan and its vast oil resources. China has a veto-wielding permanent seat on the United Nations Security Council and has successfully blocked any harsh sanctions against Sudan. Russia has tended to back China, and the two nations have resisted efforts by the other three permanent members—the United States, Great Britain, and France—to press for tougher measures.

As the United States and Europe sought to sanction Khartoum for its actions in Darfur, China poured an estimated $15 billion into Sudan and gave it an interest-free $13 million loan to help rebuild the presidential palace and a $2 billion loan to help cover its budget deficit. China's state-owned China National Petroleum Corporation (CNPC) has invested at least $5 billion in Sudan's oil industry. Sudan's profits from its CNPC deals gave it the funds to purchase attack helicopters, armored vehicles, and small arms from China—the very weapons that Khartoum uses to carry out its deadly campaign in Darfur.[27]

In return, China receives a steady supply of oil from Sudan, about 7 percent of its total oil needs. More than half, and perhaps as much as 80 percent, of Sudan's oil exports go to China.[28] This cozy relationship between oil and arms has led activists to call for a boycott of the 2008 Olympics in Beijing, dubbed the "Genocide Olympics" by human rights activists. The pressure from activists led movie director Steven Spielberg to resign from his role as artistic adviser to the games.

Sudan is far from the only place where China is actively advancing an energy-driven foreign policy. Oil can also account for China's more lenient stances on Iran and Saudi Arabia. And in 2004, China extended a $2 billion line of credit to Angola at only 1.5 percent interest over seventeen years to finance infrastructure construction by Chinese companies. China provided Angola with another $3 billion in credit in 2006. It has also offered grants and low- or no-interest loans for pharmaceuticals and health programs in Nigeria and Kenya. Chinese officials call these "loans for oil" and believe that such aid helps to convince local governments and people that "China can play a positive role in their country's economic development."[29]

America's current policy is to wag its finger at China and tell China not to make foreign policy decisions based on oil, even if the United States sometimes does. The failure of this approach is obvious. Instead, the United States should help China and other aspiring nations to adopt clean technologies, thus leapfrogging the polluting twentieth-century model they're headed for. Otherwise, this win-lose competition for resources could potentially fuel future conflicts when different countries respond to internal pressures from their own people for better lives and more chances at economic advancement.

Currently much of the economic growth in China and India is fueled by an energy policy that is dependent on a zero-sum global scramble for energy resources that pollute the environment. Ordinary people who are working to lift themselves out of poverty and into a decent life in the developing world have increased overall global energy demand. This has driven up prices and hurt the economic livelihood of people like Randy Bobula in Michigan. The United States needs to lead worldwide efforts to accept the new realities of global energy and recognize that prosperity and energy security at home is directly linked to prosperity and energy security in other countries.

The Threat from America's Addiction
to Dirty Energy

Former vice president Al Gore has been ridiculed over the years for his fixation on global warming. During the 1992 campaign, Gore was mocked by the presidential candidate George H. W. Bush as the "ozone man." The popular cartoon show *South Park* ran an episode portraying Gore as a modern-day Chicken Little.[30] But as vice president, he made the issue a priority and managed to put the Clinton administration's stamp on the 1997 Kyoto Protocol. In October 2007, Gore was awarded the Nobel Peace Prize, together with the UN's Intergovernmental Panel on Climate Change (IPCC).[31]

Global warming is a threat to the world's prosperity. Rising temperatures will cause more violent storms and more dislocation of people; in many parts of the world, it threatens our very way of life. The coastlines of New York and Florida could be inundated. But people in the developing world will be hit hardest, with vast swaths of land submerged under water. For instance, the World Bank estimates that a rise of one meter in sea levels would force 60 million people in developing countries to abandon their homes. One-tenth of the population living in river delta areas in Egypt and Vietnam would be displaced. As much as half of Bangladesh's rice lands would be flooded, forcing 30 million people to flee. More than 10 percent of urban areas and 7 percent of agricultural lands would be lost.[32] As the largest contributor to today's global warming, the United States risks taking much of the blame. There is still time to stop the worst effects of global warming, but only if the United States leads a global effort to address the threat.

Although a number of naturally occurring factors influence the global climate, the IPCC concluded in February 2007 that warming was "unequivocal" and that it is "very likely" (greater than 90 percent certainty) that most of the warming since the mid-twentieth century is due to human activity.[33] Global warming occurs when significant amounts of greenhouse gases are pumped into the atmosphere from the burning of oil, coal, and natural gas.[34] Deforestation, such as in Brazil, also contributes to the planet's hotter temperatures. Temperatures have been rising at a historically rapid pace, and NASA's Goddard Institute ranked 2005 as the warmest year on record. Globally, all ten of the warmest years on record have been since 1990.[35]

Together, the combustion of coal and petroleum emitted four times as much carbon dioxide as did natural gas.[36] Because they are also the world's cheapest energy sources, current trends indicate that the use of such fuels will continue to rise over the next generation.

While most politicians focus on U.S. dependency on oil, Americans get half of their electricity from coal-fired plants, each of which produces about 3 million tons of carbon dioxide per year. Coal-burning power plants are being built at the rate of about two per week worldwide, and coal is expected to surpass oil as the largest source of carbon dioxide emissions by 2010.[37] The extraction and the use of coal as a fuel result in many environmental problems, such as mountaintop removal, water pollution, and air pollution, but the main global threat is coal's contribution to global warming.

Natural gas is plentiful and burns more cleanly than coal or petroleum does and provides a little more than 20 percent of U.S. energy needs. It fuels much of the U.S. electric power and industrial sectors and heats more than half of all the homes in the United States. The cleanest sources of energy in terms of greenhouse gases, however, are nuclear power and renewable sources such as solar, wind, and ethanol. Nuclear energy provides 6.5 percent of the world's energy needs and 16 percent of the world's electricity, including 20 percent of U.S. electricity. One rarely hears laudatory words about the French from U.S. politicians, but even the solidly conservative senator John McCain has asked, if "France can produce 80 percent of its electricity with nuclear power, why can't we?"[38]

Nuclear power could eventually displace coal as a fuel, but a major effort must be undertaken to address the unsolved nuclear problems: safety risks, proliferation concerns, and waste storage. Political opposition to nuclear power remains strong in the United States, and it has been three decades since a new nuclear power plant was approved for construction. For most Americans, talk of nuclear power revives fearful memories of the near meltdown of the Three Mile Island plant located a few miles from Harrisburg, Pennsylvania, in 1979.

But with global warming and soaring energy costs, nuclear power is back on the table. President Bush's Global Nuclear Energy Partnership envisions nuclear power at the center of the effort to make energy clean by helping developing nations to obtain secure, cost-effective, and proliferation-resistant nuclear power. The goal, as President Bush described it, is to give developing nations "a reliable source of zero-emissions energy." James Connaughton, the chair of Bush's Council on Environmental Quality, has ambitious plans for nuclear power plants: "Today we have 400. . . . As we go forward . . . is the globe prepared to develop in advance what could be a need for 1,000 to 2,500 nuclear power plants?"[39]

The United States has 104 nuclear power plants at present. But in September 2007, NRG Energy, Inc., of New Jersey and the South Texas Project Nuclear Operating Company filed an application to build two new nuclear power reactors at the South Texas Project nuclear power station site. This is the first full nuclear plant license application in the United States in three decades. Federal tax incentives and loan guarantees played a pivotal role and were the "whole reason" the companies moved to build the new plants, said David Crane, NRG's president and CEO.[40] If the United States is going to meet its growing energy demand in part by expanding nuclear power, the government will need to get involved by financing the initiative; the start-up costs for new plants are high. It is far from clear whether such public support can be garnered.

Although operating costs are low for nuclear power plants, nuclear power is economically unpalatable to many energy companies due to the significant expenses associated with starting new plants. Experts estimate that nuclear power is more expensive over its lifetime than either natural gas or coal,[41] and that nuclear power will cost a full cent more per kilowatt-hour than comparable gas and coal plants.[42] Building new nuclear power plants also takes time. The cycle of assessing environmental impact, obtaining licensing from the Nuclear Regulatory Commission, and constructing a plant takes ten to fifteen years.[43] Thus, even if nuclear power's safety, cost, security, and environmental problems can be solved, nuclear power at best offers only a medium- to long-term solution to the energy crisis.

Small-government conservatism, with its focus on deregulation, could expose the United States to unnecessary risks if nuclear power is expanded without safeguards. The challenges associated with nuclear power plants are significant, and solving them will not be easy. The possibility of catastrophic accidents occurring and the subsequent release of radioactive material must be addressed. There are real proliferation risks as well, especially regarding the storage areas in places such as the former states of the Soviet Union and Pakistan. There is also a question of where to contain the waste. In the United States, nuclear waste will be buried in the controversial Yucca Mountain site.

Renewable energy—solar, wind, ethanol, and other sources that can be replenished—are increasingly popular in America. The actress Daryl Hannah built herself a house that runs largely on solar energy, corporate jets are under pressure to be "carbon neutral," and *The Daily Show with Jon Stewart* poked fun at Nantucket's not-in-my-backyard (NIMBY) attitude regarding a proposed wind farm in Nantucket Sound. This NIMBY problem pervades much of the energy debate, especially regarding the storage of nuclear waste.

As appealing as renewable sources of energy are, they still make up only a negligible portion of U.S. energy. Only 0.4 percent of today's energy is geothermal, solar, or wind. Hydropower is only 2.2 percent. Proponents of renewable energy sources argue that with the right government support of new technologies and research, renewable energy could provide 50 percent of U.S. energy needs by 2030 and as much as 80 percent by 2050.[44] Yet most analysts agree that over the next twenty years, the use of alternative fuels—particularly in the transportation sector—will remain modest, barring any dramatic new technological advances.[45]

Developing renewable energy technology will not be cheap, but it is imperative that the United States does so. The most ambitious cost estimate is by the International Energy Agency (IEA), which argued that as much as $17 trillion will be needed for new global energy development over the next twenty-five years.[46] Certainly, the United States is failing to make an adequate investment. In fiscal year (FY) 2007, the Energy Department allocated only $159 million to solar research and development, $303 million to nuclear energy, $427 million to coal, and $167 million to other fossil fuel research and development.[47] In contrast, the FY 2007 budget for the National Missile Defense program was $8.9 billion, on top of $9.4 billion that was budgeted in the previous fiscal year.

If the United States fails to move to cleaner sources of energy, there is no doubt that the rest of the world's population will suffer the consequences of global warming. Rising temperatures are already affecting the Earth, in ways that include longer warm seasons, melting glaciers, and more violent storms. In North America, rising temperatures have led to more intense and frequent wildfires, the spread of crop pests, and an increase in shellfish disease. Since the 1950s, average temperatures in Alaska have increased by almost 4 degrees Fahrenheit. There has also been extensive thawing of the permafrost that underlies most of the state, putting at risk billions of dollars in capital investments in oil and gas pipeline infrastructure.

To avoid the worst effects of global warming, experts estimate that industrialized nations must reduce their greenhouse gas emissions 60 to 80 percent by 2050.[48] Others have suggested that even steeper cuts are needed, and sooner. The earlier action is taken, the better. If action to reduce emissions is delayed by twenty years, rates of emission reduction may need to be three to seven times greater to meet the same target. Delays of even five years can be significant. The only way to reduce global emissions is by a return to negotiations for another global treaty to set and achieve reduction targets.

In December 2007, delegates from 187 countries met in Bali, Indonesia, to discuss a new and more comprehensive framework to replace the Kyoto Protocol. Although it attended the talks, the United States was still largely dragging its feet. It refused to offer a clear commitment to reduce its emissions and even rejected setting provisional targets for reductions in greenhouse gases. But the issue continues to unfold and the 2007 climate talks set a goal of negotiating a new greenhouse gas reduction agreement by 2012.

Reviving American Leadership on Global Warming

Like other international challenges to our security and prosperity that require collective action, such as stopping the spread of dangerous weapons and promoting increased trade, global warming demands global action. Yet efforts are stalled because of a lack of American leadership. The United States must reverse course.

Six months after taking office, President George Bush strode into the Rose Garden and declared the Kyoto Protocol on global warming dead, calling it "fatally flawed in fundamental ways."[49] Since that time, President Bush has undermined the treaty, resisted efforts to place mandatory controls on emissions, and thwarted international efforts to develop bold policies to address the crisis. Instead, his plan is to rely on advancements in technologies, nuclear energy, and cleaner coal. Critics of Bush's approach believe that the only way forward is to adopt legally binding targets for emissions reductions, as was done under the Kyoto Protocol.

The 1997 Kyoto Protocol, which set binding targets to reduce emissions below 1990 levels by 2012, legally entered into force on February 16, 2005, after Russia ratified the treaty. More than 174 countries, including every industrialized nation except the United States, have ratified the Kyoto Protocol. Many have already begun to make progress toward meeting their emissions targets.[50] The protocol divides governments into two general categories: developed countries and developing countries. At the time, the developed countries were responsible for most of the greenhouse gases heating the Earth over the last two centuries of the industrialized period. Therefore, they, not the developing countries, were the ones that were required to take action.

The developing world is rapidly catching up to the United States, however; as noted previously, by 2009 China is expected to surpass the United States in per annum emissions. One of the toughest aspects of making future progress will be negotiating a new treaty that includes the reluctant developing nations, especially India and China. Another will be convincing key constituencies in the United States that global environmental controls will not weaken the U.S. economy. Neither Clinton nor Gore was able to secure ratification by the U.S. Senate for the Kyoto Protocol.

Today, the atmosphere is a free dumping ground for polluters. Most policy makers agree that the only realistic way to reduce the use of carbon dioxide–emitting forms of energy is to put a price on greenhouse gas emissions, but there is no consensus on how to do this. The option that is most supported by members of the U.S. Congress is a cap-and-trade scheme analogous to the U.S. acid rain system adopted in 1990. The other, less politically popular option is to institute a carbon tax. With a cap-and-trade system, the level of pollution is established, with an unknown price on emissions. With a carbon tax, the opposite is true: the price on emissions is set, but the effect on emissions levels is not.[51]

Advocates for reducing greenhouse gas emissions worldwide generally agree that mandatory policy controls are a sine qua non of progress. The Bush administration has opposed any mandatory policy to contain and reduce national greenhouse gas emissions. Rather, the Bush policy set a voluntary "greenhouse gas intensity" target for the nation, a policy trick that would actually allow emissions to increase. The 18 percent reduction in emissions intensity by 2012 that the policy calls for would allow actual emissions to increase 12 percent during that period.

The Bush administration has consistently undermined international efforts to achieve bolder action. For instance, at the Gleneagles G-8 meeting in 2005, the United States watered down language on funding commitments and targets proposed by the other G-8 members. The United States again blocked G-8 consensus at a 2007 meeting of G-8 environmental ministers. This time, it objected to a carbon trading market and language regarding the economic interests of developing countries in environmental protection.

During the September 2007 General Assembly gathering in New York, UN Secretary General Ban Ki-moon convened a High Level

Event on Climate Change. Eighty leaders at the meeting called for a comprehensive process and a new framework to replace Kyoto by 2009, with a breakthrough at the United Nations Climate Change Conference held in Bali in December 2007. Bush skipped the UN's meeting on the issue and instead hosted his own meeting of representatives of seventeen major economies, plus the United Nations.[52] At the meeting, he pledged to host another meeting in the summer of 2008 and to seek agreement on voluntary goals for emission reductions by 2009.

While the Bush administration resists effective global measures, the European Union and local governments are setting the international pace on climate change and energy issues. The leaders of the EU member nations agreed in March 2007 to cut carbon dioxide emissions 20 percent from 1990 levels by 2020 (or 30 percent, if other developed nations follow suit), to raise to 20 percent their share of renewable energy use by 2020, to have 10 percent of their transport fuel coming from biofuels by 2020, and to phase out incandescent lightbulbs by 2010. States and cities across the United States are setting their own caps on greenhouse gases and are determining fuel-efficiency standards for automobiles. Such efforts by New York City mayor Michael R. Bloomberg and California's governor Arnold Schwarzenegger landed them on the cover of *Time* magazine, with the headline, "Who Needs Washington?" and an article titled, "The New Action Heroes."[53]

The developing world needs to do its part as well. Officials complain about "green imperialism," arguing that developed countries are seeking to hold developing countries back through onerous environmental regulations. As Brazilian president Inacio Lula da Silva said in 2007, "Everyone knows that the rich countries are responsible for 60 percent of the gas emissions. . . . We don't accept the idea that the emerging nations are the ones who have to make sacrifices, because poverty itself is already a sacrifice."[54] Indian prime minister Manmohan Singh has expressed similar views, positing a false choice between economic growth and efforts to combat global warming. While the developed world must do more to reduce global warming, that is no excuse for inaction by developing countries.

As demonstrated in the December 2007 agreement in Bali, there is a growing consensus in the developed world, if not in Washington, that a new post–Kyoto Protocol must be in place well before Kyoto expires in 2012. "By 2009, we will need a common understanding that all developed countries need to be playing on the same field, with quantitative mitigation targets, and that major developing countries need to be playing on a matching field, one which involves recognition and positive incentives for their measurable action," said a South African minister attending the UN conference in September 2007.[55] The meeting in Bali helped build momentum for a new agreement on greenhouse gas reduction, but ultimately achieving a new global deal will depend on leadership from the next U.S. president.

The Way Forward to a Clean and Prosperous World

Today, the dangers of failing to stem the effects of global warming are clear. Hurricanes are getting stronger, droughts and wildfires occur more often, sea levels are rising, and more than a million species face possible extinction. The science is also clear: the gas, the coal, and the oil we burn put too much carbon dioxide and other gases into the Earth's atmosphere. Those trapped gases are putting our planet—and us—at risk. The United States must lead the fight against global warming, both at home and abroad. More states, cities, and businesses across the country will have to join in the effort. The world expects no less from the United States, and it shouldn't have to.

The economic cost of inaction will only continue to grow. Not only is it getting more expensive to reach oil reserves, the growing demand for energy will further drive up prices. These higher costs will reduce America's economic growth and prosperity. For instance, a $25 per barrel increase in oil prices reduces real income by about 1 percent of GDP.[56] In fact, one study estimates that inaction could cost 5 to 20 percent of global GDP each year, compared to the 1 percent of GDP that it would cost to reduce greenhouse gas emissions.[57]

We can take steps now that will make our energy more afford-able, safe, and clean. The United States must establish a national policy on climate change and then lead other nations in adopting a new international treaty to reduce global greenhouse gas emis-sions. By taking bold action now, the United States can help to ensure that a transition to cleaner energy will be a win-win for Americans, for people throughout the developing world, and for this planet. In doing so, we must also recognize that our foreign policy and our energy policy are now mutually dependent. The United States must get both of them right for Americans to be safe and prosperous. That means using less Arab oil and an end to the free pass that many of the world's oil-rich nations have in shunning the global rules against unfair subsidies and corruption.

It is time for America to end its addiction to fossil fuel energy and to enter the following energy policy rehabilitation program:

STOP: Stonewalling on meaningful legislation that would reduce greenhouse gas emissions. The United States must establish a man-datory national policy that will first stabilize and then reduce its greenhouse gas emissions. The policy must include a target for meaningful and achievable long-term reductions in emissions. To avoid dangerous climate change, the target recommended by scien-tists is a 60 to 90 percent reduction below 1990 levels by 2050.[58] Key to this will be putting a price on greenhouse gas emissions to rectify the market failure that has left the atmosphere a free dumping ground. Such an effort will also require Americans to reduce their consumption of oil, gas, and coal, especially for transportation, through mandatory regulations for more efficient vehicles. The December 2007 legislation passed by Congress to raise fuel standards is a belated step in the right direction. Taking the lead on something the whole world needs will result in more benefits than merely thicker ice caps and safer beach communities.

START: Spearheading negotiations for a post–Kyoto Protocol global climate framework. The first step in leading the world again is to actually *lead*. The United States must return to the international negotiating process and guide the effort to devise an affordable, mandatory, and equitable post–Kyoto Protocol global framework for reducing climate change risks. Ideally, the deal reached in Bali should be accelerated and lead to a new agreement that should be in place by 2010, two years before the Kyoto Protocol expires. The new agreement must contain meaningful, mandatory targets. The United States cannot solve climate change on its own, but the rest of the world cannot solve climate change without the United States. President Bush may make some progress in working with the coalition of key nations that he brought together in September 2007, particularly because the group includes China and India. Only twenty-five countries account for 83 percent of the global emissions of greenhouse gases. If the United States can get them to agree on a way forward, progress will be possible. But only a mandatory global agreement that includes the developing countries will be sufficient to stop the rise in the world's temperatures.

STOP: Making exceptions to every rule for oil-exporting nations. The bargain the United States has had with corrupt Arab regimes to ignore their repressive systems in exchange for cheap oil should have ended on 9/11. But today, countries with oil, from Saudi Arabia to Sudan and Nigeria to Venezuela, don't have to play by the rules. And importing oil from such unstable parts of the world puts Americans at risk. The United States must begin to side with the citizens of the world, not with the oppressive regimes that rule them. We should work to diversify our energy resources while working with other leading powers to promote reform in these repressive countries. (And invading these countries to take control of their oil supply or promote democracy is not the way to do it.)

START: Leading the world in innovation again, with electric cars and alternative fuels. We need a national, well-funded program for energy security, efficiency, and alternative energy sources. In 2007, Congress voted to create the Advanced Research Project Agency for Energy (ARPA-E) to develop new energy technologies and strategies. Modeled after a Defense Advanced Research Projects Agency that was begun in response to the Soviet launching of Sputnik in 1957, ARPA-E will support out-of-the-box research to help move the United States away from fossil fuels and into renewable sources of energy.[59] This new agency, signed into law by President Bush in August 2007, must hit the ground running. As part of the effort, the U.S. government must provide the financial incentives that are needed to stimulate research, development, and deployment of cleaner, more efficient technologies far above the ARPA-E budget. The government must also eliminate misaligned incentives and barriers to taking action, such as removing the 54 cents per gallon tariff on imported ethanol. Beyond the environmental benefits, perfecting and then exporting these technologies will be both lucrative and laudable.

STOP: Putting the costs of America's energy addiction on the backs of the poor. The U.S. government must do a better job of providing assistance to Americans who are struggling to heat and cool their homes and fill up their gas tanks. People who are hurt by rising energy costs need income relief, such as an expansion of the Low Income Heating and Electricity Program. But America's middle class would also benefit from more fuel-efficient cars and must have access to renewable, cleaner sources of energy. Some Americans may even be willing to put up windmills in their backyards. Abroad, it is the developing countries that are hurt the most by the rising costs of energy. The United States must lead an effort to support the world's poorest countries in their climate change–adaptation efforts. Sharing our own technological progress can help many countries avoid the worst effects of industrialization. Africa, for instance, is blessed with vast renewable energy sources, which, if developed properly, can help the continent skip over the worst polluting phases of development. Such an effort will be crucial in any post–Kyoto Protocol negotiations to bring developing countries into the next climate change regime.

START: Developing a global energy-management system. Create a global system to manage the world's energy supplies, and keep it fair and secure. As the energy needs of the developing world expand, devising a set of rules that apply to all equally will be crucial in managing shortages, maintaining adequate stockpiles, ensuring the security of supply routes, and improving the flow of information. The International Energy Agency, set up by the Organization for Economic Cooperation and Development (OECD) countries to track energy markets after the oil shocks of the early 1970s, should be expanded, especially to include China and India. There should be an improved flow of information about world markets and energy prospects. As part of this system, a new global network of trade and investment would be created, with a transparent set of rules.

Without a major breakthrough in technology or a vast change in political attitudes, the United States and the world will remain dependent on the two most polluting sources of energy: oil and coal. That means our children will breathe polluted air, face soaring oil bills, and remain dependent on uncertain energy supplies. We must act now to change course and put the next generation on a better, more prosperous path.

The United States can change global warming and its addiction to oil and other dirty fossil fuels. If we act boldly, Randy Bobula and millions of other Americans will have a better chance of living their middle-class dreams, and billions around the world will have healthier and more secure and prosperous lives.

five

Winning the World Over by Eliminating Nuclear Weapons

In November 2002, Lieutenant Commander Steve Brock, a thirty-four-year-old navy officer, and much of the U.S. Navy Seventh Fleet staff were on their way from Japan to Hawaii for meetings with the U.S. Pacific Command when they got the word about "a big development" that was important to the fleet. Staff members were to return immediately to the flagship, USS *Blue Ridge*, to execute an important round-the-clock counterproliferation operation. Post-9/11, this had to be big.

Brock and his shipmates returned immediately to Japan and the USS *Blue Ridge* and joined the frenetic effort to locate the target: the *So San*, an unmarked North Korean shipping vessel that U.S. intelligence believed was carrying dangerous materials to Yemen. The vessel had left a port in Nampo with no identifying marks on it, raising a red flag for U.S. officials who were on the lookout for illegal transfers of weapons of mass destruction.

President George W. Bush had charged that "North Korea is a regime armed with missiles and weapons of mass destruction, while starving its citizens," when he named Pyongyang as part of the "axis of evil" in his 2002 State of the Union address. Any shipment headed for the Middle East could mean trouble. "North Korea doesn't like to hear me say it, but they continue to be the largest proliferators of missiles and ballistic technology on the face of the earth," said the Secretary of Defense Donald Rumsfeld.[1] Following the attacks on September 11, 2001, the Bush administration wanted to develop new ways to keep the world's most deadly weapons out of the hands of terrorists and state sponsors of terror. The administration was shifting away from multinational arms control efforts and instead focusing on preventive war and regime change, which included preparing to overthrow the Iraqi regime. It had also initiated a new program, the Proliferation Security Initiative (PSI), to stop shipments of dangerous materials on the high seas.

To intercept the *So San*, Lieutenant Commander Brock's theater commander ordered the use of all necessary resources—aircraft and ships—in a 24/7 effort to find and track the vessel. Once they found it, they were to wait for further instructions. The navy team faced a monumental task in trying to plot the vessel's probable course. The farther the *So San* sailed away from North Korea, the more unknown variables came into play. The navy team knew the time frame and the destination—the North Korean ship had left port in Nampo in early November en route to Yemen—but they did not know which direction it would take or how fast it was going. The list of unknowns was long: Would it make port calls in China? Would it load or drop off cargo along the way?

"With every passing hour, the circle became bigger and bigger," said Brock. The *So San* would have to pass through certain choke points on its course to Yemen, such as Singapore's Malacca Straits. But even in the straits, it would be like finding a needle in a haystack. More than fifty thousand vessels—nearly a quarter of the world's sea trade—passed through the straits each year. As Brock described the challenge, "It's like being at a football game, with thousands of people walking quickly by and you have to recognize the average-looking guy with blond hair."[2]

The crew spent Thanksgiving on watch. Ships and aircraft were pulled away from their routine missions, and finding the *So San* became a primary focus of the entire fleet. Commanders adroitly apportioned and deployed additional resources while still running daily operations in the U.S. military's largest area of operations. And the search went on. "Days and days of just pulling your hair out," Brock remembered. "Everyone had a theory of how to find it."

Finally, in early December, a navy surveillance plane sent in images that matched the ship they were seeking. Because the pilots had spotted many similar-looking vessels, they needed the team on the *Blue Ridge* to identify it. After the navy team carefully pored over the photographs, shouts and high fives went around the control center; they had succeeded in their mission.

Back in Washington, officials decided to turn to America's close ally Spain for help in seizing the vessel. On Monday, December 9, two Spanish vessels circled the ship in international waters about six hundred miles off the coast of Yemen in the Gulf of Aden and fired warning shots. When the *So San* ignored the shots, a Spanish frigate fired at it, damaging its mast. Then, in a daring raid, a helicopter hovered over the *So San* and Spanish marines jumped on board the ship. U.S. troops arrived shortly afterward and, together with the Spanish troops, found 15 disassembled Scud missiles and 85 drums of an "undetermined" chemical, even though the ship's cargo manifest listed only 40,000 sacks of cement.[3] The soldiers had done their job. As it would turn out, Washington had not.

The Prosperity Agenda Can Get the World to Follow the United States

The *So San* effort was part of the Bush administration's new approach to arms control: turning away from formal international agreements and tough diplomacy and instead seeking coalitions of the willing or simply going it alone to counter the threat of weapons of mass destruction. Such an approach has not worked because the threats are global and success depends on a global solution.

"The gravest danger facing America and the world is outlaw regimes that seek and possess nuclear, chemical, and biological weapons," President Bush declared in his 2003 State of the Union address. The only way for the United States to remain safe is for the rest of the world to join it in securing and eventually ridding the world of these dangerous materials. The paradox of the Bush approach to stopping the spread of nuclear weapons through a doctrine of preemption is that it actually made other countries feel more threatened and created greater incentives for them to acquire nuclear weapons.

The world wants physical safety, such as freedom from war and disease. People want economic opportunities to secure decent lives and the right to choose their own leaders. They want to be able to heat their homes and breathe clean air. The more the world sees America delivering on those challenges—ensuring the world's prosperity—the more it will be willing to join in the effort to keep weapons of mass destruction from the hands of terrorists. That is why promoting a prosperity agenda is so important. As Mohamed ElBaradei, the head of the International Atomic Energy Agency, said when he accepted the 2005 Nobel Peace Prize, "Today, with globalization bringing us ever closer together, if we choose to ignore the insecurities of some, they will soon become the insecurities of all. Equally, with the spread of advanced science and technology, as long as some of us choose to rely on nuclear weapons, we continue to risk that these same weapons will become increasingly attractive to others."[4]

To date, the failure to promote a prosperity agenda abroad has undermined U.S. efforts to rein in these deadly materials. So has the U.S. refusal to advance the goal of the elimination of nuclear weapons. Simply put, we have little political capital left to convince the rest of the world to follow us. The proliferation problem is serious, urgent, and getting worse. Today, there are more nuclear states than there were when President Bush took office. North Korea became the ninth nuclear state when it tested a weapon in October 2006. It is believed to have transferred nuclear materials to Syria, triggering an Israeli preventive strike against Syria in 2007. And many believe Iran is determined to become the tenth nuclear state.[5]

The list of nuclear threats continues to grow. Sixty percent of Russia's nuclear materials are vulnerable to theft or illicit transfer. Pakistan's nuclear arsenal could be at risk should the weak government of Pervez Musharraf fall to Islamists. In response to North Korea's actions, Japan is once again considering the development of a nuclear arsenal. Arab countries, including Egypt, Saudi Arabia, and Jordan, are also thinking about building civilian nuclear reactors to mirror Iran's actions. Unless we get the world behind our efforts to reverse these trends, American security will be gravely threatened.

Not only does the world see an America failing to advance global prosperity, it sees an America not living up to its own commitments on nuclear nonproliferation and even following a double standard. Worse, it sees an America breaking down the hard-fought treaties and conventions that have largely kept the world safe from attacks involving these deadly materials. For instance, the United States is reneging on the disarmament commitment it made when it signed on to the Nuclear Non-Proliferation Treaty (NPT) in 1970. In that treaty, the United States joined the four other recognized nuclear powers in pledging to pursue measures to end the nuclear arms race, achieve nuclear disarmament, and agree on "general and complete disarmament under strict and effective international control."[6] Instead, the United States refuses to discuss disarmament and is considering the development of new types of nuclear weapons. The United States has also been accused of following a double standard in offering to provide civilian nuclear technology to India, despite India's refusal to sign the NPT or to allow inspections of its nuclear weapons facilities. The United States has similarly undermined treaties and conventions to ban nuclear testing.

We are not safe from weapons of mass destruction in part because we have failed to live up to our disarmament commitments and undermined the international rules of the road that kept us safe for decades. Rather than galvanizing the world to meet the challenge posed by these deadly weapons, the Bush administration has alienated the world. In pursuing its unilateral approach to nonproliferation, the administration also put America's most precious national security assets—young men and women like Steve Brock—in harm's way in an effort that ultimately made Americans and the rest of the world less secure. We urgently need to reverse this course.

A New Way of Doing Arms Control: We Don't Do Carrots

The chase of the *So San* was a centerpiece of the Bush administration's Proliferation Security Initiative (PSI). As Bush's undersecretary for arms control and international security Robert Joseph described it, "PSI is not a treaty-based approach. There is no formal organization with a budget or a headquarters. Rather, it is a partnership among participating states, consistent with their respective national legal authorities and international frameworks, to deter, disrupt, and prevent WMD proliferation."[7] So, rather than seek to establish new international laws governing the rights of interdiction, the administration sought to build a coalition of like-minded states that would join it.

The program has had some success in interdicting illicit shipments and in tightening the noose around would-be proliferators. The administration claims that PSI partners joined forces about two dozen times to prevent the potentially dangerous transfers of materials. It also claims that a PSI interdiction, along with the invasion of Iraq, was responsible in 2003 for exposing Libya's nuclear relationship with Pakistan and for influencing Libya to give up its nuclear program. In reality, years of tough negotiations had as much to do with Libya's decision as either PSI or the Iraq War did.

While in principle PSI is a good idea, putting it into practice proved difficult. Initially, only eleven nations signed up.[8] South Korea, Russia, China, and most of the Middle East, Africa, and Latin America refused to participate. The Bush administration did eventually gain broader international support for the program.

The European Union and the G-8 have endorsed it, and after some adept diplomacy, Bush secured a unanimous UN Security Council vote endorsing the broad PSI principles in 2004. While the UN Security Council has not endorsed PSI itself or any of its enforcement or interdiction provisions, the UN Security Council resolution requires all states to refrain from transferring WMD or their means of delivery.[9]

Today, PSI has "supporters"—currently, more than seventy nations—which are encouraged, not required, to commit to a Statement of Principles to strengthen and enforce their own non-proliferation laws, and to participate in training activities and actual interdiction operations. Programs such as PSI should be continued, expanded, and strengthened wherever possible.

But such programs are no substitute for a global system of arms control that sets up tough rules to reduce the amount of dangerous materials available for proliferation. Critics question PSI's legality under international law, claiming that it contradicts the law of freedom of movement.[10] In addition, PSI does little to address the underlying insecurities that drive countries to acquire these weapons or the financial incentives that prompt countries to sell them. PSI does not include the worst proliferators and addresses only a small part of the proliferation problem. It is simply no match for the overwhelming challenge of preventing the dangerous diversion of weapons of mass destruction.

When President Bush took office in 2001, administration officials sought to undermine the decades-old system of arms control that was designed to limit the spread of nuclear, chemical, and biological weapons. The undersecretary of state for arms control and international security John Bolton and his successor Robert Joseph took the lead in making clear the administration's disdain for, and distrust of, international arms control agreements. As Bolton admitted in early 2007, the administration "put me in charge of arms control and I don't believe in arms control."[11] He also vociferously opposed negotiations with North Korea or Iran, boasting, "I don't do carrots."[12] Thus, as the Bush administration pressed its PSI program and focused on regime change for would-be nuclear states like Iran, it weakened the very global system that is essential to keeping Americans safe.[13]

Bolton may have been the main lightning rod for the new approach, but he had the full support of the administration. As the then national security adviser Condoleezza Rice explained in 2001, the "Arms control treaties of the 1970s and 1980s came out of a peculiar, abnormal relationship between the United States and Russia . . . so the process can look different."[14] In 2003, another defense official bluntly stated, "Arms control is dead. . . . The answer to dealing with nations that harbor terrorists is not arms control; it is to go in there and disarm them."[15]

Bush officials did not trust the United Nations, international conventions, or any perceived intrusion on their ability to act as they wished. Many officials in the administration believed that the entire process of negotiating and implementing arms control treaties was both unnecessary and harmful to U.S. national security interests. In a memorandum to opinion leaders, Gary Schmitt, of the neoconservative Project for the New American Century, wrote, "Conservatives don't like arms control agreements for the simple reason that they rarely, if ever, increase U.S. security."[16] Conservatives instead argued that international conventions on nuclear, chemical, and biological weapons promoted a false sense of security because some governments did not live up to their word. They argued that such international instruments in fact made America less safe by limiting the types of weapons the United States could use in its self-defense.

Bolstered by such arguments, the administration turned instead to the use of force to address proliferation threats. Certainly, circumstances exist when the use of force may be the only way to address a proliferation concern. Israel bombed Iraq's nuclear facilities in 1981. President Bill Clinton authorized the bombing of suspected weapons sites in Iraq during the 1998 offensive Operation Desert Fox. That same year, after al-Qaeda's attacks on two U.S. embassies in Africa, the Clinton administration bombed a suspected chemical weapons facility in Sudan that was believed to be owned in part by Osama bin Laden. The Bush administration took preventive military action to a different level when it decided to invade Iraq in 2003. The Iraq War became the world's first full war to prevent the acquisition or the transfer of nuclear, biological, and chemical weapons.

It quickly became apparent that regime change was a costly way to do arms control, especially since it turned out that there were no weapons of mass destruction in Iraq. The combination of international inspectors, sanctions, and Operation Desert Fox had in fact eliminated Iraq's weapons and had contained Saddam Hussein. Although the administration recognized that arms control had changed with the end of the Cold War, it chose the wrong path for the security of America and the world.

What the world saw was a zero-sum, win-lose U.S. approach to security in the world. The United States had not only turned away from international efforts to meet other nations' basic needs; it was now shaking the foundation of nonproliferation that the world had worked so hard to achieve. In the end, the Bush administration's rejection of arms control made America less safe and pushed the world further from the very partnership that was needed to meet the proliferation challenge.

The System Works

Overall, the nonproliferation system works. In the early days of the nuclear arms race, President John F. Kennedy thought that as many as twenty-five countries would develop and possess nuclear weapons. He and his successor, Lyndon B. Johnson, used U.S. leadership to build a world system to prevent that from happening. Today, nine states have nuclear weapons—the United States, the United Kingdom, France, Russia, and China—the five recognized nuclear powers—as well as Israel, India, Pakistan, and, most recently, North Korea. While nine is too many, it is a lot better than twenty-five.

The cornerstone of the effort to stop the spread of nuclear weapons is the 1970 Nuclear Non-Proliferation Treaty (NPT), signed by 190 countries and indefinitely extended in 1995. Only India, Pakistan, and Israel have not signed it and have refused international inspection of their programs, while North Korea withdrew in 2003. The grand bargain embodied in this treaty has three pillars: nonproliferation, disarmament, and the peaceful use of nuclear technology. In the treaty, the five recognized nuclear weapon states pledged never to use nuclear weapons against non-nuclear weapon states and never to transfer nuclear weapons to other states. In a provision that is often overlooked, they also pledged to eliminate their arsenals. While the treaty calls for the "earliest possible" end to the nuclear arms race, it includes no deadline for disarmament. In return for not developing nuclear weapons of their own, the non-nuclear states can receive technological assistance with peaceful nuclear programs for producing electricity.

With near-universal membership, a strengthened NPT remains the best way to limit the spread of nuclear weapons and their materials. Although the goal to eliminate nuclear weapons remains elusive, Russia and the United States have made great strides in reducing their arsenals. Down from a Cold War height of 70,000, Russia and the United States combined now possess about 26,000 weapons, 11,000 of which are actually deployed. The two countries have agreed to reduce the number of *deployed* nuclear warheads (although not their overall total) to between 1,700 and 2,200 each by 2012.

The nuclear club also has fewer members than it did thirty years ago. According to the International Atomic Energy Agency (IAEA), the nuclear watchdog agency that is charged with verifying the peaceful use of nuclear technology, forty nations that are capable of developing nuclear bombs have refrained from doing so.[17] Since the establishment of the NPT, many more countries have given up nuclear weapons programs than have pursued them. Argentina, Belarus, Brazil, Japan, Kazakhstan, Libya, South Africa, South Korea, and Ukraine have relinquished their nuclear weapons programs to join the NPT as non–nuclear weapon states.[18] Algeria showed some interest in nuclear weapons over the years but turned away from these programs in the 1990s and is no longer considered a high-risk state.

The global system that has kept us safe from unconventional weapons is broader than the NPT, however. It involves an alphabet soup of treaties and conventions establishing global rules of the road for the governance of dangerous materials. For example, the Comprehensive Test Ban Treaty (CTBT) of 1996, signed

by 177 countries, bans all nuclear test explosions.[19] Although all
five recognized nuclear powers have signed the CTBT, China and
the United States have failed to ratify it.[20] The Biological Weapons
(BWC) and the Chemical Weapons Conventions (CWC) ban the
production or the use of such materials, and most countries now
consider using these weapons taboo.[21]

Global agreements to stop the spread of dangerous weapons
will never be perfect—some countries will continue to cheat and
violate their terms. But without these rules, the world becomes
a free-for-all, with America the main target of terrorists who
may acquire the weapons. It is imperative that we strengthen the
range of treaties and conventions. There are many proposals on
how best to do so. For instance, the respected grassroots organization the Middle Powers Initiative has laid out thirteen practical
steps that would make disarmament obligations more concrete.
Led by Senator Douglas Roche, a former Canadian ambassador
for disarmament, the initiative recommends steps such as universal signature, ratification, and implementation of the CTBT; an
immediate moratorium on nuclear testing and the production
of weapons-grade fissile materials; taking all nuclear weapons
off alert status; a total elimination of nuclear weapons; and the
removal of nuclear weapons as part of any military doctrines,
thereby rejecting any concept of "usable" nuclear weapons. It
also recommends that Russia and the United States work with the
IAEA to place their fissile materials under international control
and further reduce their nuclear arsenals in an irreversible, transparent, and verifiable way.[22]

A compelling argument for this came on the morning of August
29, 2007, when, in an extraordinary lapse of security, a group
of U.S. airmen at Minot Air Force Base in North Dakota mis-
takenly attached six missiles with nuclear warheads—each with
the destructive power of up to 150 kilotons, or ten Hiroshima
bombs—to a B-52 bomber. No one, including the flight crew,
noticed the mistake, and the B-52 bomber took off for Barksdale
Air Force Base in Louisiana. It was nearly thirty-six hours before
anyone noticed that the nuclear bombs were even missing.[23] If
this can happen in the United States, imagine what is possible in

Russia, Pakistan, or North Korea. Without secure nuclear arsenals, how long will it take for al-Qaeda to obtain a nuclear device? Condoleezza Rice was right to argue that the arms control process can look different now that the Cold War is over. But the answer is not to reject a system that works. Instead, the United States must lead a global effort to strengthen these agreements. What should now look different, however, is the role of nuclear weapons.

It is time to recognize we are less safe with nuclear weapons in the world than without them. In this new age of weapons of mass destruction and global terrorism, classic Cold War deterrence is no longer an effective strategy. The threat of a nuclear retaliatory attack will not deter terrorists as it did the Soviet Union. Today's terrorists who are seeking nuclear weapons with which to attack us do not have land, people, or national futures to protect.

In 2008, the United States must take up the call that was made two decades ago by President Ronald Reagan and Soviet president Mikhail Gorbachev to abolish all nuclear weapons. Reagan considered these weapons "totally irrational, totally inhumane, good for nothing but killing, possibly destructive of life on earth and civilization."[24] Unless and until the United States embraces their challenge, it will remain the most at risk from these dangerous weapons.

Reagan's call was seen as radical and dangerous a generation ago. Today, however, it is becoming more mainstream. In early 2007, four conservative statesmen—two Republicans, former secretaries of state Henry Kissinger and George Shultz; and two Democrats, former senator Sam Nunn and former defense secretary William Perry—published an article in the *Wall Street Journal* calling for exactly this policy. Underscoring the historic opportunity for taking the world to this next stage, the four urged a new consensus for "reversing reliance on nuclear weapons globally as a vital contribution to preventing their proliferation into potentially dangerous hands, and ultimately ending them as a threat to the world."[25] The statesmen outlined a wise package of immediate steps that the United States should take as nuclear stockpiles are reduced and eventually eliminated. As a first step, all nuclear weapons should be de-targeted and taken off their hair trigger, to ensure that there is no possibility of an accidental launch.

It is time to make nuclear weapons taboo, just as we have done with chemical and biological weapons. Such steps would help others around the world to feel more secure, reducing their need for more offensive weapons. These steps would also reduce the resentments among the nuclear have-nots that there is a separate set of rules for countries with nuclear weapons. Implementing such steps, however, will require leadership from a United States that the world trusts and wants to follow. Regrettably, the United States is moving in the wrong direction.

Undermining American Security

Rather than making the United States safer by strengthening and enforcing the nonproliferation rules of the road, Bush administration officials sought to have it "their way." That meant undermining America's safety in four key ways: failing to modernize the international organizations and treaties dealing with the world's deadliest weapons, putting new nuclear weapons and technology at the forefront of policy, moving headlong with a national missile defense system that made others in the world feel less secure, and signing a major deal with India that undermined the NPT. Each of these steps eroded America's ability to lead a global effort to reduce the threat of proliferation.

Disarmament officials from around the world gathered at the United Nations in May 2005 to strengthen the NPT as part of a review that occurs every five years. The need to strengthen the treaty was urgent. North Korea had withdrawn from the regime in 2003, and the IAEA had announced its concern that Iran was secretly building nuclear weapons. A nuclear Iran could trigger nuclear programs in Saudi Arabia, Egypt, and other Middle Eastern countries; North Korea's could lead Japan, South Korea, and Taiwan to seek them as well. Confidence in the NPT was eroding, and little progress was being made by nuclear powers to eliminate their arsenals. As Secretary of State Rice admitted, the linchpin of nonproliferation efforts was "fraying in many ways."[26]

The chair of the conference, Sergio Duarte of Brazil, had high hopes of strengthening efforts to stop the spread of weapons and reduce existing arsenals. For instance, at the last Review Conference in 2000, the United States had taken up Senator Roche's Thirteen Practical Steps for reducing and eliminating nuclear weapons, which included an end to all nuclear test explosions, a diminished role for nuclear weapons in security policy, and a reaffirmation of the goal of nuclear disarmament.[27] Such a deal was crucial to securing agreement on extending the NPT. Officials expected the United States to, at a minimum, start the NPT negotiations where it had left off five years earlier.

Instead of building on that hard-won progress, the Bush administration simply walked away not only from those commitments but also from the NPT itself. Official U.S. documents that were handed out at the session sought to erase the 2000 commitments and did not even mention the Comprehensive Test Ban Treaty. Instructions to the midlevel U.S. delegates were to focus on Iran and North Korea, something the other delegates would not do without some commitment from the United States to reduce its arsenal of nuclear weapons. Rice did not bother to attend the Review Conference, and the meeting ended in total failure. IAEA Director General Mohamed ElBaradei declared that the meeting had accomplished "absolutely nothing." Chairman Duarte was concerned that the conference had actually weakened the NPT.[28]

The Bush administration further undermined the NPT by seeking to create new nuclear warheads and to resume nuclear testing. The United States has not conducted a nuclear test since 1992. In 1995, it adopted a formal policy that testing was not necessary to ensure the reliability of nuclear weapons. Despite that policy, the Bush administration has increased U.S. readiness to resume testing and started to develop unnecessary new "replacement" warheads for the already reliable current arsenal. Until 2005, the Bush administration had sought funding for a "Robust Nuclear Earth Penetrator," the so-called nuclear bunker buster. Congress objected to the program, and the administration finally agreed to develop conventional, non-nuclear options for any such military need.

The administration's obsession with a national missile defense is also making America weaker, not stronger. President Ronald

Reagan captured the hearts of conservative Americans when he announced his goal of building a shield over the United States to protect it from Soviet intercontinental ballistic missiles (ICBMs). Strong arguments still exist for developing a missile defense system: there remains a possibility of an accidental Russian launch, China could emerge as a threat, and Iran and North Korea both have problematic nuclear programs and long-range missile delivery systems. Iran's Shahab 3 missiles, with a range of 4,500 kilometers, could easily hit Israel. North Korea's Taepodong II has a range of 3,500 to 5,500 kilometers, putting Alaska and Hawaii within range, not to mention tens of thousands of U.S. troops in South Korea and Japan.

With various conventional and unconventional nuclear-related threats to the U.S. homeland and U.S. allies, the United States needs to decide what kind of missile defense system makes the most sense and how it should be balanced against other pressing U.S. defense needs. The Pentagon's Ground-based, Mid-course Defense system (GMD), formerly called National Missile Defense, is being developed and deployed to intercept one or very few warheads launched by ICBMs against the United States. The administration requested $10.3 billion for this effort, the largest single program in the fiscal year 2008 Pentagon budget.[29] By comparison, President Clinton had budgeted $10.3 billion for fiscal years 2001–2005, aimed at ensuring that technical problems associated with missile defense were addressed before any system was deployed.

With technical issues still unresolved, President Bush pushed to deploy the system at great cost, both financially and in terms of America's relationship with Russia. Until 2007, Russian president Vladimir Putin essentially looked the other way regarding Bush's efforts to build a missile defense. Putin's response was muted when, three months after September 11, the administration gave formal notice of its withdrawal from the 1972 Anti-Ballistic Missile (ABM) Treaty.[30] The ABM Treaty had restricted the deployment of antimissile defenses, thus decreasing the odds that any superpower would attempt a first strike of nuclear weapons by leaving each side vulnerable to assured destruction.

Putin's attitude changed dramatically once the United States began to construct missile defense sites in Alaska and in Eastern Europe, in essence ringing Russia on its eastern and western frontiers. In February 2007, Putin blasted the United States, declaring, "Today we are witnessing an almost uncontained hyper use of force—military force—in international relations, force that is plunging the world into an abyss of permanent conflicts. . . . We are seeing a greater and greater disdain for the basic principles of international law."[31]

A few months later, President Putin made a surprising counteroffer in response to U.S. plans for missile defense. At the G-8 summit in Germany in June 2007, Putin proposed joint cooperation that aimed to build an inclusive regional European missile defense with Russian involvement. "We have an understanding about the common threats," Putin said at the conference.[32] The offer surprised U.S. officials, and Putin traveled to Kennebunkport, Maine, in early July to offer more details on his proposal in a private visit at the Bush family's, Walker's Point compound. Bush offered praise for Putin's proposal, calling it "very constructive and bold," and adding, "I think it's very sincere, I think it's innovative, I think it's strategic."[33]

Although U.S. officials later declared the proposal unacceptable, it may well provide a basis for developing an inclusive shield against common threats.[34] Certainly, the United States would never put its security at risk because of Russian objectives. But the system cannot yet protect America, making the confrontation with Russia at this stage unnecessary.

The administration has also made dangerous exceptions to the global rules of the road. On July 18, 2006, President George W. Bush and Indian prime minister Manmohan Singh announced a far-reaching proposal for civilian nuclear cooperation. The deal would make India the first nuclear power outside the NPT to be allowed to trade in nuclear technology. India agreed to separate its civilian and military nuclear facilities but to place only the civilian nuclear plants under international safeguards, ignoring the need to bring its nuclear weapons plants under international control. The deal would also require unprecedented exemptions to U.S. law and international export rules. Even though India was violating international norms—it refused to sign the NPT and rejected IAEA inspectors—it would be eligible to buy U.S. dual-use nuclear technology, including materials and equipment that could be used to enrich uranium or reprocess plutonium. As part of the deal, India recommitted to its nuclear testing moratorium.

The agreement's supporters argue that it will bring India closer to the United States and will balance a resurgent China. They say that it recognizes India's good record on proliferation, in contrast to the record of its neighbor Pakistan. Critics of the deal argue that there are insufficient safeguards to keep India from diverting the U.S. assistance to its clandestine nuclear program. As the nonproliferation expert Henry Sokolski observed, "We are going to be sending, or allowing others to send, fresh fuel to India—including yellowcake and lightly enriched uranium—that will free up Indian domestic sources of fuel to be solely dedicated to making many more bombs than they would otherwise have been able to make."[35] The administration concluded the deal with very little consultation with Congress or nonproliferation experts. As William Potter, the director of the Center for Nonproliferation Studies at the Monterey Institute of International Studies, noted, the agreement "bears all the signs of a top-down administrative directive specifically designed to circumvent the interagency review process and to minimize input from any remnants of the traditional nonproliferation lobby."[36]

The future of the deal is uncertain. Although the U.S. Congress has approved it, the Communist Party in India has objected to the deal. In addition, it is not clear what position the forty-five-member Nuclear Suppliers Group, an international clearing house, will take. But regardless of its eventual fate, the deal is a signal that the NPT is broken. If India can make deals with the United States without permitting inspectors in its weapons facilities, why should others allow inspectors?

It is time to rid the world of the double standard for nuclear haves and have-nots. Only through a reinvigorated NPT and the universal elimination of nuclear weapons will the United States be able to bring the world together behind a strengthened nonproliferation effort. Without security from weapons of mass destruction, the world's prosperity will suffer and the United States in particular will remain at risk.

Bullhorn Diplomacy and Passive Appeasement in North Korea and Iran

In addition to undermining the global security mechanisms that worked to prevent the spread of nuclear, chemical, and biological weapons, the Bush administration also failed to deal effectively with the two most dangerous state threats to the containment of such weapons: North Korea and Iran. Steve Andreasen, the former director for defense policy and arms control in President Clinton's National Security Council, called the lack of assertive diplomacy "passive appeasement."[37]

The Bush team came to office determined to conduct foreign policy differently from President Clinton. Officials disdainfully viewed Clinton's policies toward arms control as weak and ineffective. They accused him of failing to act "resolutely and decisively" and vowed not to repeat his 1994 Framework Agreement, which "rewarded" North Korea for nuclear blackmail. During President Bush's first term, Vice President Dick Cheney repeatedly intervened to prevent a possible deal with North Korea. He said, "I have been charged by the President with making sure that none of the tyrannies in the world are negotiated with. We don't negotiate with evil; we defeat it."[38]

And for six years they did not negotiate in any serious way. When faced with efforts by North Korea and Iran to develop their nuclear programs, the Bush administration simply refused to put any workable deal on the table. The result? Both countries moved forward on their nuclear research and missile programs essentially unfettered. North Korea tested its first nuclear weapon in October 2006 and conducted seven missile tests, including that of a long-range Taepodong II missile.

The history of negotiations with North Korea is one in which the international community has repeatedly offered incentives to

Pyongyang to rein in its nuclear programs, only to see North Korea cheat on the deal. This includes a 1985 deal to get North Korea to sign the NPT, a 1989 agreement to get Pyongyang to admit IAEA inspectors, and a 1994 deal to secure a freeze on North Korea's plutonium-based nuclear program. Opponents harshly criticized the 1994 deal because it called on the international community to provide North Korea with light-water reactors and fuel oil. But the agreement kept the North Koreans from producing plutonium and from making as many as fifty nuclear bombs.

The 1994 agreement crumbled in the late 1990s, perhaps because of its slow implementation, and at that time the North Koreans probably began a second weapons program, this one based on enriched uranium. News of this second program broke in late 2001. Relations with North Korea under the new Bush administration had already begun to deteriorate. Soon after coming to office, Bush rejected Clinton's 1994 deal and publicly demeaned South Korean president Kim Dae Jung's efforts to engage the North. In 2002, Bush included North Korea as part of his "axis of evil." He further escalated tensions when he called the North Korean leader Kim Jong-il a "pygmy" and a "spoiled child." Bush said he "loathes" Kim Jong-il and that he has a "visceral reaction to this guy." The United States for years refused to meet bilaterally with North Korea, leaving the negotiations instead to the Six Party talks between the United States, North Korea, China, Russia, South Korea, and Japan.

While the United States rejected serious negotiations, the situation deteriorated. In 2003, Pyongyang withdrew from the NPT. In January 2005, North Korean officials declared publicly for the first time that they had nuclear weapons, and in October 2006, air samples confirmed an underground nuclear explosion using plutonium.[39] The U.S. policy became a bullhorn approach: North Korea must end its nuclear program "or else."

The administration took a similar "end it or else" approach with Iran. Not surprisingly, that has not worked any better than it did with North Korea. Iran, a member of the NPT, had concluded a comprehensive safeguards agreement with the IAEA in 1974, with plans to build twenty-two civilian nuclear power reactors. In fact, the United States had provided Iran with its first research reactor in the 1960s.[40] Since that time, Iran has continued to develop its civilian nuclear energy program, claiming that it is for peaceful purposes only. Iran has even kept up IAEA inspector access to its program, although it has certainly played games with the inspectors. It was these IAEA inspectors who sounded the alarm bell that Iran may be secretly developing a weapons program when they found traces of enriched uranium on centrifuges imported from Pakistan. Iran's uranium-enrichment facility at Natanz and its heavy-water reactor near Arak had been concealed from the IAEA until 2002. At that time, Iran was led by the more moderate president Mohammad Khatami, who might have been more open to a deal than the current firebrand leader President Mahmoud Ahmadinejad is.

But as with North Korea, Bush refused allies' entreaties to negotiate a solution with Iran. Britain, France, and Germany pressed for diplomacy. Instead of negotiations, Bush rattled the sabers. In April 2006, he said that "all options are on the table" to prevent Iran from developing nuclear weapons, which would include the possibility of a military strike and perhaps even a nuclear strike. Proponents of a military strike pointed to the 1981 Israeli strike on Iraq's Osirak reactor. Vice President Cheney has openly suggested that Israel might take such a step, saying that Israel "might well decide to act first" militarily.[41]

By the summer of 2006, the administration reversed course and agreed to work with the other four nuclear powers—Britain, France, China, and Russia—and Germany to try to negotiate an agreement with Iran. In June 2006, they offered Iran a package of economic incentives and political rewards in exchange for Iran's freezing its uranium enrichment before it entered talks on its nuclear program. When Iran turned down the deal, the UN Security Council imposed some mild sanctions against Iran and demanded that it suspend its uranium enrichment.[42] In March 2007, the UN Security Council strengthened the sanctions, including banning Iranian arms exports and freezing the assets, and restricting the travel of individuals engaged in the country's proliferation-sensitive nuclear activities.[43]

By the fall of 2007, Iran was still refusing to freeze its uranium enrichment and to heed other UN Security Council demands. The Bush administration appeared to be making progress in asking for stronger sanctions from its allies when the U.S. intelligence community put out a bombshell. A December 2007 National Intelligence Estimate (NIE) reversed the intelligence community's earlier judgment that Iran was actively seeking to build nuclear weapons. Now, new information indicated that Iran had in fact stopped its nuclear weapons program in 2003. The report judged that the halt in the program was "primarily in response to increasing international scrutiny."[44] The NIE stated that Iran most likely is not capable of building a nuclear weapon until after 2015, although it cautioned an earlier date is possible.[45]

While Iran continued with its enrichment program, the fact that it was not currently seeking to build a nuclear weapon undercut calls for military action. But concern over Iran's continued enrichment program remained and in March 2008, the UN Security Council again expanded sanctions against Iran.[46] The next president will have to address the problem of Iran's nuclear program, probably with a more pragmatic partnership on the issue with Russia, which continues to provide material and technology for Iran's nuclear program.

Much time was lost because of Bush's stubborn refusal to negotiate with rogue nations. By 2007, this refusal had begun to look like a weakness, not a strength. In the 2008 presidential campaign, Democratic candidates pounced on it. For instance, Bill Richardson's headline on a fund-raising envelope sent in August 2007 had "Being stubborn is not a foreign policy," in big red letters above the address line. With the war on Iraq draining U.S. bravado and resources, the administration quietly shifted course on North Korea and agreed to negotiate a deal that is almost identical to President Clinton's much-disparaged 1994 Framework Agreement, one that would get North Korea to give up its nuclear program and return to the NPT. In October 2007, North Korea agreed to disable all of its nuclear facilities by the end of the year in exchange for 950,000 metric tons of fuel oil, or its monetary equivalent. The agreement includes a process that will remove the country's designation as a state sponsor of terrorism and will end U.S. economic sanctions.[47]

The deal isn't perfect. North Korea will most likely cheat again. It quickly missed its December 2007 deadline to disclose fully its nuclear activities, prompting conservative calls to abandon the deal. The problem is, there are no better alternatives when dealing with a reprehensible regime such as the one in North Korea. As Christopher Hill, the diplomat who negotiated the October 2007 deal, said to critics of the agreement, "People lambaste the six-party process. . . . But when asked for alternatives, even the noisiest critics fall silent."[48]

As is the case with many national security challenges, none of the options for resolution are attractive. Negotiating often requires going with the "least bad" of the available unattractive options. In the cases of both Iran and North Korea, the solutions will require the United States to work with states in the region, including Russia and China, to forge deals that are in all of their interests. As long as the United States is viewed as working against much of the world's interests, reaching those deals will be problematic and these dangers are likely to worsen.

Addressing the Leading Threats: Nuclear Terrorism and "Loose Nukes"

Although President Bush has repeatedly and forcefully warned of the danger that terrorists and outlaw regimes will gain access to nuclear technology, he has done frighteningly little to address that very threat. The gravest danger arises from terrorists' access to so-called loose nukes, or stockpiles of nuclear weapons and fissile material. Their most likely sources are storage areas in the former states of the Soviet Union and in Pakistan and fissile material kept at dozens of civilian sites in about forty countries around the world. Pakistan, with an unstable government and a looming threat from extremist Islamists, has yet to come clean on the extent of its nuclear black market, which was run by the father of the Pakistani nuclear program, Abdul Qadeer Khan. The United States has never pressed hard for a full accounting of his activities.

We know that al-Qaeda is seeking nuclear materials, and the group has explicitly announced its intent to use nuclear weapons against the United States. In August 2001, Osama bin Laden asked two former Pakistani nuclear officials for help in finding other Pakistani nuclear scientists to build a nuclear weapon. After the United States overthrew the Taliban, U.S. forces found nuclear documentation, including crude bomb designs, at an al-Qaeda safe house in Kabul.[49] Keeping the nuclear arsenal out of these dangerous hands will require the United States leading a global effort. It will necessitate the United States using its diminished political capital to convince other countries to tighten their controls, and, in many cases, the United States will have to fund the effort. It is stunning that the United States is *cutting* the very programs that could achieve this important goal.

The most effective program to secure nuclear materials is the Cooperative Threat Reduction (CTR) Agreement, commonly known as the Nunn-Lugar program. It was named after its two sponsors, Senator Sam Nunn (D-Ga.) and Senator Richard Lugar (R-Ind.). Initiated in 1991 following the collapse of the Soviet Union, it has been securing the "loose nukes" left over from the Soviet arsenal. As of 2006, the program had deactivated 6,934 nuclear warheads and destroyed 633 ICBMs, 485 ICBM silos, 80 mobile ICBM launchers, 595 submarine-launched ballistic missiles (SLBMs), 155 strategic bombers, and 30 strategic nuclear submarines. All nuclear warheads have been returned to Russia from the former Soviet republics of Belarus, Kazakhstan, and Ukraine. All strategic weapons infrastructure, including missiles and silos, has also been eliminated in Belarus and Kazakhstan and elimination is underway in Ukraine.

The program has made impressive progress but has been hampered by administrative inconsistencies and underfunding. Security upgrades are far from complete, with 46 percent of the buildings in the former Soviet Union that hold bomb-grade material still potentially vulnerable. Funding for this essential national security program has been only $5.9 billion since 1991.[50] In contrast, as noted earlier in the chapter, the National Missile Defense program was funded at more than $10 billion in fiscal year 2008 alone. To achieve the goal of securing nuclear materials, experts called for a dramatic increase in spending to $3 billion a year for the Nunn-Lugar program, and a $30 billion program over the next eight to ten years to address the threat from Russia's nuclear materials. Russia could certainly help foot part of the bill now.[51]

The international community has been active as well. In 2002, the G-8 established the Global Partnership against the Spread of Weapons and Materials of Mass Destruction, which was dedicated to preventing terrorists and those who harbor them from acquiring or developing WMD, missiles, and related equipment and technology. And at the July 2006 U.S.-Russia summit, the two presidents announced a new Global Initiative to Combat Nuclear Terrorism aimed at continuing and expanding international efforts to secure nuclear and radiological materials.

One key way to address the threat of Russia's nuclear arsenal is to reduce the size of it. In May 2002, Presidents Bush and Putin signed the Strategic Offensive Reductions Treaty, agreeing to reduce their strategic nuclear warheads by nearly two-thirds before December 31, 2012.[52] Unfortunately, the treaty contains no verification provisions (notwithstanding President Reagan's maxim of "trust but verify") and excludes nonoperational and nonstrategic warheads—the very weapons that are most vulnerable to terrorist theft or attack. Since 2002, virtually no progress has been made in addressing these deficiencies or in seeking further reductions, and even less has been accomplished in endorsing the goal of eventual disarmament.

The best way to ensure that terrorists never have access to these dangerous materials is to place the ownership and the production of them under international control and monitoring. The United States should agree to do so and should press others to do the same. An important step will be stopping the production of fissile materials and the construction of new facilities to produce them. While a number of proposals exist to do this, the best was put forward by the director general of the IAEA, Mohamed ElBaradei. It would tighten controls on the nuclear fuel process by placing it in regional centers under multilateral control. It would limit the processing of separated plutonium and production of highly enriched uranium in civilian nuclear programs by restricting such activities to those under multinational control. Any spent fuel and radioactive waste would also be disposed of under international control.[53] The United States would be smart to champion ElBaradei's proposal.

The United States stopped reprocessing nuclear waste in 1972 and has not resumed it due to cost and proliferation concerns (reprocessing is the main method of extracting plutonium from spent nuclear fuel). President Gerald Ford declared a policy of no reprocessing in 1976, which President Carter later upheld. Although President Reagan repealed the ban on reprocessing, cost and proliferation concerns stymied any further active interest in it. The Bush administration wants the United States to begin reprocessing again. In February 2006, it unveiled its plans for reprocessing U.S. and foreign nuclear waste as part of its Global Nuclear Energy Partnership (GNEP) program. The program contains several useful provisions, such as the establishment of an international fuel bank by supplier countries and the take-back of spent fuel from recipient countries.

As part of this initiative, the Bush administration plans the United States to build a full-scale commercial reprocessing plant and fast reactors to separate the fissile material that is necessary to make weapons from nuclear waste.[54] Such a step would weaken efforts to stop other countries from similarly acquiring this sensitive technology and increase the risk that bomb-grade material will be acquired by terrorists seeking to build nuclear weapons. Also, taking the position that certain countries can engage in reprocessing while others are prohibited from doing so fuels yet more concern over a double standard in U.S. proliferation policy. Besides, it is unnecessary to reprocess fuel again; there is more than enough already in storage to meet the world's energy demands.

With the threat of global warming and soaring oil prices, nuclear energy is poised for an expansion. Companies are taking advantage of the administration's nuclear-friendly environment to apply for the first license of a nuclear energy plant in decades. Although nuclear energy can provide a clean, renewable source of energy, the plants pose significant nuclear proliferation challenges. Care must be given to ensuring that the plutonium and the uranium that these plants produce are safely secured and monitored.[55]

The United States remains at risk from nuclear terrorism. For the last seven and a half years, it has taken too many steps in the wrong direction. It is time to change course and put the United States at the forefront of the effort to rid the world of nuclear weapons and toughen the rules on nonproliferation.

Geez, Why Did We Do All That?

The finale to the story about Lieutenant Commander Steve Brock and the navy's efforts to track the *So San* illustrates the limitations of the U.S. counterproliferation strategy of the last several years, which has disdained diplomacy and multilateral treaties in favor of a go-it-alone approach. Following the seizure of the North Korean vessel, U.S. and Spanish authorities were quickly immersed in a diplomatic scramble to explain their actions. The vessel had been seized in international waters, where neither country had clear authority to do so. To make matters worse, Washington's new ally in the battle against global terrorists, Yemen, wanted the Scud missiles that it had purchased from North Korea and insisted that they be delivered. Yemen had increased its counterterrorism cooperation with the United States following the October 2000 al-Qaeda bombing of the USS *Cole*, in which seventeen U.S. sailors were killed, and since 9/11 had allowed the United States to conduct military strikes and intelligence operations against al-Qaeda in its territory. In the face of Yemeni insistence that the missiles be delivered and with no clear international agreement to govern the ship's seizure, U.S. officials let the *So San* and its cargo go.

Back in Washington, officials struggled to explain why, after such a monumental effort, the Scuds were delivered anyway. The White House spokesman Ari Fleischer was forced to admit, "There is no provision under international law prohibiting Yemen from accepting delivery of missiles from North Korea." Vice President Cheney had to get involved to ensure that the missiles would not be transferred to a third party, and he secured a commitment to that effect from the president of Yemen. (However, later reports indicate the Scuds may have ended up in Libya.) When Secretary of State Colin Powell called his Spanish counterpart to thank him for Spain's participation in the interdiction, the Spaniards were understandably perplexed by the release of a ship that they had risked their soldiers' lives to seize.[56]

Back in theater, the navy team that had executed the mission discussed the larger national policy implications of the So San's release. Some scratched their heads and asked, "Geez, why did we do all that?" All agreed, however, that Washington makes the big national policy decisions, and that the job of the fleet is to successfully execute the missions assigned to it. The team had an enormous challenge and a tough task, and everyone involved was proud that the navy team had succeeded from a tactical and an operational perspective. They had done their jobs well.

Unfortunately, the Bush administration has not been doing its job of keeping America safe. It threw out the rulebook that had been carefully constructed over decades of international diplomacy, sought to go it alone, and insisted on keeping nuclear weapons a part of U.S. military strategy. The end result of this approach did not make Americans or anyone else safer. Rather, it heightened insecurities around the globe, creating greater incentives for more countries to acquire dangerous technologies. Other countries began to judge that, like the United States, they would be better off pursuing their own security interests by going it alone, rather than working collectively toward common security interests.

The Way Forward: Pulling Back from the Brink of a New Nuclear Age

Heading into the second decade of this new millennium, the world stands at a crossroads: one path leads to more countries having nuclear weapons and to increased risks of a catastrophic terrorist attack, and an alternative path seeks to restore collaborative international efforts to make the world safe by increasing safeguards on weapons and reducing their overall number.

In order to stay safe, the United States must work with the rest of the world to forge a global approach to common threats. By demonstrating that we understand and will seek to address the threats that other countries face—war, poverty, debt, environmental degradation, and disease—the United States will be better placed to convince the world to join us in addressing threats to U.S. security, especially proliferation and its potential nexus with terrorism. Such a prosperity-based agenda will provide the United States with the very political capital that it is lacking today to pursue such a course. Only when it does will America be safe and secure. The United States must therefore:

STOP: Stonewalling efforts to negotiate proliferation problems with rogue regimes. Since taking office, this administration has sought regime change over international negotiations to address today's proliferation crises. The administration invaded Iraq, only to find that there were no weapons of mass destruction. Sanctions and limited military strikes had eliminated Saddam Hussein's arsenals of deadly weapons. For six years, the administration resisted negotiating with North Korea, only to see it become a nuclear power. The Bush administration has similarly avoided negotiations with Iran, while it pursued its nuclear research program unrestrained. Across the board, the administration's tough talk of regime change simply delayed progress and strengthened the extremists.

START: Making the tough deals that will keep America safe. Only a sophisticated mix of carrots and sticks will achieve results with rogue regimes. Of course, the use of force to address a particularly imminent threat remains on the table. But only forceful negotiations with Iran, North Korea, and the next problem rogue state will achieve lasting results for U.S. security. The 2007 North Korean deal must be implemented and tightly monitored. While force remains an option, the next president must do a better job working with the international community, including Russia, to rein in Iran's program.

STOP: Undermining the nonproliferation rules of the road that have kept the United States safe. The Bush administration's attempts to erode the alphabet soup of arms control treaties and conventions have made America less, not more, secure. It has also undermined America's efforts to convince the world that it understands the need to cooperate to address common threats, and has reinforced the perception that the United States has a double standard and is not bound by international rules. Endeavors to gut the NPT and resume nuclear testing have eroded progress toward the important goal of reducing the global risk from nuclear weapons.

START: Strengthening those rules. The United States must revive its leadership to strengthen the rules of nonproliferation that have kept Americans safe. America must begin to prepare now for the next NPT Review Conference in 2010 and must make up for the opportunities that were lost in 2005. The goal should be universal membership in a strengthened and tougher NPT, getting North Korea back into the regime, and persuading India, Pakistan, and Israel to join and to allow inspections of their facilities. Stronger penalties for withdrawing from the treaty or cheating should be agreed upon. In addition to universal compliance with the CTBT, our goals should include strengthening the bans against chemical and biological weapons as well. As mentioned in other chapters, the United States must do more to address the underlying conflicts that fuel various countries' belief that a nuclear arsenal may keep them safer. We must work toward regional cooperation, especially in northeast Asia and the Middle East, to forge a global effort to reduce the security threats that motivate countries to acquire nuclear, biological, and chemical weapons.

STOP: Funding the wrong priorities. The most urgent threat is loose nukes falling into the wrong hands. Yet the United States spends ten times more on a missile defense system than on securing nuclear weapons. Although America needs a national missile defense system, it should not waste funds on deploying one that does not work. Rather, the United States should shift that funding to the more urgent priority of securing the Cold War's dangerous nuclear arsenal and press Russia to help foot the bill.

START: Securing the world's nuclear arsenals. We must make securing nuclear arsenals a higher priority. The budget for the Nunn-Lugar CTR program should be tripled. All nuclear weapons and materials must be secured and placed under IAEA supervision, including weapons in the United States, in order to encourage others to follow suit. The United States should take up and press the world to accept the IAEA's proposal to secure the materials in civilian nuclear reactors spread across forty countries. Such a program would provide a strong answer to proliferators such as North Korea and Pakistan which claim to need fuel for their economies, while making it infinitely harder for terrorists to acquire these dangerous materials. The goal would be to secure all materials and eventually to stop additional countries from entering into the uranium-enrichment business. An essential component would be to establish a mechanism to guarantee the availability of reactor fuel and the removal of spent fuel at affordable prices. Such an international arrangement would virtually eliminate any justification for states to have their own fuel cycle facilities. Any state that pursued such facilities would in effect be advertising its intent to weaponize its programs, thus triggering an international response. Another additional protocol to the NPT could be agreed upon to set up such a centralized system under the control of the IAEA, with pre–agreed on sanctions for states that seek their own facilities.

STOP: Stonewalling on disarmament. Talk of new nuclear weapons, replacement warheads, and current war plans that involve the use of nuclear weapons undermines any global efforts to keep the world safe from nuclear weapons. Keeping U.S. weapons on a hair trigger also endangers the world. Undermining the NPT and other international arms control treaties and conventions is making the world less, not more, safe.

START: Leading the way to rid the world of nuclear weapons. It is time to take up Ronald Reagan's challenge to rid the world of nuclear weapons. While the United States will never unilaterally disarm, it should lead the campaign to convince the world that we are all less safe with nuclear weapons on Earth. The United States and Russia should work to make the use of nuclear weapons taboo. They should agree to eventual disarmament and decide on a deadline for achieving that goal universally. Such an approach would also help rebuild the credibility that the United States has lost with the developing world and would convince other nations that America is abiding by the NPT. It would also strike a blow at those who challenge the "have" and "have-not" status of the treaty.

The United States must counter the belief of some countries that they need nuclear weapons to secure their borders and make their people safer. Other nations simply want the "respect" that they believe accompanies a nuclear power status. To change this dynamic, the United States must return to its commitment to disarm. As part of that effort, America must abandon efforts to build new weapons and must take the lead in ending the modernization of nuclear weapons. The United States must also end any discussion of resuming nuclear testing or producing weapons-grade fissile material. The option of using nuclear weapons must be removed from U.S. defense policy. All nuclear weapons should be de-targeted and taken off their hair trigger to ensure that there is no possibility of an accidental launch. Today, these weapons should have no use in U.S. military planning. The United States will never unilaterally disarm but it must lead the way toward eliminating the world's nuclear arsenal—an arsenal aimed primarily at the United States.

It is not fantasy to imagine a world free from the nuclear threat. But to achieve that goal, the United States will have to fulfill its part of the NPT bargain and lead others to do their share. Nothing will replace hard work and deft diplomacy in keeping Americans and people around the world safe. Promoting a prosperity agenda to address the world's threats will make efforts to secure America infinitely easier. And it will mean we will no longer be sending our sailors like Lieutenant Commander Steve Brock on wild goose chases.

six

The Hidden Threat of Global Poverty

S ome security threats shared by people around the world are deceptively commonplace, but they remain every bit as dangerous as the deadliest human-made weapons. Infectious diseases and global pandemics have just as much potential for killing millions as do nuclear weapons. In fact, since the dawn of the nuclear age, more of the world's casualties have been caused by diseases than by weapons of mass destruction. Widespread poverty can foster the conditions that lead to deadly conflict and undermine global prosperity. The United States must adopt a more comprehensive approach to global security—one that recognizes the full range of common threats that exist in this new era of globalization.

Adelard Mivumba, the young man living in the Congo whom we profiled in the introduction, knows all too well how deadly these everyday security threats are. Working hard to provide for his family, Adelard has a decent life, but his prosperity is at risk. There is a possibility of renewed war and abuse at the hands of soldiers, and the Congolese government is failing to provide for the people. When asked about the government in the Congo,

Mivumba was emphatic: "*Ça ne va pas*" (It does not work). "They don't do what they say they will," Mivumba explained. They promised raises for teachers, but they didn't do it. Promises to build roads went unfulfilled. The high salaries of parliamentarians were particularly galling. "Members of parliament make $4,000 a month, but teachers make only $60. That is not fair."[1]

Corruption is rampant, and those with power use it to enrich themselves. Although the country has held elections for president and for parliament and has a new constitution, war continues to stymie real political progress at the national level. The weak federal government in Kinshasa has little control over the national army or members of armed groups who abuse the local population. Although the country's six armed groups are in theory being integrated into the national army, various members of the government continue to back their own militias, fueling continued violence. Some of the Congo's neighbors—Angola, Rwanda, Uganda, and Sudan—continue to meddle in the country's affairs, stealing its vast resources or extending their own conflicts into Congolese territory.

An estimated 1,000 conflict-related deaths occur in the Congo each day, mostly from disease and malnutrition but from ongoing violence as well.[2] Outbreaks of waterborne diseases such as cholera are common, as are incidents of diarrhea, hepatitis A, and typhoid fever. In September 2007, one of the world's deadliest pathogens, the Ebola virus, resurfaced in central Congo, where it is believed to have originated, killing 150 people. Ebola is highly contagious, and 50 to 80 percent of Ebola victims die from internal hemorrhaging.[3]

Since its independence from Belgium in 1960, the Congo has never had a government that promoted the prosperity of its people or secured its stability. The government is incapable of providing the minimum acceptable quality of life or the most rudimentary social services. Militias still control large areas in the east, including areas around Adelard Mivumba's home of Goma. Decades of war, foreign meddling, and failed, corrupt governments have left the Congolese struggling to live decent lives. While it may seem like a faraway conflict, the Congo's problems affect American security.

Why Should We Care?

For years, moral considerations have motivated some to help the world's less fortunate, resulting in impressive charitable efforts. Now we are starting to see that America must put a higher priority on, and more resources toward, addressing the root causes of conflict, poverty, and disease. Taking steps to save more lives and boost the overall prosperity of people in other countries will help revive America's moral authority and position of leadership in the world. By helping other countries with their challenges, America will be better positioned to convince them to join it in combating its biggest threats, terrorism and proliferation. But today, we must also consider world poverty itself as a threat to America.

Global terrorism is not the direct result of poverty or lack of education. Most of the 9/11 hijackers were relatively well off and well educated. Even though poverty may not be the root of terrorism, it's the fertile soil it grows in.

Poverty breeds conflict and instability, sapping governments' power to enforce laws and control their borders. This can result in security vacuums that criminals and terror groups exploit to build havens and networks of support. Before moving to Afghanistan, Osama bin Laden built his terrorist network from Sudan, which in the 1990s was suffering from a two-decade-long civil war. Bin Laden next went to the failed state of Afghanistan, where he planned and launched the 9/11 attacks. Chaos in Iraq and Somalia has drawn al-Qaeda operatives to those countries.[4]

Al-Qaeda has already exploited conditions in Mali, Yemen, Kenya, Tanzania, and Indonesia to support its operations. The fact that Osama bin Laden based himself in Sudan and then Afghanistan is a prime example of how global terror networks can exploit poverty and lawlessness. As noted in chapter 2, state failure and poverty in developing countries allow terrorists to garner local support by setting up charitable programs to step in where governments fail. For instance, in Pakistan, Egypt, Lebanon, and the Palestinian territories, radical groups provide vast amounts of aid to the local populace.[5] In Gaza, the terrorist organization Hamas funds aid programs generously and its members were elected to government due primarily to that largesse. Hamas's ability to deliver basic services stood in sharp contrast to the corrupt and inept Palestinian Authority, controlled by the Fatah Party that Yasser Arafat left behind when he died in 2004.

When local governments stumble and the United States fails to act, our adversaries will not hesitate to fill that void.

Beyond terrorism, poverty is at the nexus of many other threats that America faces. Poverty breeds crime, creating economic incentives for drug, arms, and human trafficking. Poverty triggers environmental degradation, especially deforestation, which in turn fuels global warming. Poverty gives rise to sickness, spreading infectious diseases around the world, and making people too sick to work, thus eroding the state's ability to function. Extremists and terrorists exploit poverty and lawlessness to advance their radical agendas. Of the violent conflicts during the last two decades, most were within poor countries, not between states.[6] Societies lacking prosperity produce the most dangerous risks to America's security.

As detailed below, President George W. Bush deserves credit for the large increases in foreign assistance he devoted to combating HIV/AIDS, as well as his efforts to link aid to good governance. But his aid programs were not matched by a global effort to promote security and prosperity. President Bush stressed the link between poverty and conflict when he announced generous new aid commitments in 2002, saying, "When governments fail to meet the most basic needs of their people, these failed states can become havens for terror."[7] President Bush was correct in highlighting the danger of failed states, but unfortunately, his deeds did not match his words. Driven by a conservative ideology that undervalues the role that government plays in creating law and order and in advancing prosperity around the world, Bush squandered an opportunity after September 11 to increase global security and prosperity.

Although he increased the amount of money that was dedicated to foreign assistance, he did so in the context of a broader strategy of preemptive war, regime change, and "fighting them over there so we don't have to fight them here," which made people around the world feel less secure. The time has come to adopt a new plan that goes beyond President Bush's narrow freedom agenda—a prosperity agenda that acknowledges that America's fortunes are more closely linked to the fortunes of people on the other side of the world than ever before in human history.

Tackling poverty has bedeviled world leaders for decades. In 1977, world leaders pledged at a meeting in Argentina to bring "water and sanitation to all." They vowed in Kazakhstan in 1978 to bring "health for all" and in 1990 in Thailand to bring "education for all." These various promises were brought together in one ambitious plan at the turn of the century when the world gathered in Monterrey, Mexico, and pledged to cut poverty in half by 2015 through eight Millennium Development Goals (MDG). The world has fallen behind in meeting these goals, which centered on fighting poverty and advancing health care and education. Although some regions of the world are doing better than others, Africa continues to lag behind.

It is not just a question of money. Development aid has skyrocketed over the last decade, but people are still sick and poor. What is missing is a comprehensive global approach toward building prosperity—prosperity not in terms of a bank account but in the broader sense of succeeding among one's peers, with sound institutions to provide a healthy foundation for progress. War and corruption create poverty as readily as poverty creates war and corruption.

Prosperity requires safety, security, health, education, and an ability to provide for one's family, and these are shared social goods that the free hand of the market rarely delivers on its own. Adelard Mivumba in the Congo, for instance, will never feel prosperous as long as the threats from war and an abusive national army loom large. Hisham Kassem in Egypt will not feel prosperous as long as a corrupt old order continues to rule Egypt with an iron fist. For them, achieving prosperity and security will require bold international action to address the threat of infectious diseases, lack of education, ineffective government, and other sources of conflict. In many cases, innovative solutions can make a difference for hundreds of thousands of people. But only a global effort, led by the United States, will break the cycle of poverty for the billions who are still suffering. Patience is necessary, as most of these challenges will take at least a generation to address.

An effort of this nature will help other countries in the world realize that we are prepared to help with their problems. This in turn will help convince more people to act according to U.S. interests. At the heart of the prosperity agenda is a fundamental principle: treating others as we would like to be treated. It will take a new global compact centered on this principle, with the United States vowing to use its still considerable powers to work for the world's prosperity to keep America safe in this age of deadly global threats.

The Monumental Challenge of Expanding Prosperity

If we stand at the beginning of the twenty-first century and look back on the previous century, we see that human progress has been vast and impressive. The advances in our understanding of the natural world are almost difficult to believe. A hundred years ago, in the early 1900s, researchers were only beginning to understand the basic building blocks of our world by researching the composition of the atom. Visions of space exploration were in the realm of science fiction. Flash forward to the present, and the progress is astounding. Scientists have learned how to harness the energy from the nucleus of an atom, creating new opportunities and threats. Human beings walked on the moon, and satellites orbiting the planet keep us closely tied to events around the world. Just in the last hundred years, airplanes, televisions, high-speed trains, the Internet, and cell phones have made it possible for people to travel the Earth and communicate with one another, building international companies and institutions.

Scientific advances also created greater potential to improve the lives of people around the world. According to the International Monetary Fund (IMF), the twentieth century was a period in human history of unparalleled economic growth, with global per capita gross domestic product (GDP) increasing almost fivefold in the last hundred years.

Just since 1990, the proportion of people living in extreme poverty has dropped by more than half in East Asia, declined by nearly a quarter in South Asia, and decreased slightly in Latin America (where poverty was already lower). Since the end of World War II, some countries, such as Japan and South Korea, have virtually wiped out widespread poverty and now enjoy general prosperity.[8] Although global trade has triggered hardship in some sectors, countries that were open to trade grew about twice as fast as those closed to trade. China, India, Ireland, Spain, Portugal, South Korea, and Taiwan have all joined the global market and brought eight hundred million people out of poverty in the process.

Great strides in health care also saved millions of lives. Penicillin stopped deadly infections. Some diseases that affected millions of poor people every year, such as smallpox, river blindness, and polio, were virtually eradicated. Advances in sanitation and clean water dramatically reduced outbreaks of cholera and other waterborne diseases. Progress is particularly impressive given the explosion in the world's population, from 1.65 billion in 1900 to 6 billion in 2000.

Wealthy individuals and governments alike have stepped up to help lift people out of poverty, especially in the last decade. The major industrialized nations agreed to dramatically increase funding for HIV/AIDS treatments and to slash poor countries' debt. Some of the world's wealthiest people began to give their fortunes away, bringing new resources to official efforts to fight deadly diseases and poverty. For instance, the Bill and Melinda Gates Foundation gave more than $7.8 billion, mostly to fight infectious diseases, between 1999 and 2007. Rock stars like U2's Bono browbeat presidents and ministers of the wealthy countries to reach deeper into their pockets as well.

Despite these tremendous advances, poverty continues to exist, and the challenges ahead remain monumental. One billion people—one in six people living on Earth today—continue to live in extreme poverty, struggling on the equivalent of less than

$1 a day. One in four children in the developing world suffers from hunger. Deep pockets of poverty remain throughout Asia, Latin America, the former Soviet areas of Central Asia, and most acutely in Africa. Further reducing global poverty will require tackling some of the toughest international challenges, including the growing gap between the rich and the poor, getting development aid right, devising a better strategy for fighting the drug war, breaking down trade barriers, providing basic health services, and combating infectious diseases. In some cases, the world is on the wrong path. And fairly or not, the United States gets much of the blame.

That's because you can define progress by all we've created, or you can define it by what we've created for all. It doesn't matter how little the poorest billion lives on. It matters if they could have the opportunity to get a little more.

The least prosperous countries are facing a growing gap between the rich and the poor. Although overall global wealth is rising, the poor are not getting their share of the world's prosperity. These differences in income translate into differences in the quality of human life. In the 1800s, the income gap between the richest one-fifth of the world's population and the poorest one-fifth was 3 to 1; in 1913, it was 11 to 1; by 1992, it was 74 to 1. Today, the richest 20 percent of the world's population has 86 times more income than the poorest 20 percent.

Vast concentrations of wealth in Mexico, Russia, Venezuela, Zambia, and Brazil leave more than half of those nations' assets in the hands of just 10 percent of the population. Here in America, the richest 1 percent of the population owns more than half of the nation's wealth, and 37 million Americans live in poverty. At home and abroad, such inequality fuels resentment among the have-nots. Abroad, people blame their inept, corrupt governments—and America, too. They see an America propping up the rich, the powerful, and the corrupt, rather than helping disadvantaged people secure the most basic pillars of prosperity.

Indeed, the United States has not always gotten development aid right. During much of the 1970s and the 1980s, international financial institutions, led by the IMF, lent huge sums to the developing world, mostly for large infrastructure projects. Much of these funds were diverted by corruption or spent on large arms purchases. The IMF also issued sizable loans conditioned on a variety of belt-tightening measures for much of the developing world. It insisted on "shock therapy"—rapid economic policy shifts—to bring about fiscal reform and a reduction in government spending on social programs. Many of these measures were imposed as commodity prices fell, further squeezing the poor. Millions of people across the developing world lost their social safety nets, and America got much of the blame.

Although the debt was largely owed to the World Bank, the IMF, and other international organizations, it is a common perception that the United States, as the leading global power, controls these organizations and is therefore ultimately responsible for placing the debt burden on their backs. For instance, when the IMF cut a deal with South Korea in the mid-1990s, the people resented the strict terms that forced Seoul to open its markets and close debt-ridden financial institutions. As one South Korean businessman put it, "I am hating the U.S. as a gangster that did too much to this small country."[9] By 2000, the world's poorest fifty-three countries had debt that totaled from $300 to $400 billion, much of it dating from the 1970s. By some estimates, the world's poorest countries paid out more than $100 million a day because of these debts.[10]

The United States and the other major industrialized countries finally agreed to take action at the G-8 Summit in June 2005. They pledged to write off the entire $40 billion that the eighteen poorest countries owed to the World Bank, the IMF, and the African Development Fund. Additional efforts brought the total debt reduction to $86.5 billion in current and future debt service for twenty-four countries by late 2007.[11] Rather than provide big loans with austerity strings attached, the international financial institutions are also beginning to do a better job of demonstrating that they are on the side of the people's prosperity. They are providing funds for projects that people actually see: health clinics, vaccines, and new schools.

In Western nations, we like to see these efforts as generous, but the rest of the world does not necessarily see it that way.

To developing nations, it's as if we forced them to buy a run-down house they didn't want and then we hired a contractor they didn't like who accidentally burned the house down. In the end, we let them keep the insurance money, but developing nations think it's the least we could do.

In setting the Millennium Development Goals (MDG) in 2000, UN Secretary General Kofi Annan challenged the world to cut poverty in half by 2015. The ambitious UN program sought to:

1. Eradicate extreme poverty and hunger
2. Achieve universal primary education
3. Promote gender equality and empower women
4. Reduce child mortality
5. Improve maternal health
6. Combat HIV/AIDS, malaria, and other diseases
7. Ensure environmental sustainability
8. Develop a global partnership for development[12]

One of the key targets was for the developed world to give 0.7 percent of its gross national income to help alleviate poverty. Sadly only Norway, Luxembourg, Denmark, and Sweden have done so. The United States gives only about 0.2 percent of its income, although in dollar amounts, it is at the top.[13] Developed nations need to see this less as tithing and more as investing in making their countries more secure and prosperous by making others around the world feel more secure and prosperous. This isn't free money we'll never see again. Today's poorest nation could be the place we send tomorrow's peacekeeping troops or tomorrow's tourists and consumer goods. The right kind of aid will make the difference.

Millions Die Every Year from Preventable, Curable, or Treatable Diseases

In recent decades, the world has made important progress in reducing conflict in certain countries, and, in turn, not surprisingly, those countries have become more prosperous. Since the end of the Cold War, the number of civil wars around the globe has declined sharply. Some 100 conflicts have quietly ended since the late 1980s, and more wars have stopped than have started. Between 1991 and 2004, 28 armed struggles for self-determination went on, while 43 were contained or ended. Although the Yugoslav wars and the genocide in Rwanda stand out as horrors of the 1990s, overall, the number of genocides and politicides dropped by 80 percent between 1988 and 2001.[14] The number of refugees dropped by 45 percent between 1992 and 2003. Today's wars are also less deadly. Average battle deaths per conflict have dropped from 38,000 in 1950 to 600 today. Despite these improvements, there remain 60 ongoing conflicts around the world.[15]

The end of the Cold War removed a major source of conflict, drying up superpower arms and financial support in a variety of proxy wars in the developing world. But pent-up rivalries have emerged since the end of the superpower conflict, and threats from nonstate actors such as global terror networks have grown. The end of the U.S.-Soviet polarization paved the way for the UN to increase its peacekeeping efforts, and in the early 1990s, UN conflict prevention activities grew rapidly and were met with impressive success. Between 1987 and 1999, there was a fourfold increase in UN peacekeeping operations, which helped reduce the chances that postconflict countries would relapse into war within five years. Preventive diplomacy missions have increased sixfold.[16]

War and poverty will never be completely eradicated, but some day, there will be an end to malaria, malnutrition, and poor sanitation. Worse than war, and worsened by war, these threats could be eliminated in a generation, if we're committed.

Abysmal health conditions persist in the poorest countries and even in poor areas of middle-income countries. About one in six people in the world—more than a billion—do not have access to adequate supplies of clean water; another 40 percent, or 2.5 billion, do not have access to good sanitation. More than 1.8 million children die each year from diarrhea, and each year nearly 11 million children do not live to see their fifth birthday, even though many could be saved through basic improvements in sanitation. Conditions are exacerbated by explosive population growth, especially in poor countries. Since 1950, the population has grown 50 percent in rich countries and an astounding 250 percent in poor countries.

Many of the world's poor remain at risk from the deadliest diseases on Earth, furthering a cycle of poverty, disease, and failing governments. Sick people cannot work to help pull their societies out of poverty. Each year, millions die from HIV/AIDS, influenza, tuberculosis, malaria, yellow fever, and other viruses. New epidemics include cholera in Latin America, the plague in India, the Ebola virus in Africa, dengue fever in Asia, and the West Nile virus in the United States. Poverty contributes directly to these outbreaks because of poor medical care, a lack of health-care workers, and unsanitary conditions. Inadequate education means people do not learn about the risks and the preventive measures associated with various diseases.

The 920 million people on the continent of Africa suffer the most. Sub-Saharan Africa is home to the world's twenty poorest countries.[17] And while hundreds of thousands in Asia and Latin America have been lifted out of poverty, the prosperity trend for Africa is going in the wrong direction: the standard of living is decreasing and life expectancy is falling. Gross national income has fallen from $550 to $490 a year. Malaria still kills 1 million Africans every year. AIDS has killed 20 million Africans, with another 25 million infected. Deaths due to AIDS are expected to create a staggering 40 million orphans in Africa by 2010. People across Africa are dying as if science hadn't made any advances since the early 1900s.

The world's population doubled in the last half of the twentieth century and is now more urban. In 1950, just under one-third of the global population lived in cities, while slightly less than one-half does now.[18] The global population is expected to reach 9 billion by 2050, further exacerbating the world's sanitation and health problems. With the worsening of global warming, access to potable water will become an increasing problem for much of the world's poor. Two-thirds of the global population could have water-access problems by 2025, which will likely lead to more areas of conflict and worsened sanitary conditions.

Becoming a Nation Known for Helping Out

At 1 P.M. on a sunny day in the Rose Garden in late May 2007, President Bush stood beside the podium, holding a squirming, waving four-year-old boy, Baron, who was dressed in a traditional African shirt. The president's wife, Laura, had visited the Mothers-to-Mothers center in South Africa, which treats HIV-infected women and teaches them how to keep their unborn babies HIV-free. During that visit, Mrs. Bush met the boy's mother, Kunene Tantoh. Kunene had just discovered that she was pregnant—and HIV-positive. A normal CD4 count, which measures a person's immune cells, is between 500 and 1,500. Kunene's count was 2. She was not expected to survive.

But with the treatment Kunene received at the Mothers-to-Mothers clinic, she did survive and delivered a beautiful boy, Baron, who is free of HIV. Today, Kunene works at a Mothers facility and is a mentor to other mothers. In welcoming the family to the White House, Laura Bush said that the mother and son "stand as a symbol of hope to everyone living positively with HIV." The first lady and her husband can take some credit for their success—the Mothers clinic receives funding from one of the administration's ambitious aid programs to combat HIV/AIDS.

President Bush's war in Iraq has cast a long shadow over the things he has done for peace. The best example of this is what Bush has accomplished concerning development aid and funding for HIV/AIDS. Although he has received little credit for it, President Bush has overseen the largest increase in U.S. development assistance since the Marshall Plan. Since 2000, he has more than doubled Official Development Assistance (ODA), from $10 billion to $22.7 billion in 2006, with a peak of $27.6 billion in 2005. Iraq and Afghanistan are the largest recipients of aid, receiving $4.8 billion and $1.6 billion, respectively. Bush is doubling aid to Sub-Saharan Africa, from $4.4 billion in 2004 to $8.7 billion by 2010.[19]

Christian groups pressed Bush to engage in the global fight against HIV/AIDS. And he did. His most ambitious assistance programs focused on the battle against this deadly virus. During the visit of the Tantoh family to the White House, the president announced a doubling of the President's Emergency Plan for AIDS Relief (PEPFAR) to $30 billion by 2013 to combat the disease in the countries with the highest rates of HIV/AIDS, primarily in Africa and the Caribbean.[20] First announced in Bush's 2003 State of the Union address, the program seeks to strengthen health-care systems and to leverage programs that address malaria, tuberculosis, child and maternal health, clean water, food and nutrition, education, and other needs. PEPFAR emphasizes transitioning from an emergency to a sustainable response for treatment, prevention, and care. By 2007, PEPFAR had supported antiretroviral treatment for more than 1.1 million people.[21]

The program uses "Partnership Compacts" with host nations and nongovernmental organizations to maximize impact and sustainability. It seeks to optimize the effectiveness of resources in vital areas, such as health workforce expansion, gender equality, protection of the rights of orphans, and effective HIV counseling and testing. The president set ambitious targets, working with the private sector and faith-based and community-based organizations: treatment for nearly 2.5 million people, preventing more than 12 million new infections, and supporting care for 12 million people, including more than 5 million orphans and vulnerable children.[22] Shortly after announcing the expanded program, President Bush sent the first lady, Laura, on a trip to review the programs in Zambia, Senegal, Mali, and Mozambique.

Overall, the program is on track to meet its goals. President Bush is proud of the program and boasted of having created "the Lazarus effect," in which dying communities are being brought back to life. Of course, Bush's efforts have come under some criticism. His conservatism has shaped much of his HIV/AIDS policy, and one of his first acts was to deny aid to programs abroad that support—or even discuss—abortion. The ban hits Africa hardest and the fight against HIV/AIDS in particular. Bush's program is largely focused on an abstinence-until-marriage approach and requires all recipients to oppose prostitution. That policy limits outreach to sex workers and makes condom distribution more difficult. Educating prostitutes is a critical part of the fight to stem the spread of the disease. Brazil went so far as to reject $40 million in potential aid rather than agree to the pledge to oppose prostitution.[23]

International efforts against HIV/AIDS have been impressive as well. In 2002, an independent mechanism was set up, the Global Fund to Fight AIDS, Tuberculosis, and Malaria (the Global Fund). With support from governments, philanthropies, and corporations, the Global Fund has approved nearly $7 billion in proposals and has already allocated $3 billion to various programs, mostly in China, Ethiopia, Tanzania, and Zambia.[24] The United States is the largest contributor to the Global Fund. Member states of the Organization for Economic Cooperation and Development (OECD) and the World Bank have also dramatically increased their aid effort since 2001.[25] The World Bank has also worked with the IMF, the OECD, and the G-8 to reduce the debts of countries that are hardest hit by HIV/AIDS and other diseases.[26] Nongovernmental organizations, too, have played an increasing role in fighting poverty. There are now an estimated 60,000 AIDS-related nonprofits working on the problem.

Recently, a new ally joined the fight. During the last decade, vast funding came from a new source, with sums so large that the era has been dubbed the "Age of Generosity." Major philanthropists and rock stars have enlisted in the war against HIV/AIDS and poverty. With their agility and entrepreneurial approach, their foundations can enter niches that traditional donors may not be able or willing to address. They also have vast resources. In its first six years, the Bill and Melinda Gates Foundation gave $6.6 billion for global health programs, including $2 billion to fight tuberculosis, HIV/AIDS, and other sexually transmitted diseases. The Indian HIV/AIDS activist Winnie Singh said that Bill Gates is a celebrity in India, and his program is better known than those of the U.S. government. She explained that "the Gates Foundation is better known than the PEPFAR effort, in part because Bill and Melinda Gates come and visit here. . . . People in India see him visiting the country with his wife and they go to meet with infected children."[27] Other foundations have been very generous as well, such as the foundations of George Soros, former president Bill Clinton, and the William and Flora Hewlett Foundation. Overall, between 1995 and 2005, U.S. charitable foundation gifts tripled, while the portion of funds going to international projects jumped 80 percent. One-third of that sum was devoted to global health.[28]

Rock stars, too, have taken up the cause of global poverty with a new passion and impact. The Irish star Bob Geldof first broke into the debate in 1985 with his highly successful Live Aid concerts, which raised hundreds of millions of dollars to alleviate world hunger. Then the Irish rocker Bono of U2 took the effort to a whole new level: he became a one-man world ministry to alleviate Africa's endemic challenges of HIV/AIDS, debt, and poverty. He lobbied the heads of state and the ministers of the G-8 nations, goading them into doing more to help Africa. Using his nonprofit Debt AIDS Trade Africa (DATA) as a base, he enlisted Hollywood movie stars—George Clooney, Cameron Diaz, and Brad Pitt—to help in his effort to unify development organizations to press for change. He also teamed up with the best academics on the subject and formed a lasting partnership with the Harvard economist Jeffrey Sachs, now the director of the Earth Institute at Columbia University. Bono cornered then treasury secretary Larry Summers, telling him that the rest of the G-8 had said that they would move if he did. He also traveled to Africa in 2002 with U.S. treasury secretary Paul O'Neill. Bono even chose a passage from the Bible about shepherds and the poor to press President Bush to act. When he got his meeting with President Bush, he recited the passage he had chosen from the Gospel of Matthew: "For I was hungered, and ye gave me meat; I was thirsty, and ye gave me drink; I was a stranger, and ye took me in."[29] Bono's lobbying helped move the mountain.

At the 2005 G-8 Summit in Gleneagles, Scotland, President Bush announced that the United States would double its assistance to Sub-Saharan Africa between 2004 and 2010 to $8.67 billion, as noted previously. The G-8 heads of state also announced a comprehensive package to promote faster progress toward alleviating poverty in Africa. The leaders pledged to double the aid to fight poverty by 2010, adding $50 billion worldwide and $25 billion for Africa. They also agreed to immediately write off the debts of eighteen of the world's poorest countries, most of which are in Africa. Included in the agreement was a write-off of $17 billion of Nigeria's debt, in the biggest single debt relief deal ever. The summit also committed to end all export subsidies, provide funding for malaria treatment and polio eradication, support education and health care, and help with African peacekeeping.

Unfortunately, the leaders have since backpedaled on these commitments. For instance, at the June 2007 G-8 Summit in Heiligendamm, Germany, the G-8 leaders refused to be specific on when they would meet their $50 billion aid and debt-reduction pledges that had been made at the 2005 Gleneagles summit. Instead, they said only that they would "continue their efforts" to increase funding for AIDS treatment. Bono condemned the G-8 for "broken promises." By one estimate, only $3 billion of the $50 billion target will materialize by 2010.[30]

This Age of Generosity certainly has made a difference in combating HIV/AIDS. However, in many cases, the fundamental challenges to prosperity are not HIV/AIDS but basic structural problems of the society. For instance, the top killers today in most poor countries are maternal deaths from childbirth and children's respiratory and intestinal infections. Local hospitals, clinics, laboratories, and medical schools lack basic supplies, and there is a serious shortage of health-care workers. Corruption is also a major problem. As one official of the Joint UN Program on HIV/AIDS put it, "You need a complete package. If the government is corrupt, if everyone is stealing money, then [foreign assistance] will not work." Although it is possible to devise development programs that can work around corruption, the practice inhibits the main functions of a society, such as the economy, law and order, the enforcement of contracts, and the provision of public goods such as health and education.[31]

Lack of medical infrastructure is another structural barrier. In August 2000, the Gates Foundation, the pharmaceutical companies Merck and Bristol-Myers Squibb, and the Harvard AIDS Initiative launched an HIV/AIDS treatment program in collaboration with the Botswana government. But the group soon found that the goal of treating the nearly 300,000 infected Botswanans would first require building up the medical infrastructure in the country. The emigration of health-care workers, poor medical education, and a scarcity of laboratories and clinics meant that the group could not distribute its aid. So the consortium of philanthropists, businesses, academics, and the government set out to build that infrastructure. The Peace Corps brought in doctors and nurses, and President Bush's PEPFAR program helped build a network of HIV testing facilities. Five years later, the program finally got off the ground, with 55,000 treated so far.[32]

Fostering prosperity in Africa is a complex, long-term challenge. It will take continued generous aid levels, but most important will be getting the fundamentals right within each society. Without the basic pillars of good governance and peace, no amount of assistance can bring the people prosperity. It will require time—often a generation or two for the underlying structural problems of a society to be solved—to become a strong-enough foundation to eradicate poverty.

A New Way to Do Development

President Bush recognized the need to link aid to the fundamentals of good government, and he placed it at the heart of his signature development program, the Millennium Challenge Account (MCA). The program is built on the principle that foreign aid yields better results where sound economic policies and good governance provide an environment that is conducive to economic growth. The program targets projects in nations that govern justly, invest in their people, and follow sound and open economic principles. The MCA has signed compacts worth nearly $4 billion with thirteen countries, all under the administration of the Millennium Challenge Corporation (MCC).[33] It has also initiated threshold programs that are designed to help countries qualify for compacts, totaling $316 million with fourteen countries.[34]

The MCC seeks to reduce poverty by promoting sustainable economic growth through investments in areas such as transportation, water and industrial infrastructure, agriculture, education, private sector development, and capacity building. Countries are selected to receive assistance based on their performance in sixteen areas of good governance, including civil liberties, political rights, rule of law, control of corruption, education (including that of girls), and strategic business indicators. Recipients are also encouraged to manage and prioritize the funds themselves to ensure that the right priorities are set.

Because corruption undermines every aspect of sustainable development, MCC has made fighting corruption one of its highest priorities. Each country enters into a public compact with MCC that includes a multiyear plan for achieving development objectives and identifies the responsibilities of each partner in achieving those objectives. Programs are designed to enable sustainable progress even after funding under the compact has ended, which is always less than five years from its start date. Countries that have demonstrated significant progress toward these goals by the end of the compact may also qualify for threshold programs.[35] Although promising, the MCC has been slow to get off the ground, and much of the appropriated funds have yet to be disbursed.[36] Still, the MCA is helping to promote prosperity in key parts of Africa, such as Mali.

Mali is one of Africa's success stories. It is a small, landlocked desert country on the edge of the Sahara Desert, yet it is booming. The Libyans, the Chinese, the Islamic Development Bank, and the United States are all investing in the country's future. As one of the countries that qualifies for the MCA, Mali stands to receive nearly half a billion dollars to supplement its tiny government budget of $1.5 billion. Even Timbuktu is undergoing a revival, with the world's ancient text experts rediscovering new treasures in the closets and the drawers of local residents who have saved them over the centuries.[37]

Most of the good news about Mali's success is due to the sine qua non of progress: good government. Mali's president Amadou Toumani Toure (dubbed ATT) has built on the good work of his respected predecessor, Alpha Oumar Konare, who went on to run the African Union. The government has launched a "Struggle against Poverty," which makes agriculture and infrastructure its priorities. The focus is not to depend on aid, but rather to grow the economy and lift people out of poverty. The hope is that the country's 3.5 million farmers will become self-supporting and will expand beyond their traditional cotton crops. The Bush administration has brought in the MCA, funding a 40,000-acre irrigation project to increase the country's drought-proof farmable land by 20 percent. Villagers around Timbuktu are learning how to build irrigation canals to capture the floodwaters of the Niger River. People are reversing the emigration rate: those who had previously left the country are returning to take advantage of its revival.

Mali still has a long way to go before it becomes the breadbasket of West Africa, however. Roads and basic transportation are still far from adequate to link Mali to the world market. As one observer noted, "You can't have the cattle walk two thousand kilometers to market—they become skeletons."[38] But the Europeans and the Chinese are building roads, and the United States is redeveloping the international airport. Mali is expected to reach the Millennium Development Goal of halving poverty not by 2015, but by 2025.[39] Enabling countries beyond Mali to break the cycle of poverty will require a new compact between the developed and the developing worlds to secure the fundamentals of prosperity: aid, an end to conflict, good governance, a middle class with access to capital, and open trade. As always, achieving these fundamentals will require strong U.S. leadership.

The United States must find innovative ways to help the developing world lift itself out of poverty. One successful approach has been micro lending. The recipients of the 2006 Nobel Peace Prize, the Grameen Bank and Muhammad Yunus, have provided small loans, averaging only $180, to 22 million borrowers in forty countries. The bank now gives out $2 billion in loans, primarily to women who agree to work within peer groups and commit to basic standards of living. The repayment rate is an extraordinary 96 to 100 percent. Some are now calling for a similar program to provide financing for the developing world's growing middle class—those entrepreneurs who cannot find the $250,000 to $5 million loans they need to get their businesses off the ground and growing.[40] Other innovative approaches can help as well.

For instance, the Peruvian economist Hernando de Soto has conducted groundbreaking work in finding "dead" capital in developing countries. In other words, capital that exists in a country but is not utilized, such as state-owned plants and factories that can be used as credit for a nation's poor. De Soto estimated that there is as much as $9.3 trillion in such dead capital, which, if tapped, would dwarf all aid given since World War II to developing countries.[41]

We need to begin to think of how best to aid countries, perhaps with a type of "reverse sanction." Rather than punish bad behavior by revoking aid, trade, investment, and visas—sanctions that tend to have limited impact—we need to consider how we can use all of those things to reward what we want countries to do. Building on President Bush's MCC, we must look at how to develop a system where the international community invests in the developing world to promote all the pillars of good governance, with the full range of our powers. That would mean more visas, more education, more trade, fewer trade barriers, and more foreign investment. As long as "have-not" developing countries, such as Mali, are willing to do their part, the United States and the other "have" countries must be prepared to do theirs.

Fighting Poverty: A Global Effort

Good governments, such as that in Mali, will drive the engine of prosperity across the developing world. Supporting and expanding those success stories is crucial to advancing global prosperity. The United States must understand that this progress is critical to its own safety and prosperity. Fighting poverty must no longer be viewed as social or "missionary" work, but rather as building the foundation of a more stable and prosperous world that will help keep Americans safe. Breaking the cycle of poverty will require the United States to invest in stability and prosperity around the world. But first America needs to:

STOP: The spread of infectious diseases. Poverty will remain endemic to many developing countries as long as large swaths of their populations are killed by deadly diseases. Great strides have been made, especially in the treatment of HIV/AIDS, with credit due to President Bush and organizations such as the Bill and Melinda Gates Foundation. More must be done to make treatment available to patients who live in the developing world, to eradicate other diseases, and to address the systematic failures of these countries.

START: Helping the world to see America the way Americans do—as givers. That means putting Americans on the ground when disaster strikes, as the United States did so well during the tsunami and the Pakistani earthquakes. It also means doing its share in global development. The United States and the rest of the developing world must commit to providing the 0.7 percent of income that is suggested by the United Nations. That level would require the United States to commit about $130 billion by 2012, up from the $22.7 billion provided today. Such a level would help cut today's poverty levels in half—a wise investment, given the link between poverty and violence, and between violence and the nexus of crime, drugs, and terrorism. A country known for its generosity is also far more likely to find supporters in times of need. And it will take more than money, but rather a long-term effort, to build up the main pillars of prosperity: a functioning government that can deliver a health-care system and the other essential elements of a decent life.

STOP: Waiting for a country to completely collapse before doing something. Today's crumbling regime is tomorrow's terrorist haven or refugee crisis. It's no longer acceptable to think of a failing state as someone else's problem. It'll be America's problem soon enough.

START: Thinking about which countries the United States could help the most and help them. This means helping to stop conflicts and doing more to promote development—now. The United States must build up Africa's peacekeeping capabilities and engage more directly in pressing a resolution of the conflicts across Africa, between the Arabs and the Israelis, and within Kashmir. On development, we must help countries get the fundamentals right, such as a healthy GDP, fiscal policy, sound regulations, open markets, and good business practices. We need to develop the "reverse sanction," which we discussed earlier, meaning we should use our full superpower status to assist citizens in troubled nations in a way that directly benefits them. That way, they will trust America more and will stand behind their corrupt leaders less.

STOP: Pretending the "war on drugs" is about supply. Demand for drugs in North America and Europe fuels much of the drug trade. Yet poor people in Latin America and Asia, particularly in the cocaine-producing states of Colombia, Bolivia, and Peru, and the opium-producing Afghanistan, see America supporting a war on their livelihoods.

START: Treating the drug trade as a demand problem, too. We must, as the UN's Office on Drugs and Crime has recommended, start treating drug addiction as an investment in the health of our nations, much like treating HIV, diabetes, or TB. The war on drugs cannot be won until the demand is reduced.

STOP: Self-serving or temporary aid. We have to stop giving money with the wrong strings attached. This means no more ill-advised austerity programs or loans that can be used only to buy American goods when cheaper alternatives are available. In fact, we should start with projects that will make permanent progress—vaccines and clean water, for example—that can't be wiped away by international currency markets or siphoned off by corrupt officials.

START: Helping the middle class to help itself. Developing countries must have access to capital, or a prosperous middle class simply cannot emerge. The provision of micro financing has helped bring millions out of poverty. The United States must find a way to arrange for "middle" financing to ensure that small businesses across the developing world can survive and prosper.

The United States needs to encourage sustainable investments in basic infrastructure and human capital by creating bilateral development assistance programs. This means adopting a fundamentally different approach to investing and building functioning public sector institutions around the world—governing institutions that ensure that their countries adhere to fundamental labor and environmental standards and make sure that their citizens have the social safety net that is necessary to advance prosperity and build a global middle class. We should not turn away from private-sector growth; market competition is vital for promoting innovation and entrepreneurship. But we must invest more heavily in building institutions that root out corruption, ensure basic product standards, and make sure that the world's economic players are on more equal footing.

For America to prosper, it must consider the rest of the world's economic development to be essential for its own well-being. Only then can the United States end poverty—and make Americans truly safe and prosperous. That will occur when Adelard Mivumba and the billions of people living in poverty are safer from poverty, debt, disease, environmental degradation, and war.

seven

Globalization's Impact on Prosperity

J im and Don Kane had steady jobs working at Malden Mills, in Lawrence, Massachusetts, producing Polartec fleece fabric. The two brothers, both with high school educations, had worked in the mill for more than twenty years and were able to provide decent lives for their families, with salaries of about $50,000 per year, good health insurance, and 401(k) plans.[1] Then disaster struck. In December 1995, a fire destroyed much of the mill, and they faced the prospect of unemployment.

But they were lucky. The owner of the plant, Aaron Feuerstein, used his insurance money and an additional loan of $100 million to keep all three thousand employees on the payroll with full benefits during the three months it took to rebuild the plant. Dubbed "the mensch of Malden Mills," Feuerstein explained that he was guided by the Jewish law of the Torah. "You are not permitted to oppress the working man."[2] He ran an environmentally friendly plant, and its union workforce never had a strike. The plant eventually was repaired, and everyone went back to work.

Their luck would not last, however. In 2001, Malden Mills filed for bankruptcy protection. It faced a double whammy: the market for upscale fleece jackets had fallen off and their product had to compete with low production costs in China and other developing countries. As Jim explained, "Fleece is no longer the fashion. No one is paying $300 to $400 for a fleece jacket that costs nothing to make." Jim and Don, both in their mid-fifties, were soon let go. "After the fire," said Don, "there were money problems. The Feuerstein family tried to take the best care of us that they could. But we couldn't compete." As Jim explained it, "If you aren't making a high end commodity, labor becomes a big part of your costs. Some of the jobs went overseas, some went down south."[3]

Jim left the company and took a job with Vernon Plastics, which made swimming pool liners. He took a pay cut, just as he has with every job change since the plant closed. Jim eventually regained his old salary when he was made a lead mechanic a few years later. But that company also went bankrupt, and he had to take another job with Century Box, a box manufacturer, again at a lower salary. Don was hired back by a scaled-down Malden Mills, but at a lower salary, and then laid off again. "They let the older, more expensive guys out the door and kept the kids, paying them six dollars an hour less," explained Don. He eventually took a good job with Senmina, a company that makes circuit boards, but "That job went to China," said Don. He then took an hourly job with Century Box alongside his brother, making only $19,000 a year.

Malden Mills, like more than four hundred textile plants across the country since 1997, simply could not compete with the cheaper labor in developing countries.[4] The United States has lost about three million jobs in the manufacturing sector in the decade since 1997.[5] Many of the people who lost these jobs see the American Dream—the chance to become more prosperous and provide their families with a decent life—slipping away. And they are angry. "I'm mad as hell," said Don. "They outsourced all the jobs and are making billions on the backs of working people. It's all going to China, Taiwan, and India."

"Global trade is a race to the bottom, isn't it?" asked his brother, Jim. "The rich are getting richer and the middle class is disappearing." Today, Don works in industrial maintenance, supplying stores such as Staples and Macy's. "We don't make anything," he said. "We just service things." Recognizing that today a college education is important for job security, both brothers hope their five children will go to college. One of them has earned an associate's degree and Jim's oldest son has gone to work at Malden Mills.

Global Economic Growth and Growing Pains

Americans like the Kane brothers and their families are wrestling with the impact that growing economic integration with the rest of the world is having on their lives. Americans' economic future is in very real ways inextricably linked to the fate of others around the world. Jobs, wages, profiles, interest rates, and prices of consumer goods at home are shaped by events overseas unlike ever before. Given how open and integrated America's economy is with the rest of the world, what happens economically in other countries matters far more than it did in the past. These new dynamics make people like the Kanes understandably hesitant to endorse any plan that is built around making the rest of the world more prosperous. Still, there's a connection. Right now, the United States has the storied race to the bottom. But if America starts to export its labor standards and environmental technology, it will become a race to the future.

Today, a divided country is looking for leadership on the complex issues related to the global economy. Nearly half of all Americans—47 percent—say that the United States is being harmed by the global economy, and only 25 percent say that the global economy benefits the United States. The remaining one-fourth of Americans are uncertain about the global economy's impact on the country.[6]

Throughout this book, we have argued that in order to make Americans safer, our leaders need to promote foreign policies that make people in other countries feel more secure and prosperous.

But the United States will not be able to promote prosperity abroad while increasing numbers of people are economically threatened at home, by growing budget deficits, job insecurity, rising health-care costs, and skyrocketing gas prices. The gap between the haves and the have-nots in our own country threatens our ability to lead in the world and gives greater power to arguments that we should instead retreat from the world, erect barriers, and look inward. The challenges posed by this current phase of globalization at home and abroad are considerable, but if U.S. leaders meet them head on, rather than retreating, these new global economic trends offer an opportunity for America to advance the prosperity agenda.

This means moving forward with trade agreements that are fair as well as free and that include labor and environmental standards that are proposed in good faith. But even these standards are heavily disputed by developing countries, which sometimes see any regulations as a heavy-handed way to limit their economic growth and their ability to export. Striking the right balance between developing countries' interest in growth and America's need to ensure that trade and economic competition are fair will require real leadership through uncharted and choppy economic waters. The United States must set an example that will inspire other governments to make long-term investments in building social capital, such as reforming education systems so that workers have the ability to compete. America must help to create institutions that regulate the economy and provide additional support to people whose lives or livelihoods are threatened by the increased competition associated with globalization. To remain a leader and expand prosperity in the world, America must do a better job of managing globalization to close the growing gap between the haves and the have-nots at home and abroad.

The forces of globalization are everywhere, in trade and immigration, with an influx of cheap Chinese goods, in the transfer of Hershey Company manufacturing jobs to Mexico, or in the opening of a new Mercedes-Benz plant in Alabama. Globalization also means instantaneous connectivity, as information is now available from around the world through the Internet, cheap international calls, and twenty-four-hour cable television. These expanding global ties have advanced overall economic growth in the world.

From 2001 to 2006, the world saw faster economic growth than at any time since the early 1970s, in large part due to increased global competition.[7] Emerging economies such as India and China represent a major part of this growth: economic output from emerging economies accounts for more than half of the world's total GDP, measured as purchasing-power parity. Globalization has also lifted hundreds of millions out of poverty in China, India, and elsewhere in the developing world.[8] Global trade in goods and services rose from about $95 billion in 1955 to $12 trillion in 2005, and this increase has linked America's economic fortunes more tightly with those of other countries.[9] These new linkages mean that a growing number of developing countries will shape the economies of developed countries for years to come.

Global economic changes have major implications for America's domestic economic policy. As two analysts described it, "No matter which party you belong to, or which Big Idea or school of economic policy you subscribe to, one thing is clear: Globalization has overwhelmed Washington's ability to control the economy. . . . Whether you're a Republican supply-side tax-cutter, a Wall Street deficit hawk of either party, or a Silicon Valley techie type, your preferred levels of economic policy just don't work as well as they once did."[10] Fiscal policy proposals such as raising the minimum wage or monetary policy moves like cutting interest rates have less of a direct impact on economic events inside a country than they did twenty years ago because of global economic integration.

Such dramatic changes are daunting and can lead to fears about a loss of control over the U.S. economy. But it is important to keep two fundamentals in perspective. First, America remains an economic giant in this radically transforming global economy. Although the United States has less than 5 percent of the world's population, its economy still produces about a quarter of the world's economic growth. The U.S. economy is a tremendous force for prosperity and growth in the world. Second, overall, Americans benefit from trade and increased global economic integration. In the fall of 2007, when the housing market bubble and a credit crunch raised concerns about an economic downturn, export-driven economic growth became indispensable for keeping the U.S. economy afloat. "Exports have suddenly become a key source of growth at a time when the economy is looking for any growth it can get," said Mark Zandi, a chief economist for Moody's Economy.com.[11]

The downsides to these global economic transformations are obvious. There is little dispute that some Americans, such as the Kane brothers, are squeezed by the rise in global trade, technological advances, and competition from low wages abroad. Despite fairly strong economic growth in the United States and the world, globalization's gains have not been felt evenly by all Americans. According to the U.S. Census, real median household income fell 2.7 percent between 2000 and 2005, after increasing 15 percent from 1993 to 2000. At the same time, real wages have stagnated: from November 2001 through August 2006, average weekly earnings declined in real terms.[12]

The costs of health care, housing, tuition, gas, and food have increased substantially. As Mark Zandi described it, "For those working in the bottom half of the pay scale, they're under an enormous amount of pressure." More than a million jobs have been added back to the 2.6 million lost since Mr. Bush took office, but they pay less and offer fewer benefits such as health insurance. The new jobs are concentrated in health care, food services, and temporary employment firms, all lower-paying industries. Temp agencies alone account for about a fifth of all new jobs. In addition, technology and global competition have shifted many U.S. jobs overseas, leaving less-skilled American workers struggling.[13]

In response to these new changes in the economy, some U.S. politicians and commentators have offered a set of simple but wrongheaded solutions to the complex challenge of globalization: throw up barriers to trade and foreign investment and close America's doors to immigration. When increased trade and economic ties with the rest of the world caused growing pains in other eras of U.S. history, the voices calling for isolation led the country down the wrong path, one that led to the Great Depression and to fewer opportunities for Americans.

During the last few years, such voices have again grown louder, epitomized by the CNN anchor Lou Dobbs, who rails about "exporting America," its "broken borders," and a war on the middle class.[14] In the 2004 presidential election, the Democratic presidential candidate John Kerry criticized "Benedict Arnold CEOs" and corporations that outsourced jobs overseas. Free trade agreements and progress in multilateral trade talks, which accelerated in the 1990s, have slowed. The issue was also part of the 2008 campaign, with the leading Democratic candidates questioning international trade deals. For instance, Senator Hillary Rodham Clinton (D-N.Y.) supports "smart trade" but calls for "a time out to take stock of where we are on trade. Every trade agreement has to be independently, objectively analyzed."[15]

Trade is not the only hot-button issue tied to globalization. After the September 11, 2001, attacks, concern over foreign investment spiked. When President Bush endorsed a proposed deal that would have placed a government-owned United Arab Emirates company in charge of shipping operations in major ports such as New York and New Orleans in 2006, he was met with strong opposition. "In regards to selling American ports to the United Arab Emirates, not just NO—but HELL NO," wrote the conservative representative Sue Myrick (R-N.C.) in an open letter to President Bush.[16]

These anxious and inward-looking sentiments reflect the real concerns of America's middle class that they are being pushed out of their jobs by foreign competition. Some Americans have been hit hard by a never-before-seen ability of companies to shed U.S. workers in favor of machines or workers in low-wage developing countries such as Mexico, China, and India. Jobs in Lawrence, Detroit, and Pittsburgh have moved to places like Shanghai and Mumbai or have been made unnecessary by new technologies. Downtowns across America have emptied out as manufacturing plants that used to support vibrant communities have moved to foreign lands. By one estimate, $136 billion in wages will be lost to outsourcing by 2015.[17]

The negative impact on some Americans, combined with a greater threat of lost jobs for others, raises questions about whether U.S. leadership is doing enough to manage the impact of globalization. America's overall wealth and economic growth have benefited from globalization, but not all Americans see the tangible gains in their individual lives. U.S. leaders are failing these middle-class Americans.

Instead of a zero-sum approach to facing the challenges of globalization at home and abroad, the United States needs a comprehensive strategy that helps more people feel the benefits of expanding economic ties with the rest of the world. The answer to these challenges is not to cut off imports or close U.S. borders, but rather to reconstruct the social safety net that can help Americans compete, by building their skills so that they can work in competitive industries that boost U.S. exports and Americans' wages. The answer also lies in working with other countries around the world to develop basic labor and environmental standards so that global economic competition is on a more level playing field. The United States must shape the forces that are changing the fabric of towns like Lawrence, Massachusetts, across this country and help to advance sustainable development globally.

We then return to the central problem that this book seeks to resolve. If the world isn't eager to follow us, how does America lead the world where it needs to go?

Ensuring That Globalization Advances Prosperity and Builds a Middle Class at Home

Increased globalization and technological advances during the last two decades have contributed to rising income inequalities in most regions and countries. But it is important to note that overall income growth is positive across all categories, meaning that people are better off in an absolute sense, although the gains have not been distributed equally. Those with better educations and access to credit on the whole receive more benefits from increased globalization.[18] Temporary solutions such as trade adjustment assistance can help those who are adversely affected in the short term, but the long-term solution requires governments around the world to build social capital by investing in education and a stronger social safety net with essentials such as health care.

The core challenge that lies at the heart of the next phase of globalization will be addressing these growing inequalities at home and abroad. As noted in chapter 6, this means taking steps to expand opportunities abroad for people to lift themselves up out of poverty through hard work and competition in the global economy and making sure that they are competing on a level playing field. Unlike the last few decades of the previous century, when much of the international economic agenda was focused on pushing through free market "shock therapy" reforms imposed by international institutions, today's economic agenda must focus on building new institutions that help distribute the gains from globalization more equitably. Once the world sees America helping to address its citizens' problems, America will be much better placed to convince them to follow us in meeting our challenges.

Equally important is the promotion of a prosperity agenda at home. As Americans head into the 2008 presidential elections, they do not feel prosperous or secure, even though America remains the richest, most powerful nation on earth. The value of the dollar recently hit an all-time low against the euro. With the subprime mortgage crisis, people no longer feel secure in their homes. The pace of economic growth at home slowed in 2007 and is likely to slacken further before the end of 2008. The Bush administration's budgets and tax cuts have wiped out the strong surplus that Bush inherited, accumulating $1.6 *trillion* in debt. The Congressional Budget Office (CBO) projects an additional $250 billion in debt, including war costs, for fiscal year 2008. The CBO also estimates that in 2008 federal spending will total $2.9 trillion, with revenues of only $2.7 trillion, leading to a budget deficit of $219 billion.[19]

Increasingly, other countries, such as China and wealthy Arab nations, are financing that deficit and that debt—and using their vast sovereign wealth to purchase large U.S. banks and companies. If such investments are managed wisely and transparently, they do not inherently cause a problem. But their magnitude is making Americans increasingly wary that the American economy could be vulnerable to foreign meddling.

There are increasing calls for Washington to stop globalization, suspend further talks on free trade agreements, shut off America to foreign investment, and shut U.S. borders, sending the 12 million undocumented workers in this country home. As emotionally appealing as these steps are, each of them would undermine American prosperity. We must choose a wiser course on three important issues: trade, foreign investment, and immigration.

Breaking the Free Trade Stalemate

Trade has provided lower-cost goods and services to Americans and has opened the door to economic advancement in other countries. No doubt, there are very real adjustment costs to these economic changes, but with the right leadership and policies, increased global trade is a vital component for advancing prosperity at home and abroad. A new global economic game has emerged as a result of expanding economic linkages, and better leadership is required to make sure that all of the players are competing fairly and with the same advantages.

Economic growth in other countries increases the demand for America's goods and services. Trade has grown the U.S. economy, with trade-related growth rising from about 9 percent of America's GDP in 1960 to 26 percent today.[20] All of this economic activity directly helps American workers: trade supports 31 million U.S. jobs, and workers in plants that export goods are paid up to 18 percent more on average than those in plants that do not.[21] To advance prosperity at home and abroad, U.S. policy makers must take steps to promote industries that are engines for export growth, particularly those that are on the cutting edge of innovation, such as alternative energies. In 2006, the most lucrative exports for the United States were nuclear power plants, electrical machinery, vehicles, airplanes, and medical equipment.[22] High-technology exports such as medical equipment and computer software will help the United States to advance prosperity at home by remaining fully engaged in trade abroad.

The end of the Cold War paved the way for a new approach to international trade. Rather than continue to form piecemeal trade pacts that divided world markets between the two superpowers, President Bill Clinton actively promoted global and regional trade deals such as the North American Free Trade Agreement (NAFTA), and he concluded the Uruguay Round of global trade negotiations. In 1994, the United States and other members of the Asian-Pacific Economic Cooperation (APEC) made a commitment to work toward a free trade and investment region among developed APEC member countries by 2010 and among all APEC members by 2020. In 1998, the United States, along with thirty-three other Western Hemisphere countries, formally initiated negotiations to work toward creating a Free Trade Area of the Americas (FTAA) by 2005. By 2008, however, political support had eroded for any such broad pact and progress has stalled.

These trade agreements have had mixed success and the reception from the American people has been equally mixed. There have certainly been problems with the implementation of NAFTA in environmental and labor issues, but polls indicate that a plurality of Americans (46 percent) believes that NAFTA is good for the United States. A plurality would also like to see changes to NAFTA, believing that, while business is benefiting, NAFTA can have negative impacts on American workers' jobs and wages and on the environment. Attitudes are also divided about CAFTA, with the American public showing similar concerns. Support for CAFTA would be robust, however, if key public concerns were addressed. While the polling on the issue is thin, it appears that there is slim majority support for expanding free trade to include other American countries, such as the proposed Free Trade Area of the Americas (FTAA).[23]

President Clinton further advanced the free trade cause by supporting the creation of the World Trade Organization (WTO) in 1995. He aggressively sought to enforce it, bringing an average of eleven complaints annually to the WTO dispute settlement system. Despite being unable to move the next round of global trade talks forward or to advance the hemisphere-wide FTAA, President Bush has vigorously pursued bilateral trade pacts in the four corners of the globe in diverse places such as Australia, Bahrain, and South Korea. He has sought bilateral trade agreements with many Latin American nations as well. Although trade agreements remain a source of political controversy in the United States, managed right, they can benefit our country. The Congressional Budget Office estimates, for example, that NAFTA has had a positive impact on the U.S. trade balance. Total trade between the United States, Canada, and Mexico doubled from $306 billion in 1994 to $621 billion in 2003. The expanded trade resulting from NAFTA has raised the United States' gross domestic product very slightly. The effect on the much smaller Mexican GDP has also been positive.[24]

When Americans think about global trade, China looms large, with many Americans wondering what China's emergence as a global power means for America's future. The 2008 Summer Olympics in Beijing has put China at center stage, showcasing its growing global importance. China is the second-largest trading partner of the United States (behind Canada and ahead of Mexico) and the fastest-growing market for U.S. exports. Since China entered the WTO in 2001, U.S. exports to China have grown about 150 percent, while exports to the rest of the world during the same period grew by a paltry 10 percent. U.S. exports to China are predicted to grow even further, with one study suggesting that U.S. services to China will increase to $15 billion in 2015 from around $2 billion today.[25]

Worries about China's impact on the U.S. economy are very real, however, since China does not play entirely fair when it comes to trade and economic competition. Beijing has dragged its feet in implementing some of the commitments it made as part of the WTO accession process, particularly regarding the protection of intellectual property rights and industrial policies that give preference to local firms. And a good deal of China's price advantage is the result of a variety of illegal trade practices, including export subsidies, an undervalued currency, counterfeiting and piracy, and weak health, safety, and environmental regulations.[26] China is gaining a well-earned reputation for lax standards. In 2007 alone, contaminated pet food sickened or killed up to

39,000 pets in the United States before the poisoned products were pulled off the market.[27] Millions of lead-painted children's toys from China were also recalled.

In this new complicated phase of globalization, Americans are rethinking whether increased trade ties are a good thing for America's prosperity. The challenges of expanding global economic competition in this new millennium are giving rise to understandable hesitations about what this new economic order means. Among most Americans, trade with other countries garners majority support, 59 percent in 2007. But this represents a sharp decline from 2002, when 78 percent said that trade was good for America.[28] There are growing concerns about trade's impact, and Americans have become increasingly skeptical. The share of Americans who believe that trade agreements hurt the United States rose 16 points, from 30 percent in 1999 to 46 percent in March 2007.[29] Americans are nearly evenly split when asked whether the United States should negotiate new trade agreements, stick with the ones it has, or repeal them.[30]

The main issue for many Americans is whether the United States is playing on a level field in today's global economy. Jim Kane, the former Polartec fleece plant worker in Massachusetts, reflected the mood of many in America when he said that America's leaders are not doing enough to make sure that global economic competition is fair. "If the stuff is not produced with a reasonable standard, we should tax the difference," he argued. "Companies shouldn't be able to make money on the backs of the poorest and the most unfortunate—in America or overseas."[31]

The U.S. Congress hears the public's complaints about trade's impact on American businesses and workers and has started to put the brakes on free trade agreements. The Bush administration gave a high priority to free trade agreements, completing negotiations with Chile and Singapore that had been initiated by the Clinton administration. President Bush moved forward with new agreements with Australia, Morocco, and Bahrain, but Congress became increasingly vocal in its opposition. By the time the Dominican Republic–Central American Free Trade Agreement (DR-CAFTA) was put to a vote in Congress in 2005, it received only a narrow approval, winning by a 217–215 vote in the House and 54–45 vote in the Senate. This was a slim vote margin for a relatively small trade pact, compared to the 83–15 Senate approval for permanent normal trade relations with China in 2000, the 76–24 Senate support for the World Trade Organization in 1994, and the 61–38 vote for NAFTA in 1993.

Rhetoric escalated among the sharply divided members of Congress when DR-CAFTA was narrowly approved. Senator Jay Rockefeller (D-W.V.) denounced the agreement: "CAFTA doesn't just offer the opportunity for American companies to send jobs abroad—it encourages them to do so. I'm outraged that this administration has once again turned its back on American workers."[32]

Another sign of congressional reluctance to move forward on trade issues came in 2007, when it decided not to renew fast-track trade promotion authority, which gives the president additional flexibility to negotiate free trade pacts. All of this reluctance is driven by one primary concern: that free trade agreements that lack the right labor and environmental standards will eventually harm U.S. workers.

In order to build congressional support for its shaky trade policy, the Bush administration reached an agreement with the Democratic Congress in May 2007 to do more to promote environmental and labor standards in trade agreements. It would require trading partners to enforce their own environmental laws and comply with international environmental agreements. On labor, trade pacts would have to guarantee workers the right to organize, ban child labor, and prohibit forced labor in trading-partner countries.[33] The agreement was the first major bipartisan economic deal to emerge since Democrats took control of Congress in January 2007. Although it left open whether Congress would support more free trade agreements in the remaining months of Bush's term, the agreement laid out a framework for moving forward once there was a political consensus to do so.

Just as America has become increasingly skeptical and reluctant about bilateral trade deals, global multilateral trade talks have also stalled. The Doha Round, named for the city in Qatar where the talks began in 2006, was nicknamed the "Development

Round." This ninth and most recent round of global trade talks was focused on the needs of developing countries.

The key issues in play include granting new market access for services and manufactured goods and addressing the impact of agriculture and farm subsidies. Discussions stalled largely because of disagreements over farm subsidies. Several European Union countries do not want to give up subsidy programs for farmers or fully open their markets to foreign competition in agriculture. Developing countries want the United States and the EU countries to give up farm subsidies but do not want to open up their own markets to competition, including Latin American markets such as Brazil. Finally, the United States is reluctant to do away with subsidies it provides to its own farmers, which have garnered strong support from Congress for the U.S. agricultural industry.

The global trade talks have reached a complicated juncture, and serious engagement and leadership are required to break the deadlock. Some rapidly developing countries have begun to advocate more strenuously for their own interests. Brazil has emerged as a serious leader of the "G-20" group of developing nations that has formed a power bloc in the negotiations. India has played an active role in negotiations over service industries, hoping that the agreement will lead to greater access abroad for its engineers and IT professionals. China, which stands to benefit substantially from improved market access abroad, has essentially sat on the sidelines, despite numerous calls by the United States and others for Beijing to play a more active role. While optimists take heart that the last round of negotiations, the Uruguay Round, also took a long time to negotiate (seven years), the deal is effectively stalled until a new president takes office in January 2009. It may take a Democratic president to move the talks forward. Historically, trade deals fare better under Democratic presidents, who have traditionally demonstrated a stronger commitment to labor and environmental provisions of trade pacts. They have also concluded seven of the last eight global trade rounds. The last Republican president to conclude a global trade round was Eisenhower in 1956.[34]

The collapse of the Doha Round dealt a serious blow to efforts to promote prosperity both in the United States and in the developing world. One study estimated that cutting global trade barriers by one-third, which could be done in a global trade round like Doha, would pump $177 billion per year into the U.S. economy.[35] A meaningful agreement would provide new market access for U.S. farmers and manufacturers but only as part of a difficult deal that involved cuts to U.S. farm support programs.

Countries in the developing world would benefit as well. Much of the developing world is lacking in the service and technology sectors, thus agriculture is its main source of economic growth. Failure to make progress in breaking down those barriers only serves to alienate further the developed from the developing countries, while causing economic hopes to stagnate for billions around the world who seek better lives.

Striking the Right Balance on Foreign Investment

Expanding global economic ties not only means increased trade in goods and services; it also leads to more foreign direct investment and ownership of companies that operate across borders. Foreign ownership at times raises legitimate national security concerns, as in the case of defense and technology companies that work closely with sensitive U.S. government programs, and at other times has given rise to irrational sentiments that are the exact opposite of what has made America a great country.

As noted earlier in the chapter, a public debate erupted in early 2006 over a proposed deal to transfer commercial management of certain U.S. ports to a company named Dubai Ports World that is owned by the United Arab Emirates (UAE). Despite the fact that the UAE government is a strong U.S. ally on terrorism and opposes al-Qaeda, Congress pandered to the base fears of some Americans and argued that no Arab entity, especially one with a government stake in the company, should manage a piece of U.S. infrastructure. The then chairman of the House Committee on Homeland Security Peter King said, "Having a company right out of the heartland of al Qaeda managing those ports . . . is madness."[36] The fact that al-Qaeda has no base in the UAE was apparently irrelevant.

Throughout his term in office, President Bush and other conservatives stoked fear by using phrases like "Islamo-fascism" when talking about foreign affairs. It came back to haunt them and much of America, feeding an irrational paranoia about other countries, particularly Muslim-majority countries. In this case, the UAE's firm would have employed mostly unionized American workers to run the day-to-day operations of the ports. But once the issue was in the spotlight, the facts took a backseat. At the height of the debate, fully seven in ten Americans opposed allowing this UAE company to manage operations at U.S. ports.[37] Congressional leaders ignored a plea from President Bush to support the deal, and the House of Representatives voted 348–71 for legislation that would have blocked it. The deal quietly died, as Dubai Ports World sold its U.S. operations to a division of U.S.-based AIG, and the free trade agreement that was in process with the United States fizzled.

A similar frenzy broke out in 2005 over the effort by China National Offshore Oil Corporation (CNOOC) to buy the U.S oil company Unocal Corporation. The end result was that Unocal shareholders lost a $1.5 billion premium above Chevron's bid that CNOOC had offered, while CNOOC invested elsewhere, picking up an oil company in Nigeria. Another Chinese company, Lenovo, came under scrutiny earlier the same year in its ultimately successful attempt to acquire IBM's Thinkpad division.

By 2007, the furor subsided somewhat. Overall, Americans seem to have developed a consensus that except for critical infrastructure, foreign investment in the U.S. economy will be accepted. For instance, the September 2007 decision by Borse Dubai, Abu Dhabi's government-controlled exchange, to buy a 20 percent stake in the NASDAQ caused barely a ripple. The sale to the Abu Dhabi government of a stake in the Carlyle Group, a Washington, D.C.-based buyout firm, caused little consternation. As Representative Barney Frank (D-Mass.) put it, "In the ports deal, the concern was smuggling something or someone dangerous into our ports.

What are we talking about here—smuggling someone onto a stock exchange?"[38]

Yet the scale of some of these investments is beginning to raise concerns, in particular, the vast expansion of sovereign wealth funds (SWF) over the past five years. SWFs are government investment funds, funded by foreign currency reserves but managed separately from official currency reserves. As the Council on Foreign Relations describes them, they are basically pools of money that governments invest for profit. Today, SWFs control as much as $3 trillion and could be as much as $12 trillion by 2012. The sheer size of these funds has raised concerns over whether foreign nations could gain too much political influence in American businesses and the U.S. economy.[39]

For instance, in early 2008, the government of Singapore invested $6.9 billion in Citigroup, for a 4 percent stake. Firms in Kuwait, Korea, and Japan invested $6.6 billion in Merrill Lynch. In 2007, China bought $5 billion of securities in Morgan Stanley, giving it a 9.9 percent stake in the company by 2010. Singapore, Abu Dhabi, Dubai, and Qatar are all actively purchasing large stakes in U.S. companies.[40] As the influential financier Felix Rohatyn explained, what the foreign investors are really looking for is influence on the world stage, despite their insistence otherwise.[41]

Senator Chuck Schumer (D-N.Y.) summed up the concern over the Merrill Lynch deal. "Foreign investment, in general, strengthens our economy and creates jobs. Because sovereign wealth funds, by definition, are potentially susceptible to noneconomic interests, the closer they come to exercising control and influence, the greater concerns we have."[42]

Experts are now pushing for greater international regulation of SWFs, such as an international standard for cross-border investment. Such a global standard, says Edwin M. Truman of the Peterson Institute for International Economics, could help evaluate the overall investment strategy and the governance of a fund, oversee the transparency of the fund's activity, and help allay fears over whether these funds could affect policies in the countries in which they are investing.[43]

Another concern over foreign investment is the purchase of U.S. securities by foreign governments. In recent years, foreign governments—particularly China, Japan, and a variety of Arab countries—have become major investors in the U.S. economy and purchasers of U.S. Treasury securities. As of July 2007, China held $408 billion in U.S. securities, second only to Japan's $611 billion.[44] Total foreign investment in these securities is more than $2 trillion, 44 percent of all publicly held U.S. debt. This means that the central banks of other nations lend 16 percent of the U.S. economy to us.[45] There is a small but growing concern that these foreign governments might decide to pull money out of the U.S. economy at some point, which could trigger dramatically higher interest rates and, in the worst case, lead to even further depreciations in the value of a U.S. dollar that has already seen steep declines. Democrats, for instance, have introduced legislation to trigger an alarm bell when U.S. foreign-owned debt reaches 25 percent of GDP or the trade deficit reaches 5 percent of GDP. "I believe that proposals like these need to be discussed in order to put our economic house in order," said Senator Hillary Rodham Clinton (D-N.Y.). "[We] can too easily be held hostage to the economic decisions being made in Beijing, Shanghai and Tokyo."[46]

There are, however, countervailing forces that in all likelihood will prevent that from occurring. Growing global economic interdependence is a two-way street. Foreign investors from Europe, China, India, and Japan also have a stake in U.S. economic stability, to protect their U.S. portfolio holdings and productive investments. And foreign oil producers need a stable and liquid place to invest their petrodollars. China, for instance, favors keeping America's interest rates low and the U.S. economy humming to help it maintain its own economy, which is driven by exports to the United States and Europe. Thus, it is likely that the U.S. economy will remain a preferred place of investment in the short to medium term. But over time, these other countries are likely to diversify their portfolios, and the United States may not be able to depend on the continued foreign financing of its deficit.

One country to watch is China, which is investing far beyond America. China has used its economic development at home to project power abroad, particularly in areas neglected by the United States, such as Latin America and Africa. China has more than four hundred agreements and business deals in Latin America, which serve as leverage to persuade those countries to support China in international diplomacy.[47] As noted in chapter 4, China has been especially active in Africa, developing strategic partnerships with forty-eight African countries.[48] Since the first China-Africa forum in 2000, trade between the two regions has more than doubled. There has been an equivalent amount of attention directed at diplomacy, and China has sponsored more than a hundred official meetings with African governments. The United States should carefully monitor these moves by countries like China that have recognized that economic power is an increasingly important component of projecting influence in the world.

America's national security and economic interests are best served if the next U.S. leaders turn away from the fear-based instincts of some people who want to disconnect this country from events in the rest of the world. Instead, the United States should reemerge as a leader with a program that demonstrates that economic growth halfway across the globe need not come at the cost of economic pain at home. That will require a new global compact that expands trade but ensures that the playing field is level. At home, it will take a new domestic compact that will provide the tools and the support that are necessary for Americans to compete effectively in the twenty-first century.

Meeting the Challenges and the Opportunities Posed by Immigration

Globalization has dissolved boundaries and created incentives for people to migrate to more stable and prosperous countries. When a country is less stable and prosperous than its neighbors, the flow of economic and political refugees increases. America owes its vibrancy to its tradition of welcoming immigrants. We will only continue to thrive and prosper if we continue to welcome new citizens in an open but responsible way. Sadly, America is moving away from that important foundation of its greatness.

Just as some leaders have worked to erect barriers to trade and foreign investment, there has been a growing populist movement in the United States to also create obstacles to immigration. Like trade and foreign investment, the immigration question is directly tied to the challenge of advancing economic opportunities at home and overseas.

In March and April 2006, hundreds of thousands of immigrants, legal and illegal, and their supporters rallied in more than 140 cities across the United States. They were demanding their rights, including the right to stay in this country. Under such slogans as "We are America" and "We are not criminals," marchers sought to show how immigrants, rather than taking from America, work to make America strong and deserve better respect and treatment. As these immigrant rallies took place, the CNN commentator Jack Cafferty demonized them. "The streets of our country were taken over today by people who don't belong here. . . . March through our streets and demand your rights? Excuse me? You have no rights here." He went on to suggest that the government "pull the buses up and start asking these people to show their green cards. . . . And the ones that don't have them, put them on the buses and send them home."[49]

Doctors, engineers, and other highly educated legal immigrants are also facing increasing obstacles to contributing to the economy in the United States. America's competitive economy and top-notch higher education serve as a beacon for the most innovative minds around the world. Foreign students today comprise roughly half of those who earn advanced degrees in science, engineering, and other technology-related fields.[50] Numerous high-profile and profitable U.S. companies such as Google, Sun Microsystems, eBay, YouTube, and Yahoo! were founded by immigrants. One study looked at start-up companies in the United States between 1995 and 2005 and found that wholly 25 percent were founded by foreign entrepreneurs, generating 450,000 domestic American jobs.[51] In addition, foreign nationals living in the United States were inventors of one-quarter of the international patent applications filed from the United States in 2006, up from 7.6 percent in 1998.[52]

A more intensive process of considering visa applications that was implemented after the September 11 attacks has resulted in a backlog of visas. This is making it difficult for highly educated people to continue to study and work in the United States. A 2007 study found that 1.1 million highly skilled immigrants and their families suffered from delays in getting visas.[53] The line for green cards that grant immigrants permanent residency is growing longer. A bipartisan group of thirteen governors sent a letter to Congress in late 2007 asking for increases in the number of temporary visas and green cards for highly educated immigrants.[54] "We must recognize that foreign talent has a role to play in our ability to keep companies located in our state and country," the governors wrote. Because immigrants play such a fundamental role in advancing America's prosperity, it is vitally important to address these delays. Bill Gates, in testimony before a Senate committee in 2007, warned that the United States might lose its global technological edge unless it granted more than the current 65,000 H-1B visas for foreign professionals to work in intellectually demanding U.S. jobs.[55] As the manufacturing labor market in the United States becomes increasingly technology- and skill-driven, a study by the National Association of Manufacturers found that 80 percent of the 800 manufacturing firms surveyed are experiencing a shortage of skilled labor.[56]

Such talented immigrants, who have long brought dynamism and expertise to the United States, are being discouraged—at great risk to America's prosperity. These practices may motivate the world's best and brightest to go elsewhere. Currently, the European Union is aiming to compete for these expert workers by instituting an EU "blue card" program along the lines of the American green card.[57] And as developing countries such as China, India, and Brazil continue to grow, they will more actively compete for highly skilled workers in the global marketplace.

This troublesome situation for well-educated legal immigrants is part of broader debate about immigration as a whole. America has seen a growing chorus of anti-immigrant vitriol from conservative voices. The former Republican presidential candidate Pat Buchanan wrote that militant Mexican movements are aiming, with coordination from the Mexican government, to make Los Angeles the capital of the New Aztlan.[58] The conservative commentator Bill O'Reilly denounced any quasi-legal status for illegal immigrants in this country as amnesty. He keeps a list of "sanctuary cities" on his Web site.

CNN's popular anchor Lou Dobbs has taken the anti-immigrant rhetoric to an appalling and un-American level of hysteria. Formerly the business-friendly host of *Moneyline* and the head of CNNfn, Dobbs now rails against the "greatest threats to America's way of life": outsourcing U.S. jobs and illegal immigration. On his regular segment, "Broken Borders," Dobbs decries the "army of invaders" from Mexico who are intent on reannexing parts of the Southwestern United States. Consistent themes include the hordes that come to steal America's treasure, bring deadly diseases such as leprosy and malaria into this country, and suck the U.S. welfare system dry. The middle class, he argued, "continue[s] to be assaulted by a continuing flow of cheap foreign labor into the United States and outsourcing of jobs to cheap foreign labor markets."[59] He also regularly implies that the flow is a terrorist threat. Dobbs has found an audience for his fearmongering. During the 2006 immigrant marches, viewership of *Lou Dobbs Tonight* jumped by 46 percent over the previous year, to 871,000 nightly viewers.[60]

These attacks serve only to further isolate and marginalize undocumented workers, while undermining support for a reasonable and pro–American values solution. The harsh rhetoric has helped to spawn vigilante groups that organize and patrol the border. Groups such as the Minutemen, founded by the activist Chris Simcox in Arizona, claim that they are doing the work that the Department of Homeland Security is unwilling to do to protect America.[61]

Who are these immigrants? Today, the United States has an estimated 7.2 million undocumented workers—4.9 percent of the entire U.S. labor force—or 12 million in total when these workers' family members are included. Another 500,000 arrive each year. Overall, Latin Americans make up 78 percent of the undocumented population; about half of these immigrants—more than 6 million—come from Mexico.[62] This workforce is concentrated into a large percentage of sectors that are vital to the U.S. economy. Unauthorized immigrants hold 24 percent of all farming jobs nationwide, 17 percent of cleaning jobs, 14 percent of construction jobs, and 12 percent of food preparation jobs.[63] The service sector, which consists of cleaning and food preparation, accounts for the greatest numbers of undocumented workers. Fully 31 percent of the undocumented workforce is occupied in the service sector (compared to 16 percent of the native population). One could imagine the economic impact that a mass deportation would have on the U.S. labor market, as well as on consumer prices for everything from homes to travel to tomatoes.

In fact, these undocumented workers are vital to the engine of prosperity across the United States. The Baby Boomer generation has turned sixty. As this population heads toward retirement, there are new burdens on the horizon for Social Security and Medicare, government entitlement programs that support retirees and the elderly. Immigrants are needed to boost the ratio of workers to retirees, which is tipping in favor of the elderly. As former Federal Reserve chairman Alan Greenspan has pointed out in his arguments favoring immigration, 70 percent of immigrants arrive in prime working age. The United States has not had to invest in immigrants' education, and they immediately begin to contribute toward the U.S. Social Security system. These immigrants will bolster Social Security with an estimated $500 billion during the twenty years after their arrival.[64] While anti-immigration activists claim that undocumented immigrants are a drain on U.S. social services and the tax base, in truth they contribute far more than they take out.

At the same time, native-born U.S. families are having fewer children on average than they did in generations past. Therefore, immigrants not only contribute to the U.S. economic output by entering this country's domestic labor force, but their numbers supplement the falling rate of native-born Americans who are paying into U.S. federal and state social systems. Using fake IDs, these illegal employees contribute as much as $7 billion a year to Social Security through withheld payroll taxes, although they do not have access to it because of their illegal status. There are roughly 9 million W-2s with incorrect Social Security numbers—money kept in a suspense file by the Social Security Administration (SSA). This income, based on the SSA's own expectation that three-quarters of illegal immigrants pay taxes, is so consistent that it is factored into official SSA projections.[65] As consumers, undocumented immigrants also pay all applicable sales taxes. A Congressional Budget Office report found that if proposed congressional immigration reform laws had passed in the summer of 2007, $48 billion in Social Security and tax revenue would have flowed from new immigrants and guest workers, while only $23 billion would have been spent on their services and credits over the next decade.[66]

While improving the U.S. economy, these immigrants are also helping their families and people back in their homelands. A fall 2007 report by the International Fund for Agricultural Development and the Inter-American Development Bank found that migrant workers around the globe sent more than $300 billion to their home countries in 2006, an amount that surpassed foreign development aid and direct foreign investment. These money transfers, or remittances, are helping to lift people out of poverty around the world, and represent an important contribution to global prosperity.[67]

Immigrants can also help revive small struggling communities across the United States. Pearson is one small town in Atkinson County, Georgia, that has thrived because of the influx of immigration. With a population of 8,030, Pearson is a small blue-collar community of tidy bungalows and mobile homes. It has warmly welcomed Mexican immigrants who come for the abundant agricultural work and new manufacturing jobs. By 2004, Hispanics accounted for 21 percent of the population. Hispanic-owned businesses such as bakeries and small grocery stores expand the economic pie for the community as a whole. And they contribute as consumers, too. Tommy Guthrie, of Guthrie Motors, said the new arrivals helped his business to survive.[68] Residents in Perry, Iowa, have also found their town revived by its growing Hispanic population, now at 40 percent of the 7,633 residents. "If not for Hispanics," said a grocery store owner in nearby Lenox, "this store wouldn't even exist."[69]

Yet across America, immigrants face a growing list of discriminatory laws and marginalizing treatment. For instance, in Wisconsin, new proposals would deny access to a driver's license to people without papers. One immigrant worker in Madison lamented the crackdown: "I'm really scared right now, if I get caught without a license."[70] In the fall of 2007 then New York governor Eliot Spitzer's plan to offer driver's licenses to undocumented immigrants ran into strong political opposition, with 58 percent of voters opposing the initiative. The Conservative Party ran a commercial declaring, "Along the Mexican border, we lock up illegal immigrants. In New York, Governor Spitzer wants to give them driver's licenses."[71]

Absent federal guidance, these varying and often harsh state and community-focused actions simply penalize the immigrant population while doing nothing to solve the underlying problem. A variety of bills introduced in Congress would crack down on illegal immigration without offering any path toward legal status, much less citizenship. Bills have called for criminalizing the illegal presence of, and aid to, illegal aliens; enhancing border security; and imposing heavy penalties on employers who hire or house illegal immigrants. In 2006, Congress passed the Secure Fence Act, which mandated the construction of a 700-mile-long fence along the southern U.S. border. Some states, such as California, have considered the drastic measure of banning immigrants from all public assistance, including public education. On the other side, some support the expansion of the existing H-1B visa program for skilled workers, the establishment of a temporary guest worker program, and the creation of a path to permanent residency and citizenship for qualifying illegal immigrants who are already in the country.

Some of the measures are backfiring. For instance, in 2006, the township committee in Riverside, New Jersey, passed legislation that set penalties for anyone who employed or rented to illegal immigrants. Local businesses such as restaurants and hair salons that cater to the mostly Latino immigrants were shut down, and downtown was being boarded up. "I don't think people knew there would be such an economic burden [to these restrictions on immigrants]," said Mayor George Conrad. "A lot of people did not look three years out."[72] Riverside rescinded the legislation after the local economy suffered and these practices were challenged in court.

Without federal policy to address the status of undocumented workers, the burden of social services falls disproportionately on border counties and urban municipalities that have large illegal immigrant populations. These states and municipalities are bearing a higher burden than they should. They need help from federal aid programs, in training and ultimately granting legal status to these immigrants, moving them into legitimate work environments and health-care plans where they can fully contribute to the U.S. economy.

In reality, there is no immigration crisis wrought by a treacherous illegal immigrant culture but rather an environment where the globalized economy is at work and the U.S. government is not. The problem therefore is not immigration, legal or illegal, but the failure of the U.S. government to manage immigration in a fair way that meets America's economic needs. The bottom line at this point is that the United States allows *too few* legal immigrants into the country for the jobs that the U.S. economy needs filled.

Overall, Americans understand the need for immigration but want it to be better managed. In 2006 Jim Kane retired to Arizona, where "it is all Mexican." He recognizes the need for immigration but thinks it should be better regulated. "If we are going to keep growing, pay for Medicare and Social Security, we need immigrants. But we need legal ones. First, we need to close the border, then let more people in but in an organized legal way. If we need more, bring them in, but they need to come in under the minimum wage, OSHA [Occupational Safety and Health Administration] standards and safety laws. The current system exploits the middle class because it drives down wages here and exploits the immigrants."[73]

After September 11, there was a strong spike in public attitudes against immigration, with 58 percent arguing that it should be reduced and only 30 percent saying that it should stay the same.[74] But this has leveled off, and views on immigration are about the same as they were in 2000, with 41 percent supporting the current levels of immigration and another 38 percent believing that it should be decreased. Half of all Americans (53 percent) support halting the flow of illegal immigrants and dealing with those in the United States as priorities.[75] And two thirds—68 percent—do not believe that immigrants are any more responsible for criminal activity than the native U.S. population is.[76] Americans believe that Congress should prioritize the reform of the U.S. immigration system and that a solution should address both illegal immigrants coming into this country as well as those who are already here yet remain without legal status.

But Congress and the White House are failing to act. Once a champion of a moderate compromise, President Bush has done little about the issue during his last two years in office. John McCain, whose home state of Arizona wrestles with the issue, partnered with Massachusetts senator Ted Kennedy to push for sensible and comprehensive immigration reform. Their bill called for new investment in border security and technology, coupled with a temporary visa program for undocumented workers. These visa holders would be able to apply to stay and eventually to regularize their status. But they would have to pay fines and back taxes and go to the end of the line of applicants—hardly the "amnesty" the plan's critics charge. They would also receive tamper-proof identification cards, which would reduce the use of fake Social Security cards.[77] Unfortunately, McCain backed away from the legislation after he was chastised by fellow conservatives. The issue is dead in Washington for now. Left unaddressed, the problem of illegal immigrants will leave 12 million men, women, and children at risk and in limbo. Congress and the president must come together to devise a sensible compromise along the lines proposed by Senators McCain and Kennedy.

America stands at an important crossroads in how it will address the growing challenges and opportunities resulting from a world in which every country's economic fortunes are increasingly interconnected. Immigration is a central issue that needs to be addressed to ensure that the United States preserves its prosperity, and American leaders must resolve this matter in the right way. America has been a nation of immigrants since its founding. The United States faces a pivotal choice between staying true to the values that have made it the most prosperous and free country in the world or turning its back on those values in a fearful, self-defeating attempt to build more walls.

The Way Forward: Promoting a Global Rising Tide

The anti-immigrant, antitrade, anti-investment voices in the United States are largely motivated by fear of losing control to increased global economic integration. Left unaddressed, these worries will drive America down a path where it will find itself less prosperous and less secure. Concerns about globalization at home are mirrored abroad as the gains from increased trade and technology transfers are not distributed evenly in societies; the less-educated workers, in particular, are hurt by new global economic trends.

U.S. leaders need to develop trade, foreign investment, and immigration policies that preserve American living standards. Globalization is now a fact of life, and erecting barriers to it will simply undermine Americans' prosperity in the long run. U.S. leaders need to turn away from antiforeign instincts and push for a more inclusive global economy. To make this work, U.S. leaders must recognize that certain individuals are hurt by advances in trade and globalization. The United States needs to help these individuals adjust and should boost its investments and assistance at home so that its workers have every possible advantage. We need to do a better job of managing the expanding global trade network. U.S. leadership is key to keeping it open and fair.

As the United States takes better care of Americans, it must also lead in helping others around the world share the same benefits. Global economic growth need not be a zero-sum game. Rather, Americans must understand that the economic growth of the developing world is not a threat to the United States but rather is an opportunity for us all. As we explained in chapter 6, the United States must address the challenges of the developing world—the threats of debt, poverty, disease, and conflict—in order to promote

American prosperity at home. Rising living standards abroad will also help the United States by reducing the flow of illegal immigrants, such as from Mexico, who are desperate to find jobs here. Taking these steps will help protect America from the nexus of crime, drugs, and terrorism. The more the United States can do to lift the developing world out of poverty, the more prosperous America will become from increased trade, investment, and new buyers for U.S. products around the world.

The United States must return to its original—and very American—moral values of welcoming immigrants to these shores. Keeping out the next generation of international talent will only undermine U.S. prosperity. Americans must also come together and agree on a way to address the plight of the 7 million undocumented workers—and their 5 million family members. Keeping them in legal limbo—while in the employ of American citizens—is unfair to them and is not smart for America. In the end, Americans love to compete and win. Globalization is a great challenge, but the United States needs to train better for the fight and must play to win. That means improving the ability of Americans to compete and adapt to the twenty-first-century economy with investments in reforming our education system and rebuilding the social safety net for U.S. workers.

If Washington does its job, by keeping the global rules fair, creating more opportunities, and helping those who are affected here at home, U.S. entrepreneurs and workers will do the rest. In addition, if the United States gets it right regarding the broad spectrum of international issues dealt with in this book—changing the sources of its energy, keeping Americans safe from the threat of weapons of mass destruction and terrorists, promoting democracy, and addressing the world's conflicts—Americans will be more secure and prosperous as a result.

The United States must:

STOP: Spending more than it earns as a country. The United States must get its own economic house in order and bring down its debt and deficit. America's large budget deficits are a result of our spending money we don't have. The United States needs to reduce its federal government deficit and increase overall national savings. It also must address the trade deficit—reducing trade barriers and modifying U.S. trade policies. Yet all of this will not make a serious dent in the trade deficit if we do not stop spending more than we earn.

START: Strengthening the safety net for all Americans. Getting the fundamentals right at home is the best way to give a leg up to American workers. As long as America's costly broken health-care, Medicare, and Social Security programs, lagging educational systems, and the growing gap between the rich and the poor remain, middle-class Americans will feel the squeeze. The United States must address these economic ills and adopt innovative ideas to increase national savings, such as creating private retirement accounts—universal 401(k)s—with government matching funds.[78] U.S. leaders must take steps to decrease the skyrocketing health-care costs that make American businesses less competitive and hurt the prosperity of Americans. But even if the United States achieves these fundamentals at home and abroad, millions of Americans will be thrown out of their jobs by the forces of globalization. It is not only right but in the interest of this country's prosperity to help people who are hit hard to adjust. That means a much more serious effort to assist and retrain those impacted by globalization. To address this new reality, the United States must revamp the social safety net and assistance programs for Americans. The U.S. government needs to spend significantly more than the current roughly $1 billion a year on trade adjustment assistance programs, which reach only 75,000 workers. This assistance must be universal and no longer tied to narrow conditions based on the reasons why people lose their jobs.

STOP: Thinking that trade is either a panacea or the problem. The United States cannot erect barriers to foreign trade, investment, and immigration and remain a prosperous nation. Managed correctly, each of these factors will promote Americans' wealth. Managed incorrectly, Americans will suffer from having fewer jobs, lower income, and decreased economic competitiveness. U.S. leaders must stop fearmongering and instead handle globalization the American way, by meeting the challenge head on, bringing trade barriers down, treating immigrants fairly, and managing foreign investment wisely.

Trade is not the threat that its opponents suggest, nor is it the single engine that will ensure America's long-term prosperity. There is no question that, overall, Americans and the rest of the world benefit from more international trade of goods and services. But the rapid pace of change can be frightening to the people who are most affected. And unmanaged free trade, especially when it ignores the impact that is made on labor and the environment, can hurt more people than it needs to. The challenge is to manage the global economy and its impact more wisely. If the United States addresses these problems, much of the fear about trade will recede.

START: Shaping the global trading system with renewed U.S. leadership and a revived Doha Round. New U.S. leadership is required to break the logjam on global trade talks. In order for the sides to reach a final deal, the United States will have to address its trade-distorting farm subsidy programs. It will also have to agree to new rules to allow more movement of temporary workers from developing countries into the United States. It must find some compromise that allows for both special treatment for developing countries and meaningful market access for U.S. products, and possibly change some of its "trade remedy" practices that are used to combat unfair trade practices. In return, other countries must provide meaningful market access to U.S. agricultural products, manufactured goods, and services. Each of these steps is politically very difficult for the countries involved and will take time. Success will require new efforts to take care of those affected by the new rules. The other part of promoting global prosperity is ensuring that everyone plays by the rules and that the rules are fair in the first place. Assistance will also be required for countries that need technical guidance to support transparency, good governance, respect for intellectual property rights, labor and environmental standards, and good corporate behavior. Penalties for violating the rules must be strengthened.

STOP: Scapegoating "foreigners." Throughout this country's more-than-two-hundred-year history, immigration is what kept the United States vibrant, innovative, and forward-looking. Falling victim to the fear of changes brought on by globalization and the horrors of September 11, America has veered from its core values of openness and fairness. When we lock out highly skilled and educated immigrants, we damage our competitiveness. When we lock out illegal immigrants, we force them to come here in dangerous ways and to live in fear as they work in our fields and restaurants and tend to our lawns. Both actions undermine the dynamism of the U.S. economy and violate our core American values. Simply erecting a wall does not keep immigrants out. And focusing on enforcement alone will not stop the flow as long as Americans continue to hire immigrants to make this country run. There is an immigration crisis in this country, but it is not the presence of 7 million undocumented workers. Rather, it is the failure to create a comprehensive reform package that will ensure that America has the workers it needs and that people from abroad can work here safely and fairly.

START: Encouraging the right kinds of immigration. In addition to being central to the American fabric of life, immigrant labor is a necessary component of U.S. prosperity and a result of Americans' demand for immigrant labor and the immigrants' desire for a better life. A pragmatic solution must recognize that illegal immigrants are here in this country because the U.S. economy has called them here. But undocumented immigrants feel threatened by most interactions with the government. Any comprehensive immigration plan must address two issues: (1) it must first establish a legal status and a path to citizenship for the roughly 12 million illegal immigrants in the United States; (2) it must then create a governmental entity to manage the "future flow" of immigrants into the United States to reduce illegal border crossings. In order to do this, the United States needs to be more serious about border security and workplace enforcement. America must provide a path to permanent residency and citizenship for immigrants in this country that is attainable, yet arduous enough so as not to encourage significant future illegal crossings by people who hope to benefit from a similar deal in the future. Immigrants would have to pay back taxes, become proficient in English, pay relevant fines, and be processed during a waiting period. They would be at the back of the line so as not to penalize other immigrants who have played by the rules. The United States must also find ways to bring students from abroad to study here and make sure that highly skilled immigrants can continue to contribute to American prosperity.

It is time that the United States recognizes that globalization is here to stay. Rather than retreat from this opportunity, U.S. leaders must seize it and gain from it. By turning away from America's core values—closing our doors to trade, investment, and immigration—Americans lose who we are and our very way of life. The vast majority of people in the United States understand the need to engage in the world and know that we can and must guide and influence the forces of globalization. The rest of the world faces many of the same problems that the United States does.

Only by working with other nations to advance prosperity at home and abroad will Americans thrive and be true to who we are as a country. Only then will the children and grandchildren of Jim Kane and Don Kane achieve the true, prosperous American dream.

conclusion

Prosperity: A New Vision of American Power

W hat do the Kane brothers from Lawrence, Massachusetts, have in common with Adelard Mivuma of Goma, Congo? What does Hisham Kassem in Cairo, Egypt, have in common with Randy Bobula in Iron City, Michigan? What does Winnie Singh in New Delhi, India, have in common with Adil in Islamabad, Pakistan? Why did the army captain Brian Freeman and Lieutenant Commander Steve Brock risk their lives to protect America? As Jim Kane explained it, "It's all interconnected, isn't it?"[1] During the last quarter century, the world has witnessed a tremendous transformation that has linked the fortunes and the livelihoods of people across the world more closely together than ever before.

In today's world, what happens in the Congo can have a direct impact on the lives of Americans in Massachusetts. If the United States fails to address the Congo's conflict, deadly diseases can travel from war-torn eastern Congo to the streets of towns across America. Should the Congo remain a failed state, terrorists could find in it a new safe haven from which to plan the next 9/11. Unless the United States does more to rein in weapons of mass destruction, the next attack on American soil could be even more catastrophic. When people across developing countries are denied their basic rights, a nexus of crime, drugs, and terrorism can threaten Americans here at home. Our economic prosperity suffers alongside theirs, as they will buy less of our goods and make fewer products for Americans to buy. And the world's growing dependence on dirty fuels means that global warming may one day wreak havoc on our way of life if we do not act now.

America must embrace a new vision of American power instead of the narrow "freedom agenda" pursued by the Bush administration. The United States needs new policies that promote prosperity at home and abroad. Democracy is not simply about voting in an election, and prosperity is not measured by money alone. Rather, prosperity is the ability to secure a decent life. For Adelard Mivumba, that means freedom from war and building a house with a garden. For Randy Bobula, it means the occasional steak dinner. But across the world, people want their version of the same thing: safety and security, a decent job, a good education, and a better life for their children. People everywhere are wrestling with the impact that the complex forces of globalization are having on their prosperity, their lives, their communities, and their culture. It is up to the United States to lead the way forward.

America's popularity around the world is at an all-time low. People do not see an America that helps them with their daily challenges or addresses today's threats in a way that makes them feel more secure. They see an America bogged down in war in Iraq and Afghanistan and failing to promote democracy in Egypt and Pakistan; an America that undermines the global institutions that are designed to bring medicine, food, and fuel to billions around the world. They see an America that is intent on building new nuclear weapons and retreating from the tough challenges of global trade and global warming. They see an America that tortures foreign prisoners and then lies about it.

During President George W. Bush's time in office, Americans have become less confident about U.S. leadership in the world and increasingly worried about how global security threats impact their lives: physical threats posed by terrorists and nuclear weapons, environmental threats such as global warming, and economic threats from increased globalization and economic competition from abroad.

The prosperity agenda that we put forward in this book can change global perceptions and revive the American public's confidence in America's ability to lead. Done right, it can convince billions around the world that the United States is once again spearheading the effort to provide decent lives for those still struggling around the world. At home, we need leadership that will counter the rising calls to shut U.S. borders, cut off foreign investment, and close down trade. Only such a compact will keep America secure and its citizens prosperous.

A Turning Point for American Leadership

As we move through this period of dramatic transformation, the United States is engaged in another great debate about its role in the world. September 11, the policies of the Bush administration and increased economic anxiety have left Americans wondering what their role should be and how engaged this country should be in the global challenges of today.

Debates like these have arisen at all of the pivotal turning points in our country's history. And each time, the United States has fared better when it chose to lead and engage the world. While often under the guise of other agendas, such as fighting fascism or communism, America has promoted prosperity not only at home, but also abroad. The prosperity agenda has been present throughout U.S. history—we just haven't talked about it in that way. Instead, we've relied on theoretical concepts like realism or liberal internationalism. Those ideas might be interesting to discuss in a graduate school seminar or academic journals, but when U.S. presidents are dealing with the world's events, they rarely have the luxury to talk theory. For the most part, America has benefited when U.S. leaders have approached the world pragmatically, as opposed to ideologically—the approach President Bush has used over the last seven years. And when the United States has focused on steps to advance prosperity at home by promoting prosperity overseas, America has fared much better as a country.

In the wake of World War I, the supposed "War to End All Wars," President Woodrow Wilson sought to prevent war, promote prosperity, and forge a new international consensus by creating a League of Nations. Making the case for his vision to Congress in 1918, Wilson said, "An evident principle runs through the whole program I have outlined. It is the principle of justice to all peoples and nationalities, and their right to live on equal terms of liberty and safety with one another, whether they be strong or weak."[2] Wilson failed to win over the Republican-controlled Congress. It would take another world war before his ideas took hold and shaped the international system we have today.

In the period between the two world wars, the United States retreated from its prosperity agenda. We put up trade barriers, rejected international engagements, and fell into the deepest economic depression in this nation's history. We failed to promote the prosperity of Germany and the Weimar Republic, and fascism took hold. Only after World War II, which killed more than 70 million people, including more than 400,000 Americans, did the United States return to its prosperity agenda.

Two former soldiers turned Wilson's ideals into reality: a former army captain who had fought the Germans in France during World War I, Harry S. Truman, and his successor Dwight D. Eisenhower, a former general who commanded troops in World War II. Together, one a Democrat, the other a Republican, they constructed a new web of international institutions, including the World Bank and the International Monetary Fund, to help bring people around the world out of poverty. They established the foundations to reduce trade barriers and paved the way for the establishment of the World Trade Organization.

These leaders understood that the United States cannot afford to retreat from the world and build walls against global forces. They understood that this country's interests were best advanced when the United States led. They understood that America was safer if the world was more prosperous. As President Truman said in his inaugural address, "The American people desire, and are determined to work for, a world in which all nations and all peoples are free to govern themselves as they see fit, and to achieve a decent and satisfying life."[3]

The Cold War soon divided the world into two camps, with the Iron Curtain cutting off much of Europe and the United States and the Soviet Union engaged in a bloody and costly competition for and against communism. While the United States embarked on a number of military adventures in the name of fighting communism, it also promoted a prosperity agenda to keep America safe. President John F. Kennedy, in particular, understood the need for U.S. leadership and engagement and knew that America's security would be enhanced by helping the world's poor. In his 1961 inaugural address, Kennedy declared, "To those people in the huts and villages of half the globe struggling to break the bonds of mass misery, we pledge our best efforts to help them help themselves, for whatever period is required—not because the Communists may be doing it, not because we seek their votes, but because it is right. If a free society cannot help the many who are poor, it cannot save the few who are rich."[4]

Kennedy used a variety of America's strengths to promote prosperity in the developing world. Since then, thousands of Peace Corps volunteers have traveled to help millions in small villages across the globe learn how to read, write, farm, and build basic infrastructure. Kennedy also initiated a number of other efforts aimed at building American leadership in development assistance, such as creating government organizations like the U.S. Agency for International Development, which remains one of the key agencies providing economic and development assistance around the world today.

A lot has happened since those tumultuous days. The United States sank itself deeper into an ill-fated war in Vietnam and pulled out of its post-Vietnam doldrums under Ronald Reagan, who inspired many Americans and people around the world by boldly calling for advances in freedom as he stood at the Berlin Wall and said, "Mr. Gorbachev, tear down this wall." The Iron

Curtain fell, the old order of East versus West collapsed, and America struggled to find a new paradigm, one that moved beyond the containment of communism.

Academics debated whether this was the end of history, and others posited that a clash of civilizations would dominate the future of geopolitics. The old debate between realism and balance-of-power politics, on the one hand, and Wilsonian, liberal internationalism, on the other, reemerged. A new ideology of neoconservatism, forged in the 1970s, sought to blend some elements of liberal internationalism, including making the world safe for democracy, with the display of raw U.S. power as a force for change and good in the world. Bill Clinton engaged these neoconservatives, and many supported him in the 1992 election. During his two terms in office, President Clinton understood how to use American leadership to lessen conflict, combat proliferation, reduce trade barriers, and promote democracy. He understood the connection between fighting terrorism and the necessity that the world's poor see the United States as being on their side. And he understood how to use international institutions to support America's interests and share the world's burdens.

By 2000, the neocons had turned to George Bush. After 9/11, they sold him on their vision of how to respond to the attacks. Their approach, based on U.S. supremacy, the primacy of the use of force, and disdain for negotiations and international institutions, took the United States away from the prosperity agenda. The superpower myth—that the United States can go it alone, primarily with military means—has made America less safe and the world less prosperous. President Bush spoke often about spreading freedom and democracy, but the world saw an America that failed to promote those ideals on the ground. As the world's poor struggled with the impact of globalization, they saw their prosperity threatened by greater poverty, debt, disease, conflict, and environmental degradation. They saw an America that was AWOL in meeting those challenges, one that had veered away from the global effort to promote universal prosperity and security. In response, the world has turned away from America.

Back to Basics: The Need for a New Global Compact

Somewhere along the way—among the great debates over hard power versus soft power, over how to address the forces of global integration, local disintegration, and personal anxiety—we forgot the basics. We dropped the focus on prosperity that throughout our history has made America more secure and prosperous. We must once again reorient our policy to reflect the fact that the vast majority of people want a life of basic order and decency, one that gives them the opportunity to fulfill their families' basic needs and a greater chance at happiness.

As Americans look beyond the tumultuous opening years of this new millennium, they see a world of increased threats. Some see economic competition from other countries and worry that free trade will take away their jobs and their livelihoods. They are nervous that too much foreign investment in America's businesses will undermine their control of the U.S. economy and that the falling dollar will make them less prosperous. The instinct to turn inward and throw up barriers to keep out the world has grown, as seen in today's emotional debates over immigration, trade, and foreign investment. Others see the very real threats posed by global terror networks and the spread of nuclear, chemical, and biological weapons and worry whether the government has the ability to address these dangers. Many also look at the growing challenges posed by global warming and the degradation of the environment and understand that the world is entering a new phase.

A new set of U.S. leaders will need to take a levelheaded look at these emerging threats and listen to the real anxieties of the American people. They will then need to lead the country back to the path that has made the United States an unrivaled power and a force for good in the world. As the torch is passed to the next administration, U.S. leaders will need to work with the leaders of other global powers—both the traditional powers in Europe and emerging powers such as China and India—to forge a new compact between the haves and the have-nots, between the developed and the developing world.

Much as did Wilson, Truman, Eisenhower, Kennedy, and Clinton before them, these new leaders must recognize that America's security and prosperity depend upon the needs and the interests of others. The villager struggling to build a home for his family in the midst of chaos in the Congo may not care about Osama bin Laden or weapons of mass destruction, but if he and his government understand that the United States is working to address the things he does care about—escaping poverty, having access to clean water, avoiding infectious diseases, and seeing an end to the violence—they will be more receptive to U.S. demands to ensure that the Congo does not become the next safe haven for another bin Laden.

Today's solutions require recognition by the developed and the developing world of the threats that others face and a commitment to work to address them. Whether you are in New York City and are worried about being attacked by terrorists who might have nuclear weapons or in Goma, worried about the resumption of war, your security depends on other nations' engagement in those very challenges.

Former UN Secretary General Kofi Annan tried to get the world to recognize this mutual interdependence at the UN World Summit in 2005. He saw the gap in threat perceptions between the developing and the developed worlds. For the United States, these threats were primarily terrorism and weapons of mass destruction; for the developing world, it was the threat of underdevelopment, poverty, debt, HIV/AIDS, and other infectious diseases. Annan suggested that it was time that Americans recognize that the developing world is not going to do a lot to crack down on terrorists and proliferators until the United States helps them to meet their own challenges. Annan again called for the developed world to commit 0.7 percent of its gross national income to development, to ease trade barriers, and to slash debt in exchange for a commitment by the developing world to implement good governance and take substantial steps to end income for terrorists and weapons proliferation. These steps were part of the effort to reach the UN's Millennium Development Goals by 2015. The world turned him down.

Such a "new compact" would build trust between the developed and the developing worlds to meet the mutual challenges of the twenty-first century. In 2005, the United States was not prepared to dramatically increase its investments in development or disarmament; the developing world was not prepared to move beyond its 1960s mentality and implement serious nonproliferation and antiterrorism measures. But for both the developed and the developing world to achieve stability and lasting prosperity, such an approach will be essential. And the commitment to such a drive for worldwide prosperity will not happen without American leadership.

The next U.S. president must take up that effort with renewed energy. He or she must set a goal for completing such a compact before the end of his or her first term in office. Only when the developing world again trusts the United States will it join Americans in the fight against global terrorism and nuclear proliferation. Despite the recent spike in anti-Americanism, the world still looks to America to show it the way, in part because much of the world still believes in the principles on which this country was founded.

America was not founded on a particular set of religious beliefs and is not based on race or ethnicity. The foundation for its greatness sits firmly on a set of principles and ideals laid out in the Declaration of Independence and the Constitution. It is captured by the notion of the American dream: the opportunity for advancement and a chance to make one's life better. And for other people in the world to achieve a similar prosperity, they need U.S. leadership on the issues covered in this book: promoting democracy; achieving a reliable, affordable, and invulnerable supply of energy; securing a stable and sustainable Iraq; reducing the threats of terrorism and proliferation; ameliorating extreme poverty in the world; and resolving the world's worst conflicts in the Middle East, Africa, and Asia.

Recognizing that these separate challenges are intertwined—that advances on one front require progress on others—is crucial to reviving U.S. leadership and forging this new global compact. For example, the United States will not be able to lead in fulfilling the NPT promise of nuclear disarmament if it does not work with others to help resolve the India-Pakistan conflict. America cannot make significant progress in the fight against global terrorists until it recognizes that the U.S. military presence in Iraq is one of al-Qaeda's principal recruitment tools. America cannot promote global trade without securing prosperity for America's poor and middle class.

The United States has tried to go it alone on several fronts for the last few years, and its own stability—as well as the world's—has suffered. Toward the end of his second term, President Bush began to realize that preemptive war, making threats, and undermining global institutions were doing little to advance U.S. security and the global common good. With this realization, he sent his top diplomat to forge an imperfect but tangible deal that pulled the Korean peninsula back from the brink of conflict after North Korea tested a nuclear weapon and a number of long-range missiles. Bush began to recognize the need to engage Iraq's neighbors in securing stability there. But America needs to do more than tinker at the margins with the challenges it faces. The United States must choose the path of prosperity and lead the effort to forge a new compact to achieve it at home and abroad.

To revive the American public's support for continued engagement in the world, the next president must be honest about the threats and must keep partisan politics out of the debate over America's role in the world today. Creating false links between Iraq and al-Qaeda, lying about the use of torture, and hyping the progress in Iraq all undermine the faith of the American people in their government. In addition, the next president—and all of America's leaders—must resist the temptation to use national security as a wedge issue in domestic politics. Accusing the Democratic Party of "defeatism, isolationism, and blaming America first" does not advance the country's interests. America needs to have a robust debate about its role in the world, but it must shy away from the type of partisanship that divides the country and makes Americans less supportive of committed engagement in the world.

The United States faces a critical choice as it moves beyond the Bush administration and looks to the future. One way forward is the path carved out by conservatives and the particular brand of neoconservatism that would have America shun international engagement and seek to use its strength to bend the world to its will. The United States could continue to try to impose American-style democracy and free trade on other countries with little regard to how this affected the lives of ordinary people globally, but this path is failing America.

A second possibility is one that shuns America's leadership role in the world and follows the advice of those who say that Americans should only take care of their own, closing U.S. borders to immigrants, trade, and foreign investment. Such a path would also weaken America, robbing it of the vibrant labor, innovation, and diversity that have kept it strong and prosperous.

The final alternative—and the best chance to revive America's power and prosperity in the twenty-first century—is the one outlined in this book: a foreign policy based on the promotion of prosperity. After seven difficult and lean years, the United States needs to go back to this basic goal and once again become a force for good in the world. America needs to lead, rather than bully, other countries. It needs to recognize that leadership means marshaling the support of others to advance the common good. The United States must recognize that when Adelard Mivumba feels safe from war and Randy Bobula can afford to heat his home, Americans will prosper.

NOTES

Introduction

1. Adelard Mivumba, phone interview with Nancy Soderberg, September 28, 2007, and e-mail exchange with Soderberg, October 3, 2007.
2. Lydia Polgreen, "Congo's Death Rate Remains Unchanged Since War Ended in 2003, Survey Shows," *New York Times*, January 23, 2008.
3. *USA Today*/Gallup poll of 1,005 adults nationwide, conducted July 21–23, 2006. Only 4 percent said that the world was less dangerous than at other times in their lives, and 20 percent said it was about the same.
4. Pew Research Center for the People and the Press, "Trends in Political Values and Core Attitudes: 1987–2007: Political Landscape More Favorable to Democrats," March 22, 2007.
5. Ibid.
6. Scott Bittle and Jonathan Rochkind, "Loss of Faith: Public's Belief in Effective Solutions Eroding," *Public Agenda's Confidence in Foreign Policy Index*, vol. 5 (Fall 2007).
7. Pew Global Attitudes Project, "World Publics Welcome Global Trade—but Not Immigration," October 4, 2007.
8. Pew Global Attitudes Project, "Global Unease with Major World Powers," June 27, 2007.
9. Ibid.
10. Ibid.
11. Pew Global Attitudes Project, "A Rising Tide Lifts Mood in Developing World," July 24, 2007, pewglobal.org/reports/pdf/257.pdf, accessed December 1, 2007.

Chapter 1. Making Up for Lost Time in Iraq

1. Ernesto Londono, "Quest to Heal Iraqi Boy Became a Final Mission," *Washington Post*, February 15, 2006.
2. Colin Pascual, an officer who served with Captain Brian Freeman in Iraq in 2006, in an interview with Brian Katulis, August 20, 2007.
3. Colin Pascual, interview with Brian Katulis.
4. Ibid.
5. Doug Smith, "Army Reserve Captain Brian Freeman, 31, Temecula; Abducted, Executed in Iraq," *Los Angeles Times*, March 11, 2007. The incident was recounted by Senator Christopher Dodd in early 2007.
6. Associated Press, "Widow of Abducted Soldier Gives to Iraqi Boy," February 27, 2007.
7. For detailed descriptions of the Bush administration's mistakes in post-Saddam Iraq, see Thomas Ricks, *Fiasco: The American Military Adventure in Iraq* (New York: Penguin, 2006); Bob Woodward, *State of Denial: Bush at War, Part III* (New York: Simon & Schuster, 2006); Rajiv Chandrasekaran, *Imperial Life in the Emerald City: Inside Iraq's Green Zone* (New York: Knopf, 2006); George Packer, *The Assassins' Gate: America in Iraq* (New York: Farrar, Straus and Giroux, 2005); and Nancy Soderberg, *The Superpower Myth* (Hoboken: John Wiley & Sons, 2005).
8. Thomas Melia and Brian Katulis, "Iraqis Discuss Their Country's Future: Post-War Perspectives from the Iraqi Street," *National Democratic Institute Report*, July 28, 2003.

9. Oxford Research International poll conducted with 2,737 Iraqis in face-to-face interviews, February 7–28, 2004, sponsored by ABC News, the BBC, the NHK in Japan, and the German broadcasting network Der Spiegel.

10. Kenneth Katzman, *Iraq: Post-Saddam Governance and Security*, Congressional Research Service, July 13, 2007.

11. Nina Serafino, Curt Tarnoff, and Dick K. Nanto, *U.S. Occupation Assistance: Iraq, Germany, and Japan Compared*, Congressional Research Service, March 23, 2006.

12. ABC News/BBC/NHK Poll, "Iraqis' Surge Assessment: Few See Security Gains," September 10, 2007.

13. Peter Foster, "America's Rebuilding of Iraq Is in Chaos, Say British," *London Daily Telegraph*, June 17, 2003.

14. Reuters, "Only Six Fluent in Arabic at US Iraq Embassy—Panel," December 6, 2006.

15. Rajiv Chandrasekaran, "Attacks Force Retreat from Wide-Ranging Plans for Iraq," *Washington Post*, December 23, 2003.

16. Robert Looney, "Neoliberalism in a Conflict State: The Viability of Economic Shock Therapy in Iraq," *Strategic Insights* 3, no. 6 (June 2004); and Bathsheba Crocker, "Reconstructing Iraq's Economy," *Washington Quarterly* (Autumn 2004).

17. Deborah Amos, "Keeping the Peace in Mosul," National Public Radio, October 8, 2003, www.npr.org/templates/story/story.php?storyId=1459447, accessed October 27, 2007.

18. Ibid.

19. "Our New Man in Baghdad," *The Week*, February 2, 2007; also cited in Rick Atkinson, *In the Company of Soldiers: A Chronicle of Combat* (New York: Henry Holt, 2004), p. 303.

20. Michael R. Gordon, "101st Airborne Scores Success in Northern Iraq," *New York Times*, September 4, 2003.

21. Dexter Filkins, "Biggest Task for U.S. General Is Training Iraqis to Fight Iraqis," *New York Times*, June 27, 2004.

22. Jonathan Weisman, "GOP Finding Iraq War Request a Tough Sell," *Washington Post*, October 1, 2003.

23. Amos, "Keeping the Peace in Mosul."

24. United Nations Security Council Resolution 1483 of May 2003 had formally recognized the United States and its coalition allies as an occupying force.

25. Gordon, "101st Airborne Scores Success in Northern Iraq."

26. Major John Freeburg and Sergeant First Class Jess T. Todd, "The 101st Airborne Division in Iraq: Televising Freedom," *Military Review* (November–December 2004).

27. Filkins, "Biggest Task for U.S. General Is Training Iraqis to Fight Iraqis."

28. Freeburg and Todd, "The 101st Airborne Division in Iraq: Televising Freedom."

29. Bill Glauber, "'Iraqi Idol' Is on the Air," *Chicago Tribune*, January 20, 2004.

30. Ibid.

31. Richard Oppel Jr. and James Glanz, "More Iraqi Army Dead Found in Mosul; 2 Clerics Slain," *New York Times*, November 23, 2004.

32. John Nagl, David Petraeus, James Amos, and Sarah Sewall, *The U.S. Army/Marine Corps Counterinsurgency Field Manual*, 2007.

33. Glenn Kessler and Bradley Graham, "Rice's Rebuilding Plan Hits Snags; Pentagon and Foggy Bottom Debate Funding, Staffing of Teams," *Washington Post*, January 15, 2006.

34. Steven Komarow, "Iraq Reconstruction Plan Draws Criticism Following Delays; State Department Says Initiative Is Moving Forward," *USA Today*, March 7, 2006.

35. Rajiv Chandrasekaran, "Iraq Rebuilding Short on Qualified Civilians," *Washington Post*, February 24, 2007.

36. James Glanz, "Rebuilding Teams Would Swell under Bush's New Iraq Plan," *New York Times*, January 15, 2007.

37. U.S. Department of State, "Overview of Provincial Reconstruction Teams' Mission in Iraq," July 13, 2007, usinfo.state.gov/xarchives/display.html?p=texttrans-english &y=2007&m=July&x=20070713125440eaifas0.4880182, accessed October 27, 2007.

38. James Glanz, "Head of Reconstruction Teams in Iraq Reports Little Progress throughout Country,"*New York Times*, October 19, 2007.

39. Special Inspector for Iraq Reconstruction, *Report to Congress*, October 30, 2006, p. 78; and James Glanz and David Rohde, "In a Dispute, Army Cancels Rebuilding Contract in Iraq,"*New York Times*, May 13, 2006.

40. James Glanz and Eric Schmitt, "Iraq Weapons Are a Focus of Criminal Investigations," *New York Times*, August 28, 2007.

Chapter 2. The Centerpiece of the Battle against Terrorism

1. Adil, interviewed in Islamabad by Samina Ahmed of the International Crisis Group for this book, October 10, 2007.

2. Bruce Reidel, "Pakistan Case Study," unpublished draft, Stanford/Brookings/NYU Joint Project, August 2007.

3. Much of this chapter draws on the excellent research of Caroline Wadhams and Leah F. Greenberg of the Center for American Progress. The authors thank them for their help and review of this chapter.

4. Adil, interviewed by Ahmed.

5. Craig Cohen and Derek Chollet, "When $10 Billion Is Not Enough: Rethinking U.S. Strategy toward Pakistan,"*Washington Quarterly* (Spring 2007).

6. Jane Perlez, "Aid to Pakistan in Tribal Areas Raises Concerns,"*New York Times*, July 16, 2007, www.nytimes.com/2007/07/16/world/asia/16pakistan.html?ei=5070 &en=af5a58d6e0afdaeb&ex=1187150400&pagewanted=print, accessed October 27, 2007.

7. Intel Center, "al-Qaeda Messaging Statistics (QMS)," September 9, 2007, www .intelcenter.com/QMS-PUB-v3-3.pdf, accessed October 27, 2007.

8. Craig Whitlock, "The New Al-Qaeda Central: Far from Declining, the Network Has Rebuilt, with Fresh Faces and a Vigorous Media Arm," Washington Post Foreign Service, September 9, 2007, p. A1.

9. International Crisis Group, "Elections, Democracy and Stability in Pakistan,"*Asia Report*, no. 137.

10. "The Last Battle,"*Economist*, August 7, 2007, www.economist.com/world/asia/ displaystory.cfm?story_id=9449034, accessed October 27, 2007.

11. Taimoor Shah and Carlotta Gall, "Pakistani Leader to Attend Tribal Gathering," *New York Times*, August 11, 2007, select.nytimes.com/search/restricted/article?res =FB0C12FD3C5F0C728DDDA10894DF404482, accessed October 27, 2007.

12. CNN.com/Asia, "Sharif Return Ends in Deportation," September 10, 2007, www .cnn.com/2007/WORLD/asiapcf/09/10/pakistan.sharif/index.html?iref=newssearch, accessed October 27, 2007.

13. Adil, interviewed by Ahmed.

14. Ibid.

15. David Rohde, Carlotta Gall, Eric Schmitt, and David Sanger, "U.S. Officials See Waste in Billions Sent to Pakistan,"*New York Times*, December 24, 2007, www .nytimes.com/2007/12/24/world/asia/24military.html?_r=2&hp=&oref=slogin& pagewanted=print&oref=slogin, accessed January 28, 2008.

16. Husain Haqqani and Kenneth Ballen, "Our Friends the Pakistanis,"*Wall Street Journal*, December 15, 2005.

17. Rebecca Lyman, "Pakistan: Poverty Unveiled," World Vision, meero.worldvision. org/sf_pakistan.php, accessed October 27, 2007.

18. Attributed to retired General John Abizaid, the former commander of the U.S. Central Command, September 17, 2007.

19. Caroline Drees, "U.S. Designates Al-Manar TV as 'Terrorist,'" Reuters, December 18, 2004. For Nasrallah quotes, see Anthony Shadid, "Armed with Iran's Millions, Fighters Turn to Rebuilding," *Washington Post,* August 16, 2006; John Kifner, "Hezbollah Leads Work to Rebuild, Gaining Stature," *New York Times,* August 16, 2006. For the full text of Nasrallah's speech, see a reproduction from BBC Monitoring at arabist.net/archives/2006/08/16/nasrallahs-speech-full-text/, accessed October 27, 2007.

20. BBC News, "Middle East Crisis: Facts and Figures," August 31, 2006, news.bbc. co.uk/2/hi/middle_east/5257128.stm, accessed October 27, 2007; and Israel Ministry of Foreign Affairs, "Israel-Hizbullah conflict: Victims of Rocket Attacks and IDF Casualties," July 12, 2006, www.mfa.gov.il/MFA/Terrorism-+Obstacle+to+Peace/ Terrorism+from+Lebanon-+Hizbullah/Israel-Hizbullah+conflict-+Victims+of+ rocket+attacks+and+IDF+casualties+July-Aug+2006.htm, accessed October 27, 2007.

21. Shadid, "Armed with Iran's Millions, Fighters Turn to Rebuilding"; Kifner, "Hezbollah Leads Work to Rebuild, Gaining Stature."

22. Shadid, "Armed with Iran's Millions, Fighters Turn to Rebuilding."

23. Robert F. Worth and Hassan M. Fattah, "Relief Agencies Find Hezbollah Hard to Avoid,"*New York Times*, August 23, 2006.

24. Nora Boustany, "Lebanon Offers Aid for Rebuilding,"*Washington Post,* August 31, 2006, A18.

25. Shadid, "Armed with Iran's Millions, Fighters Turn to Rebuilding."

26. Joshua Mitnick, "Rocketing Up the Charts,"*Jewish Week*, September 22, 2006.

27. National Intelligence Council, *The Terrorist Threat to the US Homeland*, July 17, 2007, www.dni.gov/press_releases/20070717_release.pdf, p. 6, accessed October 27, 2007.

28. Pew Global Attitudes Project, "Global Opinion Trends 2002–2007: A Rising Tide Lifts Mood in the Developing World," July 24, 2007, pewglobal.org/reports/ pdf/257.pdf, accessed October 27, 2007.

29. Bluma Zuckerbrot-Finkelstein, "Kindergartens and Killing: A Guide to Hamas," *St. Louis Jewish Light*, March 13, 1996, www.adl.org/PresRele/IslEX_61/2694_ 61.asp, accessed October 27, 2007; and Matthew Levitt and Jamie Chosak, "Undermining Hamas and Empowering Moderates by Filling the Humanitarian Void," September 7, 2005, www.washingtoninstitute.org/templateC05.php?CID= 2366, accessed October 27, 2007.

30. United Nations, *Human Development Report 2000; Trends in Human Development and Per Capita Income.*

31. Nimrod Raphaeli, "Saudi Arabia: A Brief Guide to Its Politics and Problems," September, 2003, http://meria.idc.ac.il/journal/2003/issue3/jv7n3a2.html, accessed October 27, 2007.

32. *The CIA World Fact Book*, "Saudi Arabia," www.cia.gov/library/publications/the-world-factbook/geos/sa.html, accessed October 27, 2007.

33. Raphaeli, "Saudi Arabia: A Brief Guide to Its Politics and Problems."

34. Ned Parker, "Saudis' Role in Iraq Insurgency Outlined," *Los Angeles Times*, July 15, 2007, www.latimes.com/news/nationworld/world/la-fg-saudi15jul15,0,3132262.story?coll=la-home-center, accessed October 27, 2007.

35. Michael Slackman, "Saudis Arrest 172 in Anti-Terror Sweep,"*New York Times*, April 27, 2007, www.nytimes.com/2007/04/27/world/middleeast/27cnd-Saudi.html?ex=1335326400&en=e547eadf46301c02&ei=5088&partner=rssnyt&emc=rss, accessed October 27, 2007.

36. U.S. State Department, "Country Reports: Middle East and North Africa Overview," *Country Reports on Terrorism 2006*, April 30, 2007, www.state.gov/s/ct/rls/crt/2006/82733.htm, accessed October 27, 2007.

37. Lee S. Wolosky, testimony before the U.S. House of Representatives Committee on Foreign Affairs, September 18, 2007.

38. Glenn R. Simpson, "Well Connected, a Saudi Mogul Skirts Sanctions,"*Wall Street Journal*, August 29, 2007, online.wsj.com/article/SB118835025334911761.html, accessed October 27, 2007.

39. Wolosky, testimony before the U.S. House of Representatives Committee on Foreign Affairs.

40. International Crisis Group, *Saudi Arabia Backgrounder: Who Are the Islamists?* Middle East Report No. 31, September 21, 2004.

41. Peter Brookes and Julianne Smith, "Course Corrections in America's War on Terror," *Stanley Foundation*, May 2007, pp. 3–4.

42. See *The Cost of Iraq, Afghanistan, and Other Global War on Terror Operations since 9/11*, CRS Report for Congress, July 16, 2007, www.fas.org/sgp/crs/natsec/RL33110.pdf, accessed October 27, 2007.

43. Josh Meyer, "In Terrorism Fight, Diplomacy Gets Shortchanged,"*Los Angeles Times*, March 19, 2007.

44. National Intelligence Council, *The Terrorist Threat to the US Homeland*.

45. Bruce Hoffman, "Combating Al Qaeda and the Militant Islamic Threat," testimony presented to the House Armed Services Committee, Subcommittee on Terrorism, Unconventional Threats and Capabilities, February 16, 2006, www.globalsecurity.org/security/library/congress/2006_h/060216-hoffman.pdf, accessed October 27, 2007.

46. U.S. State Department, "Country Reports: East Asia and Pacific Overview," *Country Reports on Terrorism 2006*, April 30, 2007, www.state.gov/s/ct/rls/crt/2006/82731.htm, accessed October 27, 2007

47. E-mail exchange between the terrorism expert Bruce Hoffman of the RAND Corporation and Nancy Soderberg, August 19, 2007.

48. Craig S. Smith, "Toll in Bombings in Algeria Rises to 33; Manhunt Begins," *New York Times*, April 13, 2007, select.nytimes.com/search/restricted/article?res=F00D13FA385B0C708DDDAD0894DF404482, accessed October 27, 2007.

49. United Nations Development Programme, *Human Development Report 2006: Country Table: Afghanistan* (2006), available at hdr.undp.org/hdr2006/statistics/countries/data_sheets/cty_ds_AFG.html, accessed October 27, 2007.

50. Barry R. McCaffrey, *Academic Report—Trip to Afghanistan and Pakistan*, West Point: United States Military Academy, June 3, 2006, p. 4, www.washingtonspeakers.com/prod_images/pdfs/McCaffreyBarry.VisitToAfghanistan.05.06.pdf, accessed October 27, 2007.

51. U.S. government official e-mail to Nancy Soderberg, November 16, 2007.
52. Matthew Weaver, "Afghan Death Toll Soars to 8,000 Last Year," *Guardian,* March 11, 2008, www.guardian.co.uk/world/2008/mar/11afghanistan.unitednations, accessed April 2, 2008.
53. Much of the information in this section comes from an unpublished paper and discussions with Caroline Wadhams of the Center for American Progress, July 2007. The authors are grateful for her assistance.
54. Barnett Rubin, "Saving Afghanistan," *Foreign Affairs* (January–February 2007), www.foreignaffairs.org/20070101faessay86105/barnett-r-rubin/saving-afghanistan .html?mode=print, accessed October 27, 2007.
55. Fifteen thousand U.S. troops are under NATO-ISAF.
56. Kenneth Katzman, "Afghanistan: Post-War Governance, Security, and US Policy" (Washington, DC: Congressional Research Service, June 21, 2007), p. 33, www .fas.org/sgp/crs/row/RL30588.pdf, accessed October 27, 2007.
57. Center for American Progress, "CAP Event Proposes a New Strategy for Afghanistan," November 7, 2007, www.americanprogress.org/issues/2007/11/afghanistan_event .html, accessed January 20, 2008.
58. Ibid.
59. Peter Bergen, testimony before the House Foreign Affairs Committee, February 15, 2007, www.newamerica.net/publications/resources/2007/peter_bergens_ afghanistan_testimony_before_the_house_committee_on_foreign_affairs, accessed October 27, 2007.
60. U.S. Department of State, "The United States and International Development: Partnering for Growth," August 6, 2007, www.state.gov/r/pa/prs/ps/2007/aug/90348 .htm, accessed October 27, 2007; David Rohde and David E. Sanger, "How a 'Good War' in Afghanistan Went Bad," *New York Times,* August 12, 2007, www.nytimes .com/2007/08/12/world/asia/12afghan.html, accessed October 27, 2007.
61. IRIN News, "Afghanistan: Room for Humanitarian Manoeuvre Diminishing— ICRC," June 14, 2007, www.irinnews.org/Report.aspx?ReportId=72728, accessed October 27, 2007.
62. Craig Smith, "Police Try to Fathom Belgian's Path to Terror," *International Herald Tribune,* December 6, 2005.
63. Paul Belien, "Belgian Export: Suicide Bombers," *Brussels Journal,* November 30, 2005, www.brusselsjournal.com/node/530, accessed October 27, 2007.
64. David Masci, "An Uncertain Road: Muslims and the Future of Europe," *The Pew Forum on Religion and Public Life,* October 2005, pewforum.org/publications/ reports/muslims-europe-2005.pdf, accessed October 27, 2007.
65. Robert S. Leiken, quoting the French academic Gilles Kepel in "Europe's Angry Muslims," *Foreign Affairs* (July–August 2005).
66. Pew Research Center, "Muslims in America," May 22, 2007.
67. Matt Weaver, "US Wants British Pakistanis to Have Entry Visas," May 2, 2007, *Guardian Unlimited,* www.guardian.co.uk/terrorism/story/0,,2070680,00.html, accessed October 27, 2007.
68. David J. Kilcullen, "New Paradigms for the 21st Century Conflict," usinfo.state .gov/journals/itps/0507/ijpe/kilcullen.htm, accessed January 26, 2008.
69. Meyer, "In Terrorism Fight, Diplomacy Gets Shortchanged."
70. U.S. Central Command, "Combined Joint Task Force—Horn of Africa Fact Sheet," July 2007, www.hoa.centcom.mil/resources/english/facts.asp, accessed October 27, 2007.
71. Ibid.

72. Nicholas D. Kristof, "Aid Workers with Guns,"*New York Times*, April 3, 2007, www
    .hoa.centcom.mil/story/english/article.asp?id=20070310-006, accessed October 27,
    2007.
73. Ginny Hill, "Military Focuses on Development in Africa," *Christian Science
    Monitor,* June 22, 2007, www.csmonitor.com/2007/0622/p07s02-woaf.html,
    accessed October 27, 2007.
74. U.S. Department of State, *Counterterrorism Newsletter*, July–October 2006.
75. Text of President Bush's address to the nation, September 11, 2006, CQ
    Transcriptions.

Chapter 3. Freedom Stumbles without Prosperity

1. Alexander Motyl, "Democracy Is Alive in Ukraine," September 12, 2005, www
    .opendemocracy.net/democracy-ukraine/alive_2822.jsp, accessed October 30, 2007.
2. Adrian Karatnycky, "Ukraine's Orange Revolution,"*Foreign Affairs* (March–April
    2005).
3. Ibid.
4. Vitaliy Moroz, telephone interview and e-mail exchanges with Brian Katulis,
    October 19, 2007.
5. Karatnycky, "Ukraine's Orange Revolution."
6. Carlos Pascual, discussion by phone with Nancy Soderberg, September 18, 2007.
7. Interview with Freedom House researchers working with Brian Katulis, July 17,
    2005, Kiev, Ukraine.
8. Interview with Freedom House researchers working with Brian Katulis on July 20,
    2005, Donetsk, Ukraine.
9. Interview with Freedom House researchers working with Brian Katulis on July 23,
    2005, Lviv, Ukraine.
10. Jason Bush, "Ukraine: What Crisis?"*BusinessWeek*, September 3, 2007.
11. Ibid.
12. Discussion by phone between Soderberg and Pascual, September 18, 2007.
13. Arch Puddington, "Freedom in the World 2007: Freedom Stagnation amid
    Pushback against Democracy," *Freedom in the World*, Freedom House (Lanham,
    Md.: Rowman & Littlefield, 2007).
14. President George W. Bush, Second Inaugural Address, January 20, 2005, www
    .whitehouse.gov/news/releases/2005/01/20050120-1.html, accessed October 30, 2007.
15. President George W. Bush, "President Addresses Nation, Discusses Iraq, War on
    Terror," June 28, 2005, www.whitehouse.gov/news/releases/2005/06/20050628-
    7.html, accessed October 30, 2007.
16. Arch Puddington, "Freedom in Retreat: Is the Tide Turning? Findings of *Freedom
    in the World 2008*," www.freedomhouse.org/uploads/fiw08launch/FIW08Overview.
    pdf, accessed January 20, 2008.
17. Mohammed Bazzi, "How Bush's War Bolstered Syria," *Salon*, May 31, 2007.
18. Eric Ellis, "Karzai: One Term Is Enough," *Fortune*, August 8, 2006.
19. "39th Annual Conference Heralds New Birth of AAIE," *Journal of the Association
    for the Advancement of International Education,* 30, no. 100 (Spring 2005), www
    .aaie.org/download/calendar/INTER%20ED%20NEWSLETTER.pdf, accessed
    October 30, 2007.
20. David de Ferranti and Anthony J. Ody, "Key Economic and Social Challenges for
    Latin America: Perspectives from Recent Studies," www.worldfund.org/assets/files/
    LitandLinks/KeyEcon&SocialChallengesforLatAm.pdf, accessed October 30, 2007.

21. Stephen Sestanovich, testimony to the Senate Committee on Foreign Relations, June 29, 2006.

22. Fred Weir, "Landslide Win Looks Likely for Putin's United Russia Party in Parliamentary Elections,"*Christian Science Monitor*, December 3, 2007, www .csmonitor.com/2007/1203/p25s04-woeu.html, accessed January 28, 2008.

23. Secretary of State Condoleezza Rice, remarks at the American University in Cairo, June 20, 2005, www.state.gov/secretary/rm/2005/48328.htm, accessed October 30, 2007.

24. Brian Katulis, "Women's Rights in Focus: Egypt," *Freedom House Special Report*, Freedom House, October 19, 2004, interviews conducted in Egypt, May 26–June 7, 2004.

25. Ibid.

26. Ibid.

27. Michael Slackman and Mona Al-Naggar, "Mubarak's Victory Orderly, but Opposition Is Still Angry," *New York Times*, September 10, 2005.

28. U.S. Department of State, *Egypt: Country Reports on Human Rights Practices 2005*, released by the Bureau of Democracy, Human Rights, and Labor at the U.S. State Department, March 8, 2006, www.state.gov/g/drl/rls/hrrpt/2005/61687.htm, accessed October 30, 2007.

29. Michael Slackman and Mona El-Naggar, "Egypt to Vote on Expanding Powers of Presidency,"*New York Times*, March 25, 2007.

30. Issandr El Amrani, telephone interview with Brian Katulis, August 15, 2007.

31. Michael Slackman, "News Analysis: In Egypt, Rice Speaks Softly,"*New York Times*, January 16, 2007.

32. Hisham Kassem, telephone interview with Brian Katulis, September 19, 2007.

33. Ibid.

34. The survey, based on a nationwide, genuinely representative sample, consisted of one-on-one interviews with 3,140 individuals conducted in all six divisions of Bangladesh from November 17 to December 31, 2003. Twelve focus groups, organized in four different divisions from January 25 to February 7, 2004, also informed the research. The integrated findings of the quantitative and qualitative research are found in *Bangladesh: Knowledge, Attitudes, and Practices, National Survey Covering Democracy and Governance Issues*, Report Submitted to the United States Agency for International Development by Associates in Rural Development, April 2004.

35. Ibid.

Chapter 4. Energy: Leading the World Where It Needs to Go

1. Randy Bobula, telephone interview with Nancy Soderberg, August 10, 2007.

2. Tom Doggett, "Pricey Gasoline Costs U.S. Consumers Extra $20 Bln," Reuters, May 22, 2007, www.reuters.com/article/topNews/idUSN2244355620070522, accessed October 28, 2007.

3. Pam Belluck and Sarah Kershaw, "With Winter Near and Heating Costs High, Many Are Taking Preventive Action," *New York Times*, October 11, 2005.

4. Gary Langer, "Poll: Traffic in the United States, A Look under the Hood of a Nation on Wheels,"*ABC News*, February 13, 2005.

5. Langer, "Poll: Traffic in the United States."

6. See Energy Information Administration, Retail Motor Gasoline and On-Highway Diesel Fuel Prices, www.eia.doe.gov/emeu/aer/txt/ptb0524.html, accessed October 28, 2007.

7. General Accounting Office, *Energy Markets: Factors That Influence Gasoline Prices,* May 22, 2007, www.gao.gov/new.items/d07902t.pdf, accessed October 28, 2007.

8. See Doggett, "Pricey Gasoline Costs U.S. Consumers Extra $20 Bln."

9. The Corporate Average Fuel Economy (CAFE) standards that govern automobile fuel efficiency were passed by Congress in 1975 as part of the Energy Policy Conservation Act, with the goal of doubling new car fuel economy in ten years. CAFE standards, which are enforced through fines for violations, increased through acts of Congress from 18 miles per gallon in 1978 (the earliest data) to 27.5 in 1985 (although these levels were lowered to 26 miles per gallon from 1986 to 1988 and to 26.5 in 1989 by the Department of Transportation), www.nhtsa .dot.gov/cars/rules/cafe/overview.htm, accessed October 28, 2007; www.epa.gov/ otaq/cert/mpg/fetrends/420r07008.pdf, accessed October 28, 2007.

10. Robert McMahon, "Vehicle Fuel Economy," Council on Foreign Relations Backgrounder, December 19, 2007, www.cfr.org/publication/12488/vehicle_fuel_ economy.html, accessed January 25, 2008.

11. Leo Lewis, "Toyota Leads Overseas Winners in US Car Market," *Times Online,* August 3, 2007, business.timesonline.co.uk/tol/business/industry_sectors/engineer ing/article2194667.ece, accessed October 28, 2007.

12. See David Shepardson, "Detroit to Delaware, Job Losses Spell Pain," *Detroit News,* February 14, 2007, www.detnews.com/apps/pbcs.dll/article?AID=/20070214/ AUTO01/702140382/1148, accessed October 28, 2007.

13. Council on Foreign Relations Task Force, "National Security Consequences of U.S. Oil Dependency," Report no. 58, October 2006, p. 14. (Referred to as CFR Energy Task Force Report further on.)

14. Osama bin Laden on December 16, 2004, cited on Set America Free, www.set americafree.org/quotes.htm, accessed October 28, 2007.

15. Energy Information Administration, "U.S. Crude Oil Imports,"tonto.eia.doe.gov/dnav/ pet/pet_move_impcus_a2_nus_epc0_im0_mbbl_a.htm, accessed October 28, 2007.

16. The Organization of the Petroleum Exporting Countries (OPEC) members include Algeria, Angola, Indonesia, Iran, Iraq, Kuwait, Libya, Nigeria, Qatar, Saudi Arabia, the United Arab Emirates, and Venezuela.

17. Council on Foreign Relations Task Force, *CFR Energy Task Force Report,* pp. 26–30.

18. Daniel Yergin, "Ensuring Energy Security,"*Foreign Affairs* 85, no. 2 (March–April 2006): 78–80.

19. Javier Blas, "Energy Industry Stymied by Cost of Development,"*Financial Times,* August 11–12, 2007, p. 5.

20. See the Department for International Development and the World Bank, "Executive Summary: Indonesia and Climate Change," March 2007, siteresources. worldbank.org/INTINDONESIA/Resources/226271-1170911056314/3428109- 1174614780539/PEACEClimateChange.pdf, accessed October 28, 2007.

21. See Jack Chang, "As Brazil's Rain Forest Burns Down, Planet Heats Up," *McClatchy,* September 8, 2007, www.mcclatchydc.com/226/story/19533.html, accessed October 28, 2007.

22. See Larry Rohter, "Brazil, Alarmed, Reconsiders Policy on Climate Change," *New York Times,* July 31, 2007, www.nytimes.com/2007/07/31/world/americas/ 31amazon.html?n=Top%2fNews%2fScience%2fTopics%2fGlobal%20Warming &pagewanted=all, accessed October 28, 2007. See also Chang, "As Brazil's Rain Forest Burns Down, Planet Heats Up."

23. See Keith Bradsher, "China to Pass U.S. in 2009 Emissions," *New York Times,* November 7, 2006, www.nytimes.com/2006/11/07/business/worldbusiness/ 07pollute.html, accessed October 28, 2007.

24. Carin Zisser, "India's Energy Crisis," Council on Foreign Relations Backgrounder, www.cfr.org/publication/12200/indias_energy_crunch.html, accessed October 28, 2007.

25. Emily Wax, "A Sacred River Endangered by Global Warming," *Washington Post*, June 17, 2007, www.washingtonpost.com/wp-dyn/content/article/2007/06/16/AR2007061600461.html, accessed October 28, 2007.

26. See Lydia Polgreen, "A Godsend for Darfur, or a Curse?" *New York Times*, July 22, 2007, www.nytimes.com/2007/07/22/weekinreview/22polgreen.html, accessed October 28, 2007.

27. Sudan Divestment Task Force, www.SudanDivestment.org, accessed in July 2007.

28. Ibid.

29. Erika S. Downs, "Brookings Foreign Policy Studies Energy Security Series: China," *Brookings Institute*, December 2006, pp. 41–42.

30. As the *South Park* expert Jake Bistrong noted, *South Park*'s situations are really just trying to get people to lighten up about real-life situations and take a break from preaching these serious issues and just laugh.

31. Much of the information in this section comes from an unpublished memo prepared by Chris Fox of Ceres. See www.ceres.org, accessed October 28, 2007.

32. Associated Press, "World Bank Study: Rising Sea Levels Could Displace Millions of World's Poor," February 13, 2007, simontay78.wordpress.com/2007/02/16/world-bank-study-rising-sea-levels-could-displace-millions-of-world%e2%80%99s-poor/, accessed October 28, 2007.

33. See the Intergovernmental Panel on Climate Change Web site, www.ipcc.ch, accessed October 28, 2007. The IPCC was set up jointly by the United Nations Environment Programme and the World Meteorological Organization in 1988 "to assess scientific, technical and socio-economic information relevant for the understanding of climate change, its potential impacts and options for adaptation and mitigation." The IPCC is not alone in its conclusions. Recently, the leading American scientific bodies with climate expertise have issued similar statements.

34. See IPCC Climate Change, 2007: The Physical Science Basis, Summary for Policymakers (2007), p. 2, www.ipcc.ch, accessed October 28, 2007. In fact, carbon dioxide in the atmosphere has risen from 280 parts per million (ppm) at the start of the Industrial Revolution in 1750 to 379 ppm in 2005. The IPCC February 2007 report on climate change science concluded that "the atmospheric concentration of carbon dioxide in 2005 (379 ppm) exceeds by far the natural range over the last 650,000 years (180 to 300 ppm) as determined from ice cores." Concentrations of CO_2 could surpass 550 ppm by midcentury. And when carbon dioxide emissions go up, so does temperature. To stay below the 2°C (3.6°F) threshold, scientists project that atmospheric concentrations of carbon dioxide must stabilize at about 400–450 parts per million, although some say 450–550 ppm.

35. See Mindy Lubber, "Reducing Energy Dependence and Addressing Climate Change: Private Sector Initiatives and Response to Public Policies," *Ceres*, March 14, 2006, www.ceres.org/news/news_item.php?nid=170, accessed October 28, 2007.

36. See Energy Information Administration, "World Carbon Dioxide Emissions from the Use of Fossil Fuels," June–October 2007, www.eia.doe.gov/iea/carbon.html, accessed October 28, 2007.

37. Massachusetts Institute of Technology, *The Future of Coal: An Interdisciplinary MIT Study*, 2007, pp. ix and 49.

38. See John McCain, Speech on Energy Policy, April 23, 2007, www.johnmccain.com/Informing/News/Speeches/13bc1d97-4ca5-49dd-9805-1297872571ed.htm, accessed October 28, 2007.

39. See "Climate Wrangle on the Potomac: Bush Hosts Major Economies," *Environment News Service*, NRG Applies for First U.S. Nuclear Power License in 29 Years,"*Environment News Service,* September 28, 2007, www.ens-newswire.com/ens/sep2007/2007-09-28-03.asp, accessed October 28, 2007.

40. See "NRG Applies for First U.S. Nuclear Power License in 29 Years,"*Environment News Service,* September 25, 2007, www.ens-newswire.com/ens/sep2007/2007-09-25-091.asp, accessed October 28, 2007.

41. Massachusetts Institute of Technology, *The Future of Nuclear Power*, 2003, web.mit.edu/nuclearpower/pdf/nuclearpower-full.pdf, accessed October 28, 2007.

42. Congressional Research Service, "Nuclear Power: Outlook for New U.S. Reactors," March 9, 2007, fas.org/sgp/crs/misc/RL33442.pdf, accessed October 28, 2007.

43. Ibid.

44. See Greenpeace and European Renewable Energy Council, *Energy Revolution: A Blueprint for Solving Global Warming,* January 2007; and American Solar Energy Society, Charles F. Kutscher, ed., *Tackling Climate Change in the U.S.: Potential Carbon Emissions Reductions from Energy Efficiency and Renewable Energy by 2030,* January 2007.

45. Energy Information Administration, *International Energy Outlook 2007,* p. 19, www.eia.doe.gov/oiaf/ieo/index.html, accessed January 28, 2008.

46. Yergin, "Ensuring Energy Security," p. 79.

47. Andrew C. Revkin and Matthew L. Wald, "Solar Power Captures Imagination, Not Money," *New York Times*, July 16, 2007, p. A10.

48. See "Mandatory U.S. Greenhouse Gas Cap Wins New Corporate Supporters," *Environment News Service,* May 8, 2007, www.ens-newswire.com/ens/may2007/2007-05-08-01.asp, accessed October 28, 2007.

49. President Bush Discusses Global Climate Change," press release, June 11, 2007, www.whitehouse.gov/news/releases/2001/06/20010611-2.html, accessed October 28, 2007.

50. See United Nations Framework Convention on Climate Change, "Kyoto Protocol, Status of Ratification," unfccc.int/kyoto_protocol/background/status_of_ratification/items/2613.php, accessed October 28, 2007. Australia's new prime minister Kevin Rudd signed the protocol in December 2007 in his first official act.

51. Rob Shapiro, "Addressing the Risks of Climate Change: The Environmental Effectiveness and Economic Efficiency of Emissions Caps and Tradable Permits, Compared to Carbon Taxes," paper published by the American Consumer Institute, 2007, www.sonecon.com, accessed October 28, 2007. For another good discussion of the pros and cons of the two systems, see William D. Nordhaus, "Life after Kyoto: Alternative Approaches to Global Warming Policies," National Bureau of Economic Research, Working Paper 11889, December 2005.

52. Those invited included Australia, Brazil, Canada, China, the European Union, France, Germany, Indonesia, India, Italy, Japan, Mexico, Russia, South Africa, South Korea, and the United Kingdom, plus the United Nations. See "Climate Change Wrangle on the Potomac: Bush Hosts Major Economies," Environment News Service, September 28, 2007, www.ens-newswire.com/ens/sep2007/2007-09-28-03.asp, accessed October 28, 2007.

53. Michael Grunwald, "The New Action Heroes,"*Time,* June 25, 2007, pp. 34–37.

54. See Larry Rohter, "Brazil, Alarmed, Reconsiders Policy on Climate Change," *New York Times,* July 31, 2007, www.nytimes.com/2007/07/31/world/americas/31amazon.html, accessed October 28, 2007.

55. See "Climate Change Wrangle on the Potomac: Bush Hosts Major Economies," Environment News Service, September 28, 2007, www.ens-newswire.com/ens/sep2007/2007-09-28-03.asp, accessed October 28, 2007.

56. Council on Foreign Relations Task Force, *CFR Energy Task Force Report*, pp. 19–22.
57. HM Treasury, *The Stern Review on the Economics of Climate Change*, October 30, 2006, www.hm-treasury.gov.uk/independent_reviews/stern_review_economics_climate_change/stern_review_report.cfm, accessed October 28, 2007.
58. See Geothermal Energy Association, "GEA Update," March 26, 2007, www.geo-energy.org/publications/updates/2007/GEA%20Update%20March%2026%2020 07.pdf, accessed October 28, 2007.
59. Its initial budget of $300 million in FY 2008 would grow to $2 billion by FY 2012, putting it in a league with the DARPA's budget of $3 billion in FY 2008. For ARPA-E, see *H.R. 4435,* December 6, 2005, democrats.science.house.gov/Media/File/ForReleases/arpa-e_sections_3feb06.pdf, accessed October 28, 2007. For DARPA, see www.arpa.mil/body/pdf/FY08_budg_est.pdf, accessed October 28, 2007.

Chapter 5. Winning the World Over by Eliminating Nuclear Weapons

1. Brian Knowlton, "Yemen Demands Return of Its Missiles: North Korean Ship Seized with Scuds," *International Herald Tribune*, December 12, 2002.
2. Lieutenant Commander Brock, telephone interview with Nancy Soderberg, March 1, 2007.
3. Brian Knowlton, "Ship Allowed to Take North Korea Scuds on to Yemeni Port: U.S. Frees Freighter Carrying Missiles,"*International Herald Tribune*, December 12, 2002.
4. Mohamed ElBaradei, Nobel Lecture, December 10, 2005, nobelprize.org/nobel_prizes/peace/laureates/2005/elbaradei-lecture-en.html, accessed October 28, 2007.
5. In addition to the five original nuclear powers (the United States, England, France, China, and Russia), Israel, India, Pakistan, and North Korea have nuclear weapons.
6. See Article VI of the Nuclear Non-Proliferation Treaty, www.fas.org/nuke/control/npt/text/npt2.htm, October 8, 2007, accessed October 28, 2007. The other four recognized nuclear powers were China, Britain, France, and the Soviet Union. Today, Israel, Pakistan, India, and North Korea are also nuclear powers. Israel, Pakistan, and India have not signed the NPT. North Korea withdrew from it in January 2003.
7. Robert Joseph, "Transforming Our Counterproliferation Efforts in the Asia Region—August 15, 2005," remarks to the Institute of Defense and Strategic Studies, Singapore.
8. Acronym Institute for Disarmament Diplomacy, "Proliferation Security Initiative (PSI) Meeting, Paris, September 3–4, 2003," www.acronym.org.uk/docs/0309/doc06.htm, October 8, 2007, accessed October 28, 2007. The eleven core signatories included Australia, France, Germany, Italy, Japan, the Netherlands, Poland, Portugal, Spain, the United Kingdom, and the United States.
9. See UN Security Council 1540. PSI participants agree to the following principles: Undertake effective measures, either alone or in concert with other states, for interdicting the transfer or transport of WMD, their delivery systems, and related materials; Adopt streamlined procedures for rapid exchange of relevant information; Work to strengthen their relevant national legal authorities to accomplish these objectives and work to strengthen international law and frameworks; Not transport or assist in the transport of any cargoes of WMD, their delivery systems or related materials to or from countries or groups of proliferation concern; Board and search any suspect vessels flying their flags in their internal waters, territorial seas, or areas beyond the territorial seas of any other state; Consent under the appropriate circumstances to the boarding and searching of their own flag vessels

by other states, and to the seizure of such WMD-related cargoes; Stop and/or search suspect vessels in their internal waters, territorial seas, or contiguous zones, and enforce conditions on suspect vessels entering or leaving their ports, internal waters, or territorial seas; Require suspect aircraft that are transiting their airspace to land for inspection and seize any such cargoes, and deny aircraft transit rights through their airspace; Prevent their ports, airfields, or other facilities from being used as transshipment points for WMD-related cargo.

10. Alex Rodriguez, "Russia Balks at Search Request: U.S. Wants Ships, Planes Stopped," *Chicago Tribune*, January 31, 2004.

11. John Bolton, interview with Jon Stewart on the *Daily Show*, March 20, 2007.

12. BBC News, "Profile: John Bolton,"news.bbc.co.uk/1/hi/world/americas/4327185 .stm, accessed October 28, 2007.

13. The authors want to thank Jofi Joseph in the office of Senator Robert Casey and Andy Grotto of the Center for American Progress for their careful review of this chapter and for their constructive criticisms. We also want to thank Deepti Choubey for the research she provided for this chapter.

14. Condoleezza Rice, interview on CBS's *Face the Nation*, July 29, 2001.

15. Thomas Barnett, the deputy director of the Department of Defense's Office of Force Transformation, quoted in Amy Svitak, "A Decades-Long Policy Shifts," *Armed Forces Journal* (September 2003): 12.

16. Gary Schmitt, Defense Memorandum to Opinion Leaders, December 13, 2001, newamericancentury.org/defense-20011213.htm, accessed October 28, 2007.

17. Mohamed ElBaradei, "Towards a Safer World,"*Economist*, October 16, 2003.

18. Out of these, only South Africa and the three former Soviet states actually had bombs. Japan is believed to have pursued a nuclear weapons program during World War II.

19. Preparatory Commission for the Comprehensive Nuclear-Test Ban Treaty Organization, "Membership," www.ctbto.org, accessed October 28, 2007.

20. The CTBT replaces the Partial Test Ban Treaty of 1963, which applied to all non-underground nuclear tests. The CTBT will not enter into force until it receives the signatures of these three countries and is ratified by thirteen additional nations, including the two members of the permanent five (P-5) not yet on board, China and the United States. Israel is another treaty signatory that has failed to ratify the agreement. And India, Pakistan, and North Korea, which have all conducted nuclear weapons tests since 1996, have refused to sign the treaty. The Clinton administration pressed hard for it, but it fell 19 votes short of the 67 needed for Senate ratification. The Republican-controlled Congress argued that the United States might need to test nuclear weapons to ensure the safety and reliability of the stockpile.

21. It was, in fact, the first President Bush who agreed to ban chemical weapons in 1991 and started to negotiate the CWC, now with 180 members. The United States and Russia are destroying their stockpiles of 70,000 tons combined.

22. See the Middle Powers Initiative, "Advancing the NPT 13 Practical Steps," www .gsinstitute.org/mpi/pubs/13steps_0403.pdf, accessed October 28, 2007. Launched in March 1998, the Middle Powers Initiative (MPI) is a carefully focused and coordinated campaign by a network of international citizen organizations to encourage the leaders of the Nuclear Weapon States (NWS) to break free from their Cold War mind-set and move rapidly to a nuclear weapon–free world. See the Lawyers' Committee on Nuclear Policy, Inc., "MPI: Middle Powers Initiative,"www.lcnp .org/mpi/index.htm, October 8, 2007, accessed October 28, 2007.

23. Joby Warrick and Walter Pincus, "Missteps in the Bunker," *Washington Post*, September 23, 2007. See also Barbara Starr, "Air Force Investigates Mistaken

Transport of Nuclear Warheads," September 6, 2007, www.cnn.com/2007/US/09/05/loose.nukes, accessed October 28, 2007.

24. Max M. Kampelman, "Zero Nuclear Weapons," British American Security Information Council, July 10, 2007, www.basicint.org/nuclear/kampelman.htm, accessed October 28, 2007.

25. George P. Shultz, William J. Perry, Henry A. Kissinger, and Sam Nunn, "A World Free of Nuclear Weapons," *Wall Street Journal*, January 4, 2007.

26. David Sanger and Daniel B. Schneider, "Month of Talks Fails to Bolster Nuclear Treaty," *New York Times*, May 28, 2005.

27. See the Middle Powers Initiative, "Advancing the NPT 13 Practical Steps."

28. Sanger and Schneider, "Month of Talks Fails to Bolster Nuclear Treaty."

29. Democratic Policy Committee, S.1547, The National Defense Authorization Act for Fiscal Year 2008, democrats.senate.gov/dpc/dpc-new.cfm?doc_name=lb-110-1-108, accessed October 28, 2007.

30. The Russians did, however, indicate that they would no longer feel bound by their START II commitments.

31. Vladimir Putin, Speech at the 43rd Munich Conference on Security Policy, February 10, 2007.

32. CNN.com, "Surprise Offer Defuses U.S.-Russia Missile Spat," June 7, 2007, www.cnn.com/2007/WORLD/europe/06/07/bush.putin/index.html, accessed February 14, 2008.

33. Peter Baker, "Putin Proposes Broader Cooperation on Missile Defense," *Washington Post*, July 3, 2007.

34. Thom Hanker, "Russian Radar in Azerbaijan Is Unacceptable, Missile Defense Chief Says," *International Herald Tribune*, September 18, 2007, www.iht.com/articles/2007/09/18/europe/missile.php, accessed January 21, 2008.

35. See Esther Pan, "The U.S.–India Nuclear Deal," www.cfr.org/publication/9663/#5, accessed January 21, 2008.

36. Ibid.

37. Steve Andreasen, "Bush's Passive Appeasement," *Los Angeles Times*, May 31, 2005.

38. Warren P. Stroebel, "Administration Struggles to Find Right Approach to N. Korea Talks," Knight Ridder, December 20, 2003.

39. Thom Shanker and David E. Sanger, "North Korean Fuel Identified as Plutonium," *New York Times*, October 17, 2006.

40. David Albright, "An Iranian Bomb?" *Bulletin of Atomic Scientists* (January 1995).

41. Jim VandeHei, "Cheney Warns of Iran as a Nuclear Threat," *Washington Post*, January 21, 2005.

42. George Jahn, "Security Council Members Meet on Iraq," Associated Press, ap.google.com/article/ALeqM5jHz-Bz3Pa0Ivga_oNIvTbrBoIN7QD8U6JGIG1, accessed January 21, 2008.

43. See UNSC Resolution 1747, available at http://www.un.org/News/Press/docs/2007/sc8980.doc.htm, accessed January 21, 2008.

44. Mark Mazzetti, "U.S. Finds Iran Halted Its Nuclear Arms Effort in 2003," *New York Times*, December 4, 2007, www.nytimes.com/2007/12/04/world/middleeast/04intel.html?ref=Washington, accessed January 21, 2008.

45. "Iran: Nuclear Intentions and Capabilities," National Intelligence Estimate, National Intelligence Council, November 2007, www.dni.gov/press_releases/20071203_release.pdf, accessed January 21, 2008.

46. See "UN Resolution 1803 Passes on March 3, 2008," daccessdds.UN.org/doc/UNDOC/GEN/N08/257/81/PDF/N0825781.pdf?openElement, accessed March 17, 2008.

47. Helene Cooper, "North Koreans Agree to Disable Nuclear Facilities,"*New York Times,* October 4, 2007.

48. Ibid.

49. Susan B. Glasser and Kamran Khan, "Pakistan Continues Probe of Nuclear Scientists,"*Washington Post,* November 14, 2001; Farhad Manjoo, "Osama's Nuclear Plans Half-Baked,"*Wired,* November 20, 2001.

50. See Defense Threat Reduction Agency Public Affairs, "Cooperative Threat Reduction Program," www.dtra.mil/newsservices/fact_sheets/fs_includes/pdf/CTR%20Program .pdf, accessed October 28, 2007.

51. See Howard Baker and Lloyd Cutler, "A Report Card on the Department of Energy's Nonproliferation Programs with Russia," www.stimson.org/ctr/pdf/ BakerCutlerReport2001.pdf, accessed October 28, 2007.

52. See Office of the Press Secretary, "Fact Sheet: Treaty on Strategic Offensive Reductions," January 10, 2001, www.whitehouse.gov/news/releases/2002/05/200 20524-23.html, accessed October 28, 2007.

53. ElBaradei, "Towards a Safer World."

54. Fissile means that an element can sustain a chain reaction. For example, U238— the most common form of uranium—is fissionable (it will fission when bombarded with neutrons) but not fissile (it won't sustain a chain reaction).

55. See chapter 4 for a more detailed discussion of nuclear power. Some countries that have used highly enriched uranium (HEU) in civilian research reactors include Kyrgyzstan, Chile, Colombia, Iran, Kazakhstan, Libya, the Philippines, Romania, and Uzbekistan.

56. CNN.com, "US Lets Scud Ship Sail to Yemen," December 12, 2002, archives. cnn.com/2002/WORLD/asiapcf/east/12/11/us.missile.ship/, accessed October 28, 2007.

Chapter 6. The Hidden Threat of Global Poverty

1. Adelard Mivumba, phone interview with Nancy Soderberg, September 28, 2007.

2. International Crisis Group, *Democratic Republic of the Congo,* www.crisisgroup .org/home/index.cfm?id=1174&l=1, accessed November 3, 2007.

3. Geffrey Gettleman, "A Fatal Outbreak in Congo Is Ascribed Partly to Ebola,"*New York Times,* September 12, 2007, p. A13.

4. For instance, according to the International Crisis Group, terrorists have taken advantage of the state's collapse to attack neighboring countries and transit agents and matériel. Prior to the 2006 Ethiopian invasion, the country was a refuge for the al-Qaeda team that bombed a Kenyan resort in 2002 and tried to down an Israeli aircraft. See "Somalia's Islamists," Africa Report No, 100, December 12, 2005.

5. Susan Rice, "The Threat of Global Poverty,"*National Interest,* Spring 2006, p. 79.

6. Carnegie Commission on Preventing Deadly Conflict, *Preventing Deadly Conflict, Final Report,* Carnegie Corporation of New York, 1997, wwics.si.edu/subsites/ ccpdc/pubs/rept97/finfr.htm, accessed November 3, 2007.

7. Tim Weiner, "More Entreaties in Monterrey for More Aid to the Poor,"*New York Times,* March 22, 2002, p. A10.

8. The International Bank for Reconstruction and Development, The World Bank, "The Coming Globalization," in *Global Economic Prospects: Managing the Next Wave of Globalization, 2007,* www-wds.worldbank.org/external/default/ WDSContentServer/IW3P/IB/2006/12/06/000112742_20061206155022/addi tional/GEP_029-066.pdf, accessed November 3, 2007.

9. Don Kirk, "Politicians Denounce Strict Terms of Bailout: IMF's Conditions Breed Resentment in Seoul,"*International Herald Tribune,* December 5, 1997, www.iht .com/articles/1997/12/05/won.t_4.php?page=1, accessed November 3, 2007.

10. Jubilee Debt Campaign, "The Basics about Debt," www.jubileedebtcampaign.org .uk/?lid=98, accessed November 3, 2007. Jubilee Debt Campaign uses the figure 54 for the poorest countries. In the interest of consistency, we use 53.

11. U.S. Department of State, "The United States and International Development: Partnering for Growth," August 6, 2007, www.state.gov/r/pa/prs/ps/2007/ aug/90348.htm#uno, accessed November 3, 2007.

12. See the UN Millennium Development Goals, www.un.org/millenniumgoals/, accessed February 13, 2008.

13. Anup Shah, "US and Foreign Aid Assistance," in *Global Issues,* April 8, 2007, www .globalissues.org/TradeRelated/Debt/USAid.asp#ForeignAidNumbersinCharts andGraphs, accessed November 3, 2007.

14. A politicide is a gradual but systematic attempt to exterminate an independent political entity.

15. See the Human Security Report, www.humansecurityreport.info/HSR2005_PDF/ Overview.pdf, accessed November 3, 2007.

16. Ibid.

17. The International Bank for Reconstruction and Development, The World Bank, "The Coming Globalization," in *Global Economic Prospects: Managing the Next Wave of Globalization, 2007.*

18. United Nations Department of Economic and Social Affairs, *World Population Prospects: The 2004 Revision,* www.un.org/esa/population/publications/WPP2004/ 2004Highlights_finalrevised.pdf, accessed November 3, 2007.

19. U.S. Department of State, "The United States and International Development: Partnering for Growth," August 6, 2007, www.state.gov/r/pa/prs/ps/2007/aug/90348. htm#uno, accessed November 3, 2007.

20. Current focus countries: Botswana, Cote d'Ivoire, Ethiopia, Guyana, Haiti, Kenya, Mozambique, Namibia, Nigeria, Rwanda, South Africa, Tanzania, Uganda, Vietnam, and Zambia. Bush's plan will focus the resources on those countries in Africa and the Caribbean that are the most affected. These countries are Botswana, Cote d'Ivoire, Ethiopia, Guyana, Haiti, Kenya, Mozambique, Namibia, Rwanda, South Africa, Tanzania, Uganda, and Zambia. These countries have the highest rates of HIV/AIDS and account for 70 percent of the total in all of Africa and the Caribbean.

21. U.S. Department of State, "The United States and International Development: Partnering for Growth."

22. See "President Bush Announces Five-Year, $30 Billion HIV/AIDS Plan," www .whitehouse.gov/news/releases/2007/05/print/20070530-6.html, accessed November 3, 2007.

23. Chris Breyer and Voravit Suwnvanichkij, ". . . And in Another, AIDS in Retreat," *New York Times,* August 12, 2006.

24. Laurie Garrett, "The Challenge of Global Health," *Foreign Affairs* (January– February 2007).

25. OECD aid has a strong focus on health, with member countries spending approximately $95 billion on bilateral and multilateral development assistance in 2005 (including debt relief), up from about $40 billion in 2000. About $37 billion went to Asia, $29 billion to sub-Saharan Africa, and $21 billion to the Middle East and North Africa. The World Bank has increased its funding to more than $2 billion in 2006.

26. Garrett, "The Challenge of Global Health."
27. Winnie Singh, interview with Brian Katulis, September 26, 2007, Washington, D.C.
28. Garrett, "The Challenge of Global Health."
29. James Traub, "The Statesman," *New York Times,* September 18, 2005.
30. Pan Kwan Yuk and Dave Shellock, "Asian Stocks Flat as Tokyo Takes Holiday," *Financial Times,* December 23, 2004. www.ft.com/cms/s/0/1201cc88-15ea-11dc-a7ce-000b5df10621,dwp_uuid=8806bae8-0dc4-11dc-8219-000b5df10621.html, accessed November 3, 2007.
31. Garrett, "The Challenge of Global Health."
32. Ibid.
33. The thirteen countries are: Armenia, Benin, Cape Verde, El Salvador, Georgia, Ghana, Honduras, Lesotho, Madagascar, Mali, Mozambique, Nicaragua, and Vanuatu.
34. U.S. Department of State, "The United States and International Development: Partnering for Growth."
35. For more information on the Millennium Challenge Corporation, see www.mcc.gov, accessed November 3, 2007.
36. Sheila Herrkungm and Sarah Rose, "Will the Millennium Challenge Account Be Caught in the Crosshairs?" Center for Global Development, March 30, 2007.
37. Lydia Polgreen, "Timbuktu Hopes Ancient Texts Spark a Revival," *New York Times,* August 7, 2007, www.nytimes.com/2007/08/07/world/africa/07mali.html, accessed November 3, 2007.
38. Ibid.
39. "Millennium Development Goals: The Eight Commandments," *Economist,* July 5, 2007.
40. See, for instance, Paul Collier, *The Bottom Billion: Why the Poorest Countries Are Failing and What Can Be Done about It* (New York: Oxford University Press, 2007).
41. CATO Institute, "Individual Liberty, Free Markets, and Peace, Hernando de Soto's Biography," www.cato.org/special/friedman/desoto, accessed November 3, 2007.

Chapter 7. Globalization's Impact on Prosperity

1. Jim and Don Kane, telephone interview with Nancy Soderberg, October 6, 2007. The brothers are cousins of Soderberg.
2. CBS News, "The Mensch of Malden Mills," July 6, 2003, www.cbsnews.com/stories/2003/07/03/60minutes/main561656.shtml, accessed November 3, 2007.
3. Jim and Don Kane, telephone interview with Soderberg.
4. Data from the National Council of Textile Organizations, www.ncto.org/ustextiles/closings.asp, accessed November 3, 2007.
5. Bureau of Labor Statistics, U.S. Department of Labor, www.bls.gov, accessed November 3, 2007.
6. NBC News/ *Wall Street Journal* Poll, March 2–5, 2007, 1,007 adults nationwide, www.pollingreport.com, accessed November 3, 2007.
7. "Rich Man, Poor Man," *Economist,* January 20, 2007.
8. *Globalization, Worker Insecurity, and Policy Approaches,* CRS Report for Congress, July 24, 2007.
9. Steve Schifferes, "Globalization Shakes the World," BBC News, January 21, 2007, news.bbc.co.uk/2/hi/business/6279679.stm, accessed November 3, 2007.
10. Michael Mandel with Richard Dunham, "Can Anyone Steer the Economy?" *BusinessWeek,* November 10, 2006.
11. Ron Scherer, "Surge in Exports Buoys U.S. Economy," *Christian Science Monitor,* October 17, 2007.

12. Gene Sperling, "Finding a New Consensus on Trade and Globalization," congressional testimony, January 30, 2007.

13. CBS News, "Income Gap of Poor, Rich, Widens," August 16, 2004, www.cbsnews.com/stories/2004/08/13/national/main635936.shtml, accessed January 26, 2008.

14. Lou Dobbs, *War on the Middle Class: How the Government, Big Business, and Special Interest Groups Are Waging War on the American Dream and How to Fight Back* (New York: Penguin, 2006).

15. Associated Press, "Clinton to Give Trade Deals a 'Time Out,' Contender Signals Wariness on Trade to United Auto Workers in Iowa," November 12, 2007, www.msnbc.msn.com/id/21756848/, accessed January 26, 2008.

16. Tom Raum, "Bush's Stance on Ports Deal Fuels Anger," *Boston Globe*, February 23, 2006.

17. Cited in CBS News/AP story: "Outsourcing Backlash Brewing: Executives Shift White-Collar Jobs Overseas, Politicians Take Notice," January 19, 2004, www.cbsnews.com/stories/2004/01/19/national/main594119.shtml, accessed November 3, 2007.

18. International Monetary Fund, *World Economic Outlook: Globalization and Inequality*, October 2007.

19. Congress of the United States Congresssional Budget Office, "The Budget and Economic Outlook: Fiscal Years 2008 to 2018," January 2008, www.cbo.gov./ftpdocs/89xx/doc8917/01-23-2008_BudgetOutlook.pdf, accessed January 26, 2008.

20. Christian Weller, "Economy Needs a New Engine for Economic Growth as the End of the Housing Boom Continues," April 27, 2007, www.americanprogressaction.org/pressroom/cap/statements/2007/04/weller_economic_analysis.html, accessed November 3, 2007.

21. "Trade Makes the United States Strong," *Business Roundtable*, trade.businessroundtable.org, accessed November 3, 2007.

22. Ron Scherer, "Surge in Exports Buoys U.S. Economy."

23. Americans and the World, "International Trade: NAFTA, CAFTA, FTAA," www.americans-world.org/digest/global_issues/intertrade/nafta.cfm, accessed January 26, 2008.

24. Congressional Budget Office, "The Effects of NAFTA on U.S.-Mexican Trade and GDP," May 2003, www.cbo.gov/ftpdoc.cfm?index=4247&type=0&sequence=1, accessed January 26, 2008.

25. Oxford Economics, *The Prospects for U.S.-China Services Trade and Investment, December 2006*, China Business Forum, www.chinabusinessforum.org/pdf/us-china-services-trade.pdf, accessed November 3, 2007.

26. Peter Navarro, *Report of the China Price Project*, Merage School of Business, University of California-Irvine, www.peternavarro.com/sitebuildercontent/sitebuilderfiles/chinapricereport.pdf, accessed November 3, 2007.

27. Associated Press, "Thousands of Pets Probably Sickened by Food," April 9, 2007, www.msnbc.msn.com/id/18029173/, accessed November 3, 2007.

28. Pew Global Attitudes Project, "World Publics Welcome Global Trade—But Not Immigration," October 4, 2007.

29. Cited in Raymond Ahearn, "Globalization, Worker Insecurity, and Policy Approaches," Congressional Research Service, July 24, 2007.

30. Mark Penn and Thomas Freedman, *The Emerging Politics of Globalization*, for the Democratic Leadership Council, 2007, www.dlc.org/documents/Penn_Globalization_121306.pdf, accessed November 3, 2007.

31. Jim and Don Kane, telephone interview with Soderberg, October 6, 2007.

32. "In Senate Vote, Rockefeller Opposes Central American Free Trade Agreement," www.senate.gov/~rockefeller/news/2005/pr070105.html, accessed November 3, 2007.

33. Steven R. Weisman, "Bush and Democrats in Accord on Trade Deals," May 11, 2007, www.nytimes.com/2007/05/11/business/11trade.html?_r=1&oref=slogin& pagewanted=all, accessed November 3, 2007.

34. Truman (Geneva Round I, 1947; Annecy Round, 1949; Torquay Round, 1951), Eisenhower (Geneva Round II, 1956), Kennedy (Dillon Round, 1962), Johnson (Kennedy Round, 1967), Carter (Tokyo Round, 1979), and Clinton (Uruguay Round, 1994). The current Doha Round was started in 2001. See Progressive Policy Institute, "The Last Republican President to Conclude a Multilateral Trade Agreement: Dwight D. Eisenhower,"*PPI Trade Fact of the Week*, May 29, 2002, www.ppionline.org/ppi_ci.cfm?knlgAreaID=108&subsecID=900003&contentID= 250547, accessed November 3, 2007.

35. Drusilla K. Brown, Alan V. Deardorff, and Robert M. Stern, "CGE Modeling and Analysis of Multilateral and Regional Negotiating Options," *Research Seminar in International Economics* (Ann Arbor: University of Michigan, 2001), p. 32, www .spp.umich.edu/rsie/workingpapers/wp.html, accessed November 3, 2007.

36. Peter King, "Dubai Ports Company in al-Qaida Heartland," February 20, 2006, archive.newsmax.com/archives/ic/2006/2/20/120409.shtml, accessed November 3, 2007.

37. FOX News/Opinion Dynamics Poll of 900 registered voters nationwide, conducted February 28–March 1, 2006.

38. Stephen Labaton and Julia Werdigier, "Mild Reaction in Capitol to a Dubai Nasdaq Stake," *New York Times*, September 21, 2007, p. C7.

39. Lee Hudson Teslik, "Backgrounder: Sovereign Wealth Funds," Council on Foreign Relations, January 18, 2008, www.cfr.org/publication/15251/sovereign_wealth_ funds.html?breadcrumb=%2F, accessed January 26, 2008.

40. Associated Press, "Sovereign Wealth Funds Eye US Deals," January 15, 2008, www.boston.com/business/articles/2008/01/15/sovereign_wealth_funds_eye_us_ deals/, accessed January 26, 2008.

41. Andrew Ross Sorkin, "What Money Can Buy: Influence," *New York Times*, January 22, 2008, www.nytimes.com/2008/01/22/business/22sorkin.html?_r=1&oref=slogin, accessed January 26, 2008.

42. Ibid.

43. Teslik, "Backgrounder: Sovereign Wealth Funds."

44. Includes Treasury Bills, bonds, and notes. See "Major Foreign Holders of Treasury Securities," Department of Treasury/Federal Reserve Board, January 16, 2008,www.ustreas.gov/tic/mfh.txt, accessed November 3, 2007.

45. U.S. Senate Statements and Releases, "In Remarks on Senate Floor Senator Clinton Urges Action to Address U.S. Foreign Debt and Trade Imbalance," February 28, 2007, www.senate.gov/~clinton/news/statements/record.cfm?id=269895, accessed November 3, 2007.

46. U.S. Senate Statements and Releases, "Senator Clinton Calls for Action to Address Economic Vulnerability Created by Growing Foreign-Held Debt."

47. Willy Lam, "China's Encroachment on America's Backyard," Jamestown Foundation, November 24, 2004, www.jamestown.org/publications_details.php?volume_ id=395&issue_id=3152&article_id=2368903, accessed November 3, 2007.

48. China-Africa Forum, "Beijing Summit Adopts Declaration, Highlighting China-Africa Strategic Partnership," November 5, 2006, english.focacsummit.org/2006- 11/05/content_5166.htm, accessed November 3, 2007.

49. Fairness and Accuracy in Reporting (FAIR), "CNN's Immigration Problem: Is Dobbs the Exception—or the Rule?" April 24, 2006, www.fair.org/index. php?page=2867, accessed November 3, 2007.

50. Stuart Anderson and Michaela Platzer, "American Made: The Impact of Immigrant Entrepreneurs and Professionals on U.S. Competitiveness," www.nvca.org/pdf/ AmericanMade_study.pdf, accessed November 3, 2007.

51. Donald Snyder, "Technology Firm Executives Say Immigration Barriers Hurt America," FOX News, May 30, 2007.

52. "Rise in Foreign Patent Filings in the U.S. Noted," October 16, 2007, www.eetasia .com/ART_8800483744_480100_NT_10bba180.HTM, accessed January 26, 2007.

53. Vivek Wadhwa et al., "Intellectual Property, the Immigration Backlog, and a Reverse Brain Drain: America's New Immigrant Entrepreneurs, Part III," Kauffman Foundation, August 22, 2007, papers.ssrn.com/sol3/papers.cfm?abstract_ id=1008366, accessed November 3, 2007.

54. Julia Preston, "Legal Immigrants Rally at Capitol to Protest Backlog," New York Times, September 19, 2007.

55. Snyder, "Technology Firm Executives Say Immigration Barriers Hurt America."

56. Barbara Hagenbaugh, "U.S. Manufacturers Getting Desperate for Skilled People," USA Today, December 5, 2006.

57. Jan Sliva, "EU Seeking Skilled Immigrant Workers," Business Week, September 26, 2007.

58. "Pat Buchanan Defends Controversial Immigration Comments," Hannity & Colmes, August 23, 2006.

59. Jonathan Darman, "Q&A: Lou Dobbs on Immigration and Objectivity," Newsweek, April 2, 2006.

60. Newsmax.com, "Lou Dobbs' Ratings Up at CNN," May 10, 2006, archive .newsmax.com/archives/ic/2006/5/10/104603.shtml?s=ic, accessed January 26, 2007.

61. Joseph Mathews, Crossing Arizona, a documentary film directed by Joseph Mathews and Daniel DeVivo, RAINLAKE Film, 2006.

62. Pew Hispanic Center, "Fact Sheet: The Labor Force Status of Short-Term Unauthorized Workers," April 13, 2006, pewhispanic.org/files/factsheets/16.pdf.

63. Jeffrey Passel, "The Size and Characteristics of the Unauthorized Migrant Population in the U.S.," Pew Hispanic Center, March 7, 2006.

64. National Immigration Forum, "Top 10 Immigration Myths and Facts," June 2003, www.immigrationforum.org/documents/TheJourney/MythsandFacts.pdf, accessed November 3, 2007.

65. Eduardo Porter, "Illegal Immigrants Are Bolstering Social Security with Billions," New York Times, April 5, 2005.

66. Susan Milligan, "Fiscal Lift, Burden in Immigrant Legislation," Boston Globe, June 5, 2007.

67. Karin Brulliard, "Migrants Sent Home $300 Billion in 2006," Washington Post, October 18, 2007.

68. Rachel Swarns, "In Georgia, Immigrants Unsettle Old Sense of Place," New York Times, August 4, 2006.

69. Iowa State University, "The Impact of Immigration on Small-to-Mid-Sized Iowa Communities," June 2001, www.extension.iastate.edu/Publications/PM1879.pdf, accessed January 27, 2008.

70. Steven Walters and Craig Gilbert, "Immigrants Decry License Bill," Milwaukee Journal Sentinel, May 5, 2005.

71. See www.newsday.com/news/local/politics/ny-stdmv055402575oct05,0,6002989 .story, accessed November 26, 2007.

72. Ken Belson and Jill Capuzzo, "Towns Rethink Laws against Illegal Immigrants," *New York Times*, September 26, 2007.

73. Jim and Don Kane, telephone interview with Soderberg.

74. Gallup poll, June 8–25, 2006, N = 2,032: "Thinking now about immigrants—that is, people who come from other countries to live here in the United States: In your view, should immigration be kept at its present level, increased or decreased?"

75. *USA Today*/Gallup poll, July 6–8, 2006, N = 1,014: "In your view, what should be the higher priority in dealing with the issue of illegal immigration: developing a plan for halting the flow of illegal immigrants into the U.S. or developing a plan to deal with illegal immigrants who are already in the U.S., or should both be given the same priority?"

76. Associated Press/Ipsos poll, May 15–17, 2005, N = 1,001: "Generally, do you think immigrants are more likely to be involved in criminal activity than people born here, or isn't there much difference?"

77. "Enter McCain-Kennedy," *Washington Post*, May 14, 2005, www.washington post.com/wp-dyn/content/article/2005/05/13/AR2005051301483.html, accessed November 3, 2007.

78. See, for instance, Gene Sperling's proposal at www.americanprogress.org/issues/2004/01/b289151.html, accessed November 3, 2007.

Conclusion. Prosperity: A New Vision of American Power

1. Jim and Don Kane, telephone interview with Nancy Soderberg, October 6, 2007.

2. President Woodrow Wilson's Fourteen Points, January 8, 1918, World War I Document Archives, net.lib.byu.edu/~rdh7/wwi/1918/14points.html, accessed January 27, 2007.

3. Harry S. Truman, Inaugural Address, January 20, 1949, in *From Revolution to Reconstruction: An HTML Project*, www.let.rug.nl/usa/P/ht33/speeches/truman.htm, accessed January 27, 2008.

4. John F. Kennedy, Inaugural Address, January 20, 1961, John. F. Kennedy Presidential Library and Museum, www.jfklibrary.org/Historical+Resources/Archives/Reference+Desk/Speeches/JFK/003POF03Inaugural01201961.htm, accessed January 27, 2008.

INDEX